Killing Animals

Killing Animals

THE ANIMAL STUDIES GROUP

University of Illinois Press

URBANA AND CHICAGO

© 2006 by the Board of Trustees
of the University of Illinois
All rights reserved
Manufactured in the United States of America
1 2 3 4 5 C P 6 5 4 3 2

∞ This book is printed on acid-free paper.
Library of Congress Cataloging-in-Publication Data
Killing animals / the Animal Studies Group.
p.   cm.
Includes bibliographical references and index.
ISBN-13: 978-0-252-03050-5 (cloth : alk. paper)
ISBN-10: 0-252-03050-8 (cloth : alk. paper)
ISBN-13: 978-0-252-07290-1 (pbk. : alk. paper)
ISBN-10: 0-252-07290-1 (pbk. : alk. paper)
1. Animal welfare. 2. Hunting. 3. Slaughtering and slaughter-houses.
4. Human-animal relationships. I. Animal Studies Group.
HV4711.K587   2006
179'.3—dc22   2005022117

Contents

Preface

The Animal Studies Group brings together eight British academics: Steve Baker, Jonathan Burt, Diana Donald, Erica Fudge, Garry Marvin, Robert McKay, Clare Palmer, and Chris Wilbert. They approach the field of animal studies from backgrounds in different humanities disciplines, notably contemporary visual culture, art history, early modern and modern cultural and intellectual history, anthropology, contemporary literary studies, philosophy, and human geography. All members of the group have published work in their own specialist areas and have worked to encourage interest in human-animal relations within their own fields of expertise. The aim of the Group as a whole is to go beyond the single discipline that often confines an individual and to use the knowledge of each member to further studies of animals within the humanities through creative interplay of ideas, discussion, and mutual criticism.

Killing Animals is the Group's first collective work. Each member has written an essay, taking the theme of the book as his or her starting point. What has emerged is eight very different, challenging essays. We have not attempted to adopt a house style—different disciplines, we have come to realize, require different modes of representation, different languages, and different assumptions about both the focus and the function of the essay as a form.

We have learned much from each other during the process of writing this book, not only about current debates and ideas in each of the disciplines but also about what each of us can offer to a wider debate. We hope that we have been able to communicate these insights to the reader and that the book will stimulate other studies of a similar kind. The centrality of animals in cultural history and in contemporary consciousness demands such breadth in the frame of reference within which they are studied.

The development of *Killing Animals* was very different from most essay collections. Whereas many such works originate as a series of separately planned conference papers drawn together by an editor, *Killing Animals* is a book that has been throughout a collaborative venture. Thus both the introduction and the conclusion are based on exchanges and debates among the Group as a whole.

We have not attempted to come to any single ethical understanding of our subject—this would be impossible, since there are many differences of view among us. The Group is not a campaigning organization but a group that promotes the academic study of the place of animals in human history as an autonomous and substantive field.

The Group's thanks go in particular to Liz Dulany at the University of Illinois Press for her support and to Stephanie Schwandner-Sievers for her hospitality and patience.

Killing Animals

Introduction

To give just the barest outline of the extraordinary scale of animal killing conducted by human beings in recent years, we are going to present a wide set of figures taken, to some extent at random, from various sources. Most of these, and many more sets of statistics, are easily locatable on the Internet, in government and international reports, and in many of the books referred to in the chapters of this book.

First, we can look at the statistics related to farm animals. Often they are destroyed to eliminate infections that might spread to other animals or to humans. Between April 1996 and October 2001, 5,196,247 animals were killed under the Over Thirty Month Scheme as part of the effort to control the disease BSE (bovine spongiform encephalopathy) in the United Kingdom. According to the Department of Environment, Food and Rural Affairs Disease Control System Database, 4,230,786 animals were killed as part of the effort to control foot-and-mouth disease in the United Kingdom in 2000.[1] In Hong Kong in December 1997, 1.4 million geese, ducks, and chickens were killed to prevent a "bird flu" from spreading to humans. The routine slaughter of animals for food involves even vaster numbers. Each year in the United States, 45 million turkeys are killed for Thanksgiving. Six billion broiler chickens are raised in sheds. A hog sticker in a highly industrialized factory in the United States could cut as many as 1,100 throats per hour.[2] At the time of the BSE outbreak, three-quarters of all American cattle were fed animal protein, consuming about 2 billion pounds a year, mostly the remains of other cattle.[3] In 1998, the total number of animals slaughtered for food in the United Kingdom was 883,319,000, which works out at twenty-eight animals slaughtered every second.[4] In 2002, the number of poultry slaughtered in the United Kingdom was 850,082,000, and the figure for sheep and lambs was 13,094,000.[5] Australia's kill quota for kangaroos in 2001 was 5.5 million.

Besides the consumption of animals for food, there are also vast figures for other kinds of consumption, such as clothing and display. Every year it is estimated that more than a billion animals are slaughtered for leather worldwide.[6] Buenos Aires recorded exports between 1977 and 1979 of 21,534,299 animal skins, from pumas to lizards. In 1999, it was reported that some 20,000 French cats were caught annually for their skins.[7] Between 1980 and 1985, the United States imported between 2 and 4 million reptile skins and 125 million live ornamental fish.[8] Hunting and science also use up enormous numbers of animals. In the United States in 2001, some 13 million people took part in hunting activities. The British Home Office statistics on animal experimentation for 2002 list a figure of 2,655,876 animals used.

The knock-on effects of the ornamental fish trade and the taking of fish for consumption is staggering. Stocks of large predatory fish throughout the world's oceans have dropped by 90 percent in 50 years.[9] The numbers of common shark species have dropped by 75 percent in fifteen years. Many activities are extremely wasteful of animal life, often entailing the destruction of species other than those intended to be caught. Every day some 1,700 ships worldwide set more than 20,000 miles of drift net in the open sea, entangling, apart from the catch, an estimated 308,000 seals, whales, and porpoises and, presumably, countless numbers of seabirds.[10] Up to 50 percent of a trawler's catch is unsalable and is thrown back into the sea. It takes four tons of industrially trawled fish to produce one ton of pellets to provide feed for farmed salmon.[11] For every kilo of prawns caught, another ten to twenty kilos of miscellaneous marine life is also caught. The United Kingdom produces 35 million farmed sea trout per annum for consumption.[12] The United Nations believes that over 20 million fish and half as many other forms of marine life are also caught every year for the aquarium trade, which causes immense damage to the remaining fauna and flora.[13]

These levels of killing are without precedent. But in the nineteenth century, for example, battues (large-scale shoots) of game birds and other animals produced huge kills. On October 27, 1807, fourteen guns on the Duke of Norfolk's Holkham estate shot 16 partridges, 69 pheasants, 266 hares, 171 rabbits, 8 woodcock, and 1 other unspecified bird, a total of 531 animals. One of the kings of Naples and his suite, during the same period, in a journey from Italy to Vienna, killed 5 bears, 13 wolves, 17 badgers, 354 foxes, 1,121 rabbits, 1,625 roebucks, 1,820 boars, 1,960 deer, 12,335 partridges, 15,350 pheasants, and 16,354 hares.[14] The growth of empire and of commerce and luxury trades had a big influence on animal destruction too. Between 1870 and 1920, nearly 20,000 tons of ornamental feathers entered the United Kingdom. This was a figure less than half that for France, which imported 50,000 tons between 1890 and 1930. Both estimates represent scores of millions of birds killed all around the world.[15] There are many other examples of the widespread devastation brought about by collecting or hunting for ivory, skins, and other forms of trophy.

When one begins to draw up a list (the above statistics are only a small part of a far greater picture), it is easy to see how the killing of animals takes place, and has taken place, on such a scale that is almost beyond comprehension. It is not just the statistics that are staggering but the fact that almost all areas of human life are at some point or other involved in or directly dependent on the killing of animals. These areas cover everything from science—understood in the broadest possible sense to include everything from industry to medicine and other forms of research—and food production to clothing, recreation (field sports and hunting), cosmetics, fertilizers, pet foods, jewelry, and numerous types of utensil, ornament, and decoration. This list could be further extended to include other types of human impact on the natural world: from the large-scale, such as the side effects of pollution, urban and industrial development, and the destruction of habitats, to more small-scale issues such as the slaughter of birds by cats that are kept as domestic pets.[16] This killing is ubiquitous and omnipresent: a holocaust of immense proportions. Indeed, the extent and the variety of the killing is reflected in the number of terms we use to describe these different types of death. Animals become extinct. They are also killed, gassed, electrocuted, exterminated, hunted, butchered, vivisected, shot, trapped, snared, run over, lethally injected, culled, sacrificed, slaughtered, executed, euthanized, destroyed, put down, put to sleep, and even, perhaps, murdered.

Despite this, the purposeful killing of animals, at least in most industrialized nations, is largely invisible in the public domain. It generally takes place in slaughterhouses, factories, city kill shelters, or laboratories well away from the public eye. Furthermore, the scale of animal death caused by environmental damage rarely impinges on the public consciousness, except in those rare instances of an eye-catching disaster such as the sinking of an oil tanker or the accidental spillage of toxic industrial effluent into a local river.[17] In fact, when representations of animal death do erupt into the public domain (as when they appear, say, in a film or other media), they are often accompanied by a shocked outcry—ironically, in the name of animal welfare.[18] All that this protest serves to do is to reinforce the taboos to ensure the normal invisibility of animal killing and to keep the implications of such killing even further from public consciousness. Perhaps this willful blindness explains why even the existence of statistics and other forms of evidence that indicate the scale of animal killing—easily found in accessible books and magazines or on the Internet—appears to have only limited effects.

The killing of animals is a structural feature of all human-animal relations. It reflects human power over animals at its most extreme and yet also at its most commonplace. From a historical point of view, there is nothing new about this killing; what has changed is the scope of the technology involved and the intensity of its global impact on animal species. Furthermore, humans can now bring into existence and then control and manipulate the lives of millions of animals, solely in order to kill them. The scale of this practice has no historical precedent. In spite of widespread humanitarian sensibilities, of the modern cultural and political centrality of institutions dedicated to the welfare of animals, and of the much vaunted "love of nature," public concern has hardly any impact on the scale of the killing. Indeed, in some cases humane institutions, such as those that deal with stray and homeless animals in towns and cities, actually exacerbate the killing, as one sees in the case of kill shelters. Between 8 and 12 million pets are placed in shelters in the United States each year, and of these, approximately 5 to 9 million animals are euthanized.[19]

This book explores the problematic complexity of this ultimate expression of human power over animals and does so by revealing the extraordinary diversity of killing practices and the wide variety of meanings attached to those practices. Killing an animal is rarely simply a matter of animal death. It is surrounded by a host of attitudes, ideas, perceptions, and assumptions. Humans are deeply invested in animal killing both at the level of the complicated industrial and scientific processes that are used in controlling the animal body and in the cultural forms of conduct and ritual that codify things like hunting practices, butchery, and sacrifice. Even within a given culture, these attitudes and codes can be widely varied. Certainly the taboo on visual imagery of animal death would suggest an unease and a potential of public disgust that threatens the whole edifice of killing. However, this discernible strain of discomfort is often selectively manifested in a sympathetic response to the plight of particular cases that for some reason or other capture the public imagination. For instance, the conditions of veal calves in transport were the cause of protests at British ports in 1995.[20] The overall picture is, for most people, too dark and too enmeshed in a vast network of economic and consumer interests to be seen in its entirety, let alone for it to be acted upon.

In this book, the different strands that make up the phenomenon of killing animals, both in the past and in the present, are analyzed and discussed through case studies. They examine the different issues of scale; visibility and invisibility; the different structural aspects of killing in, for instance, hunting, extermination, or slaughter; philosophical and aesthetic responses; killing in the name of humanitarianism; and so on. Given that the killing of animals is implicated in almost every aspect of human life, a cross-disciplinary approach has been adopted as the best way of illuminating some of its dimensions.

More specifically, our interest is to explore the ways in which societies past and present manage the concept of animal killing in various cultural arenas. If the fact of animal killing is as fundamental to society as the numbers of deaths suggest, then ideas of what it means to kill an animal or animals must be complex and pervasive. Such ideas have, however, yet to receive the systematic attention they deserve. It is for this reason that this book's interdisciplinary focus remains within humanities subjects broadly conceived.

Through history, many societies have demonstrated attitudes of unease about animal killing and yet at the same time pleasure in displays of cruelty, meat-eating, and hunting. As historian Erica Fudge shows in her discussion of animal baiting in the late sixteenth and seventeenth centuries, enjoyment of these kinds of spectacle did not rule out the simultaneous existence of a compassionate philosophy. The latter is exemplified by Montaigne's focus on the importance of the capacity for sentience rather than the possession of reason as a criterion for the inclusion of animals in a human moral framework. Distinctions were also made between different kinds of killing: the useful and the pleasurable. Fudge analyzes the competing moral frameworks around the animal in terms that we would recognize today. Her findings suggest that historians have underestimated the sophistication of attitudes toward animal killing in periods before the nineteenth century, which is so often said to have witnessed the birth of humanitarianism. The fact that an analysis of the different methods of killing took place in the early modern period alerts us to the fact that these methods reflected different kinds of human-animal relations, all of which were at some level defined by death.

In anthropologist Garry Marvin's analysis, domestic animals and pets have always been bred for the benefit of humans. Their death is, ideally, orderly and uncontested by the animal. In hunting, on the other hand, this type of relation between human and animal is slightly reversed. The animal offers a challenge to the hunter, and the positions of dominance and subservience are more equivocal. Here the rules of killing are different, even though the end result is often the same.

It appears that the divided attitude toward killing is partly a product of the multifaceted nature of human-animal interactions. However, differing views can also coalesce around a single issue. Art historian Diana Donald locates a strangely divided consciousness in Victorian hunting practice: on the one hand, joy in pursuing and killing an animal; on the other hand, sympathy, even passionate identification, with the victim. Given the problematic nature of the public representation of animal death discussed earlier, it is significant that Sir Edwin Landseer's pictures of dying deer aroused the same kind of mental conflict vicariously in the Victorian public. These images invite questions about the relationship between the direct experience of killing animals and the emotional effect of contemplating visual representations of it. Such images by Landseer constructed the events they purported to depict, often expressing a fatalistic belief in the universal struggle for survival in nature that effectively exculpated the human perpetrator of the hunt.

Art historian Steve Baker considers similar themes, but this time in relation to contemporary art. Baker discusses how far such art can intervene productively in current debates on the killing of animals. He focuses particularly on the problematic ethical and aesthetic status of artworks whose materials include actual dead animal bodies or body parts. As with Donald's examples, these artworks evoke diverse, often conflicting, responses and mark the fault lines of an ambivalent attitude toward animal death. For Baker, it is in the foregrounding of this ambiguity that these rather gory artworks become so compelling.

While the book as a whole emphasizes what humans do to animals, it is instructive to consider the reverse of this pattern: geographer Chris Wilbert's essay is on animals that attack humans. There has long been a fascination with this phenomenon, but it has become a particular focus of media reports in the developed world in recent years. The subject has a number of different dimensions. On the one hand, it could reflect changing spatial relations between humans and animals: how their geographical relationships shift with alterations in landscape and urbanization as well as in new forms of control. On the other hand, it could reflect a different sense of human-animal interaction in which the humans and animals are conceived as living in domains that are less exclusive of each other, risky as that may be. Here, human-animal relations are conceived in terms of the animal's resistance to killing and death.

The shift in Wilbert's essay to the animal side of human-animal relations resonates with a similar animal-centered perspective that operates, though for very different purposes, in literary critic Robert McKay's essay. McKay is concerned with literary representations of animal disease, particularly BSE. In his analysis of Deborah Levy's *Diary of a Steak* (1997), the focus is on how this fictional work has a broader bearing on cultural attitudes toward animal health crises and the relationship of these crises to wider political and ethical issues in the meat industry. The emphasis here is very much on the consequences of these catastrophes for the animals rather than for humans.

The complexities of the slaughter of animals for meat are also the subject of historian Jonathan Burt's essay, which analyzes the twentieth-century debates about ritual slaughter in the meat industry. Burt confronts the fact that despite the mechanized and dehumanized nature of the meat industry, there are still important cultural differences in methods of slaughter that produce conflicts within the industry itself. Disputes over these cultural differences, and arguments over what constitutes humane and inhumane slaughter, raise uncomfortable issues of race and religion, particularly in relation to the licensing of practices of different ethnic groups. Such decisions are especially important when the method of killing an animal constitutes a major part of a group's ethnic, cultural, or religious identity.

The difficulty in adjudicating upon "humane" and "inhumane" slaughter—one would think that the irony of the terms of such a debate would not be lost on anyone—raises a more general question: what it means to kill *in the name of humanitarianism.* Philosopher Clare Palmer explores the ethics involved in the widespread practice of painlessly killing healthy animals in animal shelters. Palmer notes that pets are frequently treated with an attitude of instrumentalism—pets are there to be enjoyed but can also be discarded when necessary. Much as they may be loved, they are like disposable goods. The paradoxes and contradictions around the "humane" killing of pets are not simply a philosophical issue of the kind raised in Palmer's dialogue with animal rights philosophers Tom Regan and Peter Singer. These contradictions are also reflected in the attitudes of animal welfare organizations that, in many ways, even if with the best of intentions, promote this instrumentalist ethos while at the same time trying to reduce the numbers of animals killed in animal shelters. Palmer offers some constructive solutions that, by exploring relevant historical and cultural relationships between humans and pets, suggest that humans have more collective responsibilities toward these animals than is widely accepted.

The essays in this book, taken together, highlight the general issues involved in the killing of animals as raised in this introduction. They also provide

specific examples, which demonstrate the complexity of attitudes and practices that are entailed. Despite the stupefying magnitude of the killing in a
global and historical sense, we must not avoid the need for an analysis of
this defining aspect of human behavior. Such an analysis could, it is hoped,
point toward a future where this killing becomes unnecessary.

Notes

1. For more details, see the Department of Environment, Food and Rural Affairs Web
site at http://www.defra.gov.uk.

2. Gail Eisnitz, *Slaughterhouse: The Shocking Tale of Greed, Neglect, and Inhumane Treatment inside the U.S. Meat Industry* (New York: Prometheus Books, 1997), plate 6. The
figures she gives for annual slaughter in the U.S. are 93 million pigs; 37 million cattle; 2
million calves; 8 million horses, goats and sheep; and 8 billion turkeys. An automated
poultry plant can process as many as 360,000 birds in a day (61, 167).

3. Eric Schlosser, *Fast Food Nation* (London: Penguin, 2002), 272.

4. See http://www.viva.org.uk.

5. See http://www.statistics.gov.org.

6. See http://www.peta.com for a range of figures and references on meat production,
fur farming, and numerous other animal related industries.

7. *The Independent,* December 10, 1999.

8. Bryan Norton, Michael Hutchins, Elizabeth Stevens, Terry Maple, eds., *Ethics on the
Ark: Zoos, Animal Welfare, and Wildlife Conservation* (Washington: Smithsonian Institution Press, 1995), 3. Although these statistics are older than some of the others quoted,
they indicate a level of extraction that has extreme long-term effects for the population
dynamics of all fauna.

9. Ransom Myers and Boris Worm, "Rapid Worldwide Depletion of Predatory Fish
Communities," *Nature* 423 (May 2003): 280–83. See also *The Guardian,* May 15, 2003.

10. These figures were researched by the World Wildlife Fund and presented to the
International Whaling Committee in June 2003.

11. Paul Brown, "The Dead Sea Cells," *The Guardian,* May 17, 2003. Brown also describes
a Dutch supertrawler, the *Helen Mary,* which is 350 feet long and capable of trawling
98,000 tons of fish in fifty days.

12. Andrew Purvis, "Farmed Fish," *The Observer,* May 11, 2003.

13. See http://www.mcbi.org, the Web site of the Marine Conservation Biology Institute.

14. William Daniels, *Rural Sports,* vol. 3 (London, 1801–13), 400; William Youatt, *The
Obligation and Extent of Humanity to Brutes* (London, 1839), 178.

15. Robin Doughty, *Feather Fashions and Bird Preservation: A Study in Nature Protection*
(Berkeley: University of California Press, 1975), 25.

16. The numbers of threatened species on the International Union for the Conservation
of Nature's Red Lists continues to rise. Between 1996 and 2000, the numbers of threatened
mammal species increased from 1096 to 1130, and the number of bird species increased
from 1107 to 1183. There has been a marked increase in the threats to primates particularly, as well as to tortoises and freshwater turtles in Southeast Asia, which are used for

both medicine and food. There has also been a marked deterioration in freshwater fish species in river systems. See http://www.iucnredlist.org. The numbers for the predation on birds by domestic cats are difficult to quantify. For the US, estimates indicate that about 1 billion birds are killed a year by cats.

17. These include tanker disasters such as the *Torrey Canyon* (1967) and the *Amoco Cadiz* (1978), which spilled 117,000 tons and 233,000 tons of crude oil respectively. The worst disaster was the *Exxon Valdez* in 1989, which spilled 11 million gallons. Estimates vary on the impact on wildlife of the *Exxon Valdez* disaster. Figures for seabirds vary between 75,000 and 250,000 deaths—35,000 carcasses were actually found. Other species such as seals, otters, whales, and fish were also heavily affected.

18. For a discussion of the tradition of avoiding or censoring depictions of animal suffering and death, see Jonathan Burt, *Animals in Film* (London: Reaktion Books, 2002).

19. See http://www.aspca.org.

20. Hilda Kean, *Animal Rights: Political and Social Change in Britain since 1800* (London: Reaktion Books, 1998), 213–14.

1 Wild Killing: Contesting the Animal in Hunting

GARRY MARVIN

In his introduction to a recent series of essays on violence from anthropological perspectives, Jon Abbink notes that violence is universal in human societies. Although he admits that this might be a trivial observation, he rightly suggests that the attempt to explain what violence is and what it does constitutes an enormous challenge. He argues that violence needs to be understood as a socially and culturally meaningful activity that shapes many aspects of human social relations:

> Violence has the effect of a "creative" or at least "constituent" force in social relations: deconstructing, redefining or reshaping a social order, whether intended or not. This is not meant as an evaluative statement as to its positive or negative value, but as an analytic one. It is only to call attention to the vital role of socially rooted and historically formed relations of power, force and dominance—also in an ideological sense—in defining social relations, effected through violent action.[1]

Such a perspective can be adapted to the issues central to this present book, for violence is a key element in the relationships between humans and animals.

The particular sort of violence we are concerned with is killing rather than other forms of the deliberate infliction of injury or physical or mental suffering on animals. It is possible to argue that the killing of animals deconstructs, redefines, or reshapes the social order between humans and animals, but it can be construed as more powerful than that. Abbink's use of the prefixes *de-* and *re-* here suggests that violence is part of breaking down and making anew in the human context; an intrusive force, a force for and of change.

However, in the case of human-animal relations, the human need and ability to kill animals and the general acceptance or tolerance of the violence of killing is fundamental to the creation of the social order between these sets of creatures; such killing constructs, defines, and shapes this order.

Huge numbers of animals, particularly those classified as domesticated, owe their very existence to the fact that they will be killed—they live primarily for this end. Humans regularly kill animals for food and for the use of other body parts. They are sacrificed and in other ways killed in religious and other ritual events; in scientific experiments; as part of pest and vermin control, for reasons of public health; as part of wildlife management practices; and in sporting events in which they compete with other animals or against humans. In some cases, it is true that the social relationship is shaped by the refusal of humans to take any part in the death of animals, as in the case of vegetarians or because of religious beliefs. In other cases, such as keeping animals for pleasure, particularly as pets, while the relationship is not predicated on killing the animal, this is often the end of the relationship when the animal is ill, infirm, or unwanted.

My central concern in this chapter is to explore the relationships between human lives and animal lives and deaths as they are enacted and expressed in hunting. Hunting has developed very differently in different periods of history and in different cultures; an analysis of this is beyond the scope of this chapter. I am also unable to engage with the rich anthropological literature that deals with the hunting practices and beliefs in those societies often loosely defined as "hunting and gathering" in which hunting to obtain meat and other animal parts is part of a necessary strategy for survival and subsistence: these will, however, be alluded to for comparative purposes. The focus here will be on hunting as a sport or as a leisure pursuit, but even here it is necessary to impose restrictions. Such hunting practices have been reported and described from the earliest histories and literatures, and it is beyond the scope of this chapter to attempt a survey of such traditions, the complexities of their forms, their possible meanings, and their different social and cultural significances. Rather than a general survey of all forms of hunting as sport, my concern here will be directed to discussing key themes in such hunting practices in the present and in particular in Europe and North America. Finally, it is important to emphasize that what follows is an *anthropological* attempt at exploring the world of hunting and understanding the nature of the relationships and engagements involved.

Many people in the modern world condemn hunting as a sport or leisure pursuit as anachronistic, unnecessary, and morally unacceptable. Positions for and against hunting have been hotly contested and debated at length in terms of animal rights and environmental ethics and at the levels of local, national, and international politics.[2] Moral judgments as to the acceptability or unacceptability of hunting do not form part of my anthropological account, which is primarily an attempt to understand and interpret a set of cultural practices.

In a book concerned with killing animals, a consideration of how the deaths of wild animals are brought about in hunting is important if we are to understand the full range of deaths inflicted on animals by humans. I will argue that other forms of killing are largely utilitarian and that those who perpetrate such killing do so within the context of working practices governed by human supremacy over the animal. In such contexts, humans can demand and command the death of the animal, which is brought about in ways that the animal is not allowed to challenge or contest. In hunting, humans might desire the death of the animal, but they cannot demand or command it; the death of the animal is not inevitable. Hunters must struggle to achieve supremacy, and the animal must have the freedom to resist the hunters' desires. As I will argue later, in hunting, the death of the animal has to be won from it rather than its life being simply taken. Central to this form of killing is the challenge that the animal presents to the hunter.

Hunting—A Cultural Pursuit

An argument that runs through much of the literature on hunting—particularly that which seeks to defend it—is that hunting is somehow inherent in or a natural part of the human condition and that human hunting is directly analogous to animal hunting or predation. The argument I will advance here is that while human hunting may, in some superficial ways, seem similar to such animal behaviors—tracking, stalking, pursuing, and killing prey—the similarity is indeed superficial. Human hunting is a cultural pursuit, not a natural practice. The naturalistic argument is normally expressed along the lines that for the vast majority of their time on earth, *Homo sapiens* have been hunters and that modern humans cannot fully escape from this heritage. The authors of such arguments then suggest that it is *natural* for people in the present to want to hunt and that they are largely following the natural instincts of being human. So, for example, Ann Causey, a widely cited author in hunting literature, quotes approvingly the view that "the will to hunt, the desire to hunt, lies deep. It is . . . inherent in man" to support her own view that "the urge to kill may be viewed as an original, essential human trait" and further that "it is impossible to believe that education alone can obliterate desire that has been developed and reinforced over millions of years."[3] I do not wish to dissect the dubious biology and evolutionary theory on which such arguments are made—this has already been effectively accomplished by others[4]—my concern is rather with the acultural and ahistorical nature of such arguments. Hunting cannot simply be explained as being triggered by something in the genetic makeup of humans nor as being motivated by a mystical link to a putative past. Human hunting is a set of cultural rather than natural practices, and it is important here to emphasize that it differs from the predation in the nonhuman animal world with which is it sometimes compared. Human hunting certainly involves predation, but predation is not the same as hunting.

Tim Ingold, in an essay in which he explores the modes of subsistence in human evolution, has carefully worked through the distinctions between hunting and predation and has argued that hunting is a special form of predation and is a uniquely human activity that "consists in reality in the *subjective intentionality* that is brought to bear on the procurement process."[5] Humans, in a similar way to animals, may engage in predation when an animal is suddenly present and they kill it; but hunting is of a different order. As Ingold argues: "Whereas the predatory sequence of pursuit and capture begins at the moment when the predator detects the presence of a potential victim, hunting can begin long before with the onset of an intentional *search* for signs of prey."[6] His point is that an animal becomes an active predator only at the moment when a potential prey presents itself, whereas "human hunting, by contrast is not spontaneous but projective; that is to say, the intention to procure game precedes the encounter with prey."[7] This notion of intention is crucial in Ingold's distinction between human hunting and animal predation. It is only where there is a deliberate search prior to predation that we have a case of hunting.

Ingold offers a short illustrative example. He imagines that he meets someone along a path (presumably in the countryside) and asks him what he is doing. The man replies that he is merely going on his way. Later, Ingold hears that the man has killed an animal that happened to cross his path. The question he then poses is whether the man was actually hunting:

> Of course not, because at the time he had no intention or expectation of procuring game. Had he had such an intention he would have replied to my initial inquiry that he was, indeed, out hunting. Thus the essence of hunting lies in the prior intention that motivates the search for game, the essence of predation lies in the behavioural events of pursuit and capture, sparked off by the presence, in the immediate environment, of target animal or its signs.[8]

The arguments of two more recent writers add to the critique of human hunting being equivalent to animal predation. Paul Veach Moriarty and Mark Woods compare the actions of a mountain lion finding and killing a deer with that of a person hunting a deer. The lion jumps on the deer and kills it by breaking its neck. It then eats its fill of the animal, including the viscera, before dragging the carcass to a safe place where it can be later consumed. The human hunter obtains a license to hunt, drives to the hunting area, and begins looking for a suitable deer that can be killed legally:

> The hunter sees a deer a hundred yards away that appears to be the correct deer as specified on the licence. He or she shoots the deer with a high-powered rifle, guts the deer (leaving the viscera as waste), tags it, hauls it to his or her vehicle, transports the deer home, carves it up in his or her garage, freezes the meat, and spends the next few months eating the deer after cooking it up on a barbecue grill or stove.[9]

The point they wish to make with this example is that both cases involve predation, but they are very different:

> Are they both instances of "natural predation" in which animals participate in some "quintessential natural process"? We maintain that the hunter in the second scenario is participating in a cultural event called "deer hunting" that differs sharply from the lion's activities in the first scenario. At every step of the deer hunting process, the person's actions are shaped by and within a cultural context (when to hunt, what to hunt, how to hunt, what hunting instruments are appropriate, etc.). Even the decision that one should hunt cannot be separated from the hunter's cultural context; deer hunting is acceptable in some cultures and unacceptable in others. There is almost nothing about the above human hunting scenario which can be separated from culture. The basic confusion is that one commits an equivocation fallacy when one claims that human hunting is a form of natural predation. Predation involves killing and consuming a live organism as a food resource for another organism; in a strict, definitional, sense human hunting can be construed as a form of carnivorous predation. But to say that human hunting is a form of *natural predation* . . . simply makes no sense.[10]

So far, these arguments have remained at the general level of hunting as being the search for, the pursuit of, and the attempt to kill animals. It is important, though, to recognize that it is impossible to describe hunting adequately in such general terms. As Roger King has warned:

> To hunt is to perform an act, localized in time and space. Yet hunting is also at the same time a social practice embedded in a broader social and political context which constitutes its meaning, its implications for nature, and the

modes of belief which surround it. The aboriginal hunter, the ancient Assyrian king, the medieval poacher, the Victorian trophy hunter, and the modern sports hunter all kill animals. It would be mistaken to suppose, however, that they all perform the same act. The weapons used, the game pursued, the reasons and justifications which they offer, the symbolic functions which their hunting performs, the legal restrictions which apply to it, and the impact on the ecological situations in which they hunt, are all different.[11]

The warning is important and well made—hunting takes a myriad of shapes and forms and will be experienced differently and have different meanings for different people in different cultures. King adds to his point about the specificities of different hunting practices when he further suggests that there is no such person as "the hunter" in general: "The hunter is never just an anonymous cipher, but a member of a particular culture, living at a particular moment in that culture's history. The hunter brings certain technologies to bear on the hunt, together with distinct beliefs and attitudes."[12]

Although it is essential to recognize these specificities, I also wish to argue that, in terms of sports hunting, it is possible to delineate some key features that all forms of sport hunting have in common and which underpin them, features that also set hunting apart from other forms of killing animals. Before proceeding with an exploration of these features, it will be useful to consider, in brief, some of the social and cultural aspects of ways of killing animals that I will categorize as "domestic killing." Other authors in this book examine in depth and detail specific forms of such killing, but it is necessary to consider some general points about such lethal practices in order to begin to understand the relationships created between humans and animals within hunting.

Domestic Killing

In order to develop further the arguments about human hunting and killing—what I am terming "wild killing"—it is necessary to offer some observations and interpretations of other forms of killing animals. My concern here is with the deaths of those animals whose lives are closely entwined with human lives.

In the modern Western world, a range of animals are kept by humans to serve largely their purposes, and as such they form part of the social and cultural world of humans in which they live under the direct control of their owners. The greatest number will be animals kept to supply humans with meat and other bodily products.[13] Others are kept in order to be used in medical and other experimental practices. Some are kept as working animals; for example, dogs are used for a wide range of tasks such as guarding, herding other animals, guiding the blind and assisting people with other disabilities, and working with the police and the armed forces. Horses work in the racing world, for the police, in riding schools, or as a means of transport. Perhaps second only to the numbers kept for food are those kept as pets, animals whose primary purpose is to form companionable bonds with their human owners.

The deaths of almost all these animals will not be as a result of natural causes but rather are a human responsibility brought about by human decisions and actions. They will be deliberately killed because they have come to the end of what is perceived to be their useful lives; in order to undergo a further transformation into, for example, meat or scientific material; or to bring about an end to what is perceived to be their suffering. These are domesticated animals which have culturized deaths brought about by human agency in human space, and, in terms of the ways they are brought about, they should be certain and guaranteed. Just as the lives of these domesticated animals are carefully controlled, so are their deaths.

The vast majority of these deaths are brought about in ways that might be classified as either mechanical or medical. The nature of mechanical death would be epitomized by the killing of domesticated livestock—cows, sheep, pigs, and poultry—in the industrial slaughterhouse and that of medical death by the killing of experimental laboratory animals or sick pet animals by lethal injection or other forms of poisoning. In all of these cases, the animals ready for death are removed from the spaces they have occupied during their lives[14] and brought to industrial or clinical spaces where there the lethal violence inflicted on them will come from professional killing specialists for whom this forms a working practice.

There are two significant transfers or movements here as the animals approach death. They are transferred from their living space to places of death that are governed by rules, routines, repetition, and predictability related to minimizing suffering but more importantly related to efficiency and hygiene. Control is fundamental here, as are certainty and inevitability. There should be no doubt as to the outcome of the process, and there should be no challenge posed by the animal; it is essentially defenseless against what will happen to it. It is not allowed any chance to resist, to struggle, or to exercise its will and attempt to escape. These must be orderly deaths.

There is also an important transference in terms of the relationships involved between the animals and humans. In the majority of cases, those who owned and lived with these animals hand over the responsibility for their deaths to others.[15] These professionals must maintain a disciplined and distanced relationship with the animals they have to kill. There is an obvious and close bodily interaction and engagement between the slaughterer and the cow killed and the vet and the animal euthanized, but there is also a significant emotional distance; this is a detached and impersonal, non-individualized relationship. Such deaths might be represented as *cold* deaths achieved through confined, clinical, and mechanical killing.[16]

In this exploration of domestic killing, there is one category of animals that has so far not been mentioned: the killing of those creatures classified as pests or vermin. Pest/vermin is a rather indeterminate classification, and what animals are considered in this way will be differently configured in different cultures and at different times. What they all share, however, is that humans regard them as transgressive animals and often, more strongly, as enemies that provoke emotional reactions ranging from annoyance or anger to repulsion and disgust. These are animals which are intrusive into human spaces and human concerns, invading cities and towns, homes and other buildings (whether urban or rural), gardens and the fields of human cultivation where they disturb the local cultural order. Humans have a conflictive relationship with pests and vermin because they are either (and sometimes both) destructive or regarded as polluting. They are destructive when they kill and eat domestic livestock or eat crops, and they are polluting when they are simply present in places where humans think they ought not to be.

The killing of vermin and pests is usually expressed in terms of destruction, removal, eradication, extermination, annihilation, or cleansing. In their assault on these animals, humans make use of a variety of weapons, traps, poisons, and other chemicals, and they may even use other animals for this purpose, for example, cats which are kept on farms to kill mice and rats. People who suffer such intrusions may attempt to kill these animals themselves. For example, in Western societies, farmers might themselves set traps, put out poison, or shoot animals that are causing them a problem. At a domestic level, gardeners put out poison to kill slugs and other creatures which eat their plants, and people who have evidence of mice in their houses may try to catch them or poison them. Here the person does not, generally, have to have specialist skills in order to kill these and other animals, but they might not have the appropriate means or the necessary knowledge and experience for going about it, and they might even find the process disagreeable. In these cases, they will hand over the responsibility to others: there is a considerable industry in which professionals are paid to kill vermin and pests.

Unlike the domestic killings discussed above in which animals are brought into specialist places of death, here the professional killers must move to the spaces in which the animals are found and attempt to kill them there; they must be removed *from* those spaces. This process usually begins with a search for the problem animals, or at least a search for the signs of their presence, before the means for killing can be put into place in ways that minimize any attempt by the animal to evade them. These are situations of disorder in which humans attempt to reimpose an order of their choosing. In terms of the motivations and emotions (annoyance, anger, repulsion, loathing, disgust) of the people who have suffered such invasions, it is possible to consider these as *hot* deaths compared with the unemotional, clinical killing considered previously. The means of killing should be efficient and effective, but it is the actual death, in and of itself, of the animal that is wished for or desired, and there is relief and satisfaction when it is accomplished.

Wild Killing

Having considered some of the key features of domestic killing, in the rest of this chapter I will concentrate on the structures of relationships between human and animals that develop in wild killing—killing that takes place in the context of hunting as a sporting or leisure practice. It is important to have set out the features of domestic killing because I wish to use them to contrast and highlight what is unique about how humans set about hunting and killing wild animals. For example, I suggested that domestic killing involved bringing domesticated animals to human spaces to be killed; that this killing was mechanical or medical; that it was controlled, orderly, and made routine; that the death was inevitable and certain; that the killing was depersonalized and emotionally distant; and that it was, in the main, carried out by professionals for whom it was work.

In contrast, I will suggest that what is significant in hunting is that the hunter enters the spaces of wild animals in order to try to find and kill them; that the animal is uncontrolled and is naturally resistant to being brought into a relationship with the human; that the killing arrives only at the end of a contest and is far from certain; that the relationship is based on unpredictability rather than routine; that the hunter develops a personal and emotionally close relationship with the prey; and, finally, that such hunting is practiced by nonprofessionals for whom this is a leisure activity.

Defining Hunting

There is a rich anthropological literature of the hunting practices of peoples rather loosely classified as "hunters and gatherers," but little anthropological attention has been paid to the hunting of wild animals in the modern world when the practices move from the domain of necessary strategies for subsistence to that of hunting as a sport. In this movement, hunting becomes set apart from the everyday, in terms of utilitarian concerns, and enters the space of play, games, sport, and other leisure activities. It becomes subject to rules and regulations that mark it as an unnecessary activity that is engaged in for the inherent pleasure of the event itself.[17] To suggest that this is a pleasurable activity is not to suggest that it is a frivolous activity, and, as will be shown later, it is also necessary to understand hunting as a complex and serious ritual activity.

A fundamental difference between hunting for food and hunting as sport lies in the nature of the contest between the hunters and the hunted. A person hunting for food must compete with the animal's abilities to escape attention, to flee, and to remain alive in order to find and kill the animal. In this situation, the hunter does not seek out that contest for its own sake; it is simply a necessary, unavoidable and natural element in the relationship between a predator and prey. Here the hunter does all in his or her power to minimize the nature of that contest in order to obtain meat in the most efficient and effective way possible. The sports hunter, however, competes in a very different way. Here the contest is deliberately sought out and elaborated. Rules, regulations, and restrictions are imposed and willingly followed to create the challenges that are fundamental for hunting to be a sporting activity.[18] The hunter competes with himself or herself in terms of attempting to successfully exercise personal hunting skills, with the environment in which hunting takes place, and, finally, with the animal which is the focus of attention. The primary interest of the sports hunter is not that of obtaining meat nor even that of merely killing an animal. Rather, it is with an immersion into the very difficulty of bringing about an encounter with the animal and with the pleasure and satisfaction that comes from successfully overcoming these self-imposed restrictions and difficulties. There is certainly the hope and an intention to kill an animal, but how that animal is found and how it is killed is far more important than the mere fact that it is killed.[19] In his essay on hunting, Spanish philosopher José Ortega y Gasset suggests that there is a crucial distinction between the killing in utilitarian hunting and the killing in sports hunting:

> In utilitarian hunting the true aim of the hunter, that which he looks for and values, is the death of the animal. Everything that goes before is purely a means to achieve this end which is its proper objective. But in sports hunting this order of means and ends is reversed. The sportsman is not interested in the death of the animal, that is not what is proposed. What interests him is every-

thing that he has had to do to bring it about, that is, to hunt. In this way the actual end is that which was previously only a means. Death is essential because without this there is no authentic hunting: the death of the animal is its natural end and finality: that of the hunt in itself, *not* that of the hunter. The hunter endeavours to achieve this death because it is the sign which gives truth to the whole hunting process, nothing more. To summarise, one does not hunt in order to kill, but rather the reverse, one kills in order to have hunted.[20]

In one of the few anthropological analyses of sports hunting, Matt Cartmill offers a succinct definition of non-utilitarian hunting:

> Hunting in the modern world is not to be understood as a practical means of latching onto some cheap protein. It is intelligible only as symbolic behaviour, like a game or religious ceremony, and the emotions that the hunt arouses can be understood only in symbolic terms. . . . Hunting is not just a matter of going out and killing any old animal, in fact very little animal-killing qualifies as hunting. A successful hunt ends in the killing of an animal, but it must be a *special* sort of animal that is killed in a *specific* way for a *particular* reason.[21]

Of primary significance here is the "special sort" of animal which is the object of attention. This must be a wild animal rather than a domesticated species. "Wild" and "domestic" might be regarded as terms relating to a generally "Western" view of animal classification, and the idea can, perhaps, be captured cross-culturally by defining those animals which are appropriate for the hunt as animals not in the regular and immediate care of humans.[22] The further refinements that Cartmill makes to his definition are connected with the form of the infliction of death and how this form of killing in hunting is different from other animal killing. The animal must be free to escape, there must be direct physical violence, it must be premeditated, and it must be at the hunter's initiative. Ortega y Gasset suggests another defining feature of hunting that is useful to add to Cartmill's definition. His suggestion is that as hunting weapons became more effective, sports hunters had to impose a voluntary restriction on their ability to kill the hunted animal in order to give it a chance to escape and so as "not to make the hunted and the hunter excessively unequal, as if going beyond a certain limit in that relationship would annihilate the essential character of the hunt, transforming it into pure slaughter and destruction."[23]

In terms of these defining features for hunting, shooting a cow in a field would not be hunting, nor would it be to drive deer into an enclosure where they were shot. The requirement of direct physical violence means that putting out poisoned meat to kill wolves is not hunting. Premeditation in hunting requires that those hunting deliberately set out with the intention of hunting prior to any actual killing. Accordingly, a hunting event can only have occurred if the hunters set out to hunt, even if they failed to kill anything, but a person who set out to drive to town and deliberately killed a rabbit sitting in the road could not be said to have hunted that rabbit. A hunting event is created at the initiative of the hunter, and a person who, when attacked by a lion, shoots it cannot claim to have hunted that lion.[24] Finally, the hunter must voluntarily restrict his or her ability to kill the chosen animals because without such a restriction, there might be little contest and little chance to compete against the natural abilities of the animal. Shooting at polar bears from a low-flying helicopter would be premeditated and instigated by the person shooting and would involve direct violence against a free wild animal, but it would not be hunting.

In a philosophical article in which he examines arguments for and against hunting, Jordan Curnutt suggests other necessary features that should be incorporated into a definition of sport hunting:

> Sport hunting is a complex activity which combines two necessary components:
>
> 1. *Physical actions:* [a] stalking, pursuing, or otherwise seeking a wild animal and [b] killing it or at least attempting to kill it.
> 2. *Psychological states:* [a] intending, planning, desiring, hoping to kill the animal pursued and [b] enjoying, grieving, feeling satisfaction, pleasure, pride, relief, etc. in the killing or the attempt.[25]

These are important features because they point to the physical relationship, attempting to close the distance, between the hunter and the prey prior to any attempt to kill it and to the emotional engagement with the *potential* prey during the search stage of hunting and with the *actual* prey at the moment of bringing about its death.

It is impossible, within the confines of a chapter, to explore fully all of these issues, and it is certainly not my intention to attempt an all-embracing definition of hunting. All of the particular elements introduced above are fundamental for understanding the general lineaments of hunting as a cultural practice, but what I want to develop here are some further issues concerning the creation of the particular relationships of engagement and disengagement between humans and animals in events of this type. In both domestic killing and wild killing, there are a series of processes that progressively close the distance between the human and the animal to the point at which the death of the animal can be achieved. However, in contrast to domestic killing, hunting is predicated both on the difficulties and effort needed to reduce that distance in order to bring about the death of an animal and on the fact that humans attempt to achieve this within a natural space into which they move rather than a cultural space into which they bring the animal. Here humans neither directly control the animals nor the environment in which they live, and both should be allowed to offer an immediate, individual and personal challenge to those who intend to hunt. It must, furthermore, be a challenge in which the hunter can be defeated.[26] Ortega y Gasset suggests that such hunting requires

> that the hunted animal has its *chance,* that it is able, in principle, to avoid capture . . . that it possess some effective means to escape from the pursuit, because hunting is precisely the series of efforts and skills which the hunter has to exercise in order to dominate, with sufficient frequency, the counter-measures of the animal which is the object of the hunt. If these counter-measures did not exist, if the inferiority of the animal were absolute . . . [then] the special event that is hunting would not exist.[27]

Success on the part of the hunter is not a key defining feature of hunting. The animal will often escape, and the hunter may return empty-handed.

All forms of sports hunting involve humans leaving the zone of human habitation to enter the wild or cultivated countryside, the zone of animal habitation.[28] Although each form of hunting has its own unique social and cultural shape and can be distinguished by its particular hunting practices, I would like to suggest that all forms of hunting can be divided in one of two types according to the ways in which their practitioners are present in the countryside. These I will define as hunting by *disturbance* and hunting by *disguise,* and in each category the relationships between the hunters and the prey are fundamentally different. Hunting by disturbance is marked by maintaining a clear distinction between the human and the animal in terms of both physical, behavioral, and emotional distance. Here the human presence in the natural world is clearly signaled and is openly intrusive. In the case of hunting by disguise, the distinction between the human and the animal becomes blurred; the hunter attempts to become animal; the physical, behavioral, and emotional distance is closed. Here the human slips, unobtrusively, rather than openly intruding, into the countryside. A deer hunter in David Mamet's *The Village* captures perfectly the need of the hunter to be absorbed into the countryside when he comments, "You have to be like it to be part of it."[29]

Hunting events of the first kind are characterized by noise and by creating disruption and movement in the area in which it takes place in order to force animals to flee. Dogs or humans might sweep noisily through a woodland, dogs will crash through the undergrowth barking as they go, and the human beaters will shout, use whistles, and bang on trees. The intention is to flush out the potential prey from the safety of the cover offered by the landscape, to get them flying or running, so that they can become targets for the hunters. This form of hunting involves no great skill in finding the animals which are the object of the hunt, although there is great skill in devising ways of forcing them to move in the direction of the hunters, but it involves a challenge in terms of being able to shoot and kill an animal that is in motion and that suddenly appears, perhaps from an unexpected direction. In the moment of its appearance, the hunter must decide whether it is an animal that may be legally or otherwise allowably killed and whether it is acceptable to take that particular shot.[30] Each form of hunting will have its own rules about safety, requirements of making an almost certain kill, and expectations associated with when and how a fatal shot may be taken. It is only if these requirements and conditions have been fulfilled that the hunter can have the satisfaction of having killed fairly and appropriately.[31]

Although I have avoided discussing the particularities of specific hunting events, it is important to mention here that there is a set of forms of hunting that have a very different structure from those mentioned above but that, nevertheless, can be classified as hunting by disturbance. These forms of hunting are characterized by the use of packs of hounds to track their prey, either by sight or scent, and in which the hunted animal is finally killed by the hounds or by a specifically designated individual once the animal has been brought to bay. In western Europe, stag, fox, hare, and mink hunting would be key examples of such forms of hunting, as would fox hunting in the United States. Many of these are also characterized by the participation of humans as horse riders who follow the hounds but who do not directly engage, individually, in any of the processes (the finding, pursuit, or killing of the prey) of hunting itself.[32] These forms of mounted hunting involve hounds being directed by a huntsman to start searching for their potential prey in a particular area, but after that the hunt develops as a relationship between the hounds and the hunted animal. The event involves disturbance in that the humans are clearly visible in the landscape and they announce their presence with ritual calls and the use of horns; the potential prey is also made aware of a threatening presence by the baying of the hounds. Once again, the intention here is to force the animal to flee, a process that allows for the central feature of this form of hunting—the contest between the hunted animal and the hounds. In the particular case of stag and other deer hunting, a human will, finally, kill the animal with a lethal shot, but in all the other cases the animal is finally caught and killed by the hounds. This form of wild killing is an animal killing. Although it has elements of a natural animal predator–animal prey relationship, this form of hunting is an entirely cultural event created, maintained, and controlled by humans and expressive of a human engagement with the natural world.[33]

I argued above that all forms of hunting involve a movement toward the animal and an entry into the natural habitat of the animal, but those forms of hunting that can be classified as hunting by deceit require a movement of another order toward the animal. Hunting events of this kind are characterized by the human attempting to remain unobtrusive and undetected in the landscape in order to find, follow, and approach the hunted animal. This is a close, direct, and personal engagement between the human and the animal; it is not, however, an *open* engagement. Although the hunter does not in any way cease to be human, he or she must adopt many of the ways of a wild animal—a process that Ortega y Gasset intriguingly refers to as "being open to the animal" and "vacations from the human condition."[34] The hunter must disguise or camouflage the human shape and presence by means of clothes that allow him or her to blend into the environment, to become one with it, to be able to see without being seen.

Unlike the forms of hunting discussed above that depend on creating movement or flight, this form of hunting depends on stillness. Here, movement has to be disguised; the hunter must learn to walk silently, with stealth, or to sit in wait without moving at all, perhaps in a "hide." Human presence is also carried on the air and lingers on the track that the human intruder has taken. The hunter must understand how the air is moving and how to remain downwind of the quarry.[35] All of this understanding and skill based on sight, hearing, and smell is instinctual to the animal, part of its repertoire for survival, and the human must become equally adept in using such senses when hunting. The hunter must be fully alert to the animal in order not to alert the animal itself, to attempt to be absent, a nonpresence, to the eyes, ears, and noses of others in order to defeat the animal. This form of hunting depends essentially on deceit and an out-animaling of the animal.[36] The hunter needs to close the gap as silently and secretly as possible—a characteristic of other predator/prey relationships. The moment of the lethal shot is entirely human—no animal can kill at a distance—but that moment cannot arrive unless the hunter has been successful in becoming partly animal.

It was argued earlier that a defining feature of domestic killing was its orderliness and inevitability achieved—in part—through the continuous control that humans exert over the animals whose deaths are brought about in this way. In contrast, the killing brought about in hunting is disorderly and certainly not inevitable, because it is based on the lack of continuous control of wild animals by humans. The death of a wild animal in the hunt must be achieved in very different ways from those in which the death of a domestic animal is achieved. In an important sense, its death must be won from the animal rather than being simply imposed on it. The wild animal must be able to escape from desires and decisions of the hunter who seeks to kill it; it must be able to refuse to give up or surrender its life. Unlike its domestic counterpart, which is forced to remain passive as it approaches its death, the wild animal must be given the opportunity to remain an active and re-active agent. Possible and actual failure, both in terms of failing to find a suitable animal and failing to kill that animal when it is found, is essential to sports hunting. It is the only occasional success of a completed hunt, compared with the many failures when hunting, that makes that success significant and valued by the hunter. As Ortega y Gasset again comments, "The attraction of hunting is that it must always be problematic."[37]

I have described the deaths in domestic killing as cold deaths and those of vermin as hot deaths. Here I would like to suggest the term "passionate deaths" as one to describe the killing of animals in hunting. Once again, this refers to the human rather than the animal condition, to the nature of the death that is brought about by the human rather than to the animal experience of that death. The hunter commits himself or herself intensely and fully to the visceral and emotional pleasures of hunting. This is not utilitarian work but a passionate pursuit in which the animal is sacrificed to the pleasure of that passion. In domestic killing, the human creates a distance between himself or herself and both the animal and the processes of killing the animal. The professional killer is distanced personally or emotionally from the death of each individual animal, whereas a personal and emotional connectivity is a defining feature of the relationship between the hunter and hunted, and I would argue that it even obtains in that short moment when a hunter aims at a particular pheasant. At the moment of aiming and pulling the trigger, that individual bird is the hunter's bird. This connectivity is even greater when the hunter has successfully found, followed, and then killed a particular animal—a success, and a relationship, that is often marked by having a photograph taken with the dead animal or by having its head or entire body mounted as a trophy. In death, the hunted animal belongs fully to the hunter, and being recognized as ultimately and individually responsible for the death of that particular animal is a significant constitutive feature of the relationship between them.

I suggested at the beginning of this chapter that the killing of animals by humans is a fundamental aspect of the creation of the social order between them—an order characterized by the dominance of humans and the enforced control and submission of animals. The processes and practices of hunting are a culturally created challenge to this normal order of things. Wild animals are free from the constraints of an enduring and engaged life with humans—they resist humans by remaining hidden or distant, refusing to form a close relationship with them.[38] The challenge that hunters set themselves is to attempt to bring about an engagement with the wild animal, to create a relationship where none existed. It is a relationship that might last only a few moments or a few hours, but it is one that, for both humans and animals, is highly emotionally charged, although those emotions will be differently configured, experienced, and expressed. Finally, I would suggest that hunting can be interpreted as a ritual event that celebrates the wild animal and the human attempt to engage with it and one in which the animal is sacrificed as the culmination of that celebration. Perhaps of all forms of animal death dealt with in this book, this is the only form of death that is actively celebrated rather than being merely brought about.

Notes

I would like to express my thanks to friends and colleagues, particularly Bill Andrewes, John Corbin, Donna Landry, Nigel Rothfels, and Mark Woods, who have taken the time to help with comments, criticisms, and suggestions. Many thanks also to friends and colleagues in the Animal Studies Group who have suggested ways of improving and clarifying arguments. I am particularly grateful to Stephanie Schwandner-Sievers, who was always able to spy the game when I was lost in the woods.

1. Jon Abbink, "Preface: Violation and Violence as Cultural Phenomena," in Göran Aijmer and Jon Abbink, eds., *Meanings of Violence: A Cross Cultural Perspective* (Oxford and New York: Berg, 2000), xii.

2. For a view of how the debate of some of the key issues has developed over last couple of decades, see R. Loftin, "The Morality of Hunting," *Environmental Ethics* 6 (1984): 241–50; Ann Causey, "On the Morality of Hunting," *Environmental Ethics* 11 (1989): 327–43; M. Bekoff and D. Jamieson, "Sport Hunting as an Instinct: Another Evolutionary 'Just-So-Story'?," *Environmental Ethics* 13 (1991): 375–78; Roger King, "Environmental Ethics and the Case for Hunting," *Environmental Ethics* 13 (1991): 59–85; Matt Cartmill, *A View to a Death in the Morning: Hunting and Nature through History* (Cambridge: Harvard University Press, 1993); N. Hettinger, "Valuing Predation in Rolston's Environmental Ethics: Bambi Lovers versus Tree Huggers," *Environmental Ethics* 16 (1994): 3–20; T. Kerasote, *Blood Ties: Nature, Culture and the Hunt* (New York: Kodansha International, 1994); J. Posewitz, *Beyond Fair Chase: The Ethic and Tradition of Hunting* (Helena, Mont.: Falcon Publishers, Inc., 1994); J. Swan, *In Defence of Hunting* (San Francisco: HarperSanFrancisco, 1995); Jordan Curnutt, "How to Argue for and against Sport Hunting," *Journal of Social Philosophy* 27, no. 2 (1996): 65–89; B. Luke, "A Critical Analysis of Hunters' Ethics," *Environmental Ethics* 19 (1997): 25–44; F. Wood, "Against Cartmill on Hunting: Kinship with Animals and the Midcentric Fallacy," *Philosophy in the Contem-*

porary World 4 (1997): 56–60; Roger Scruton, "From a View to a Death: Culture, Nature and the Huntsman's Art," *Environmental Values* 6 (1997): 471–81; Paul Veach Moriarty and Mark Woods, "Hunting ≠ Predation," *Environmental Ethics* 18 (1997): 391–404; C. List, "Is Hunting a Right Thing?" *Environmental Ethics* 19 (1997): 405–16; C. List, "On the Moral Significance of a Hunting Ethic," *Ethics and the Environment* 3 (1998): 157–75; J. Kawall, "Is (Merely) Stalking Sentient Animals Morally Wrong?," *Journal of Applied Philosophy* 17 (2000): 195–204; and A. Gunn, "Environmental Ethics and Trophy Hunting," *Ethics and the Environment* 6 (2001): 68–95.

3. Causey, "On the Morality of Hunting," 337, 339. For an early and a later philosophical perspective on issues related to the primal myth of hunting, see José Ortega y Gasset, *La Caza y Los Toros* (Madrid: Revista de Occidente, 1968); and Scruton, "From a View to a Death," 471–81; but also R. Caras, *Death as a Way of Life* (Boston: Little Brown, 1970); and P. Shepard, *The Tender Carnivore and the Sacred Game* (Athens: University of Georgia Press, 1998).

4. See, for example, Bekoff and Jamieson, "Sport Hunting as an Instinct."

5. Tim Ingold, *The Appropriation of Nature: Essays on Human Ecology and Social Relations* (Manchester: Manchester University Press, 1986), 79.

6. Ibid., 90. It is not clear from his argument here whether Ingold would allow that an animal might engage in some form of intentional search for signs of prey. For example, it might be claimed that a lion walking across the savanna might be scanning the environment for signs of potential prey.

7. Ibid.

8. Ibid., 91.

9. Moriarty and Woods, "Hunting ≠ Predation," 399.

10. Ibid., 400.

11. King, "Environmental Ethics," 62.

12. Ibid., 70.

13. I have left out of the analysis here one case that is positioned between domestic killing and wild killing. Industrial fishing involves capturing huge numbers of wild creatures for domestic consumption. Such fishing is a mechanical "harvesting" of fish which are then not killed individually but rather allowed to die out of their natural element.

14. Exception would be animals which have lived out their lives in laboratories and are finally killed there.

15. There are, of course, exceptions—for example, the farmer who kills a rabbit, chicken, or even a pig for his or her own consumption (Dimitris Theodossopoulos offers a detailed example of this in a Greek farming community; see *Troubles with Turtles: Cultural Understandings of the Environment on a Greek Island* [Oxford and New York: Berghahn Books, 2003], chap. 6) and those who kill vermin themselves.

16. A fuller account of such killing and deaths would need a more complex analysis of the nature of the violence involved in each. The violence involved into the confinement of animals in the slaughterhouse and the sorts of tools used to kill them is of a different order from the confinement and control of animals in the laboratory or surgery and the instruments used to bring about their deaths. Attention would also have to be paid to the skills and techniques necessary for efficient and effective killing.

17. This is not to suggest that nothing is produced in this form of hunting, and many

hunted animals are converted into meat. The point here is that in most cases, the production of such meat is not a necessary form of providing essential food for the hunter.

18. This is not to suggest that hunting for food is simply a wearisome task, and the anthropological literature suggests that those who hunt for food derive considerable pleasure from the activity. I also do not wish to suggest that sports hunters do not sometimes break the rules, regulations, and restrictions that make hunting a form of sport rather than unrestricted slaughter.

19. I am excluding from this analysis the forms of hunting that might be involved in culling as part of a wildlife management strategy or the killing of wild animals (not classified as vermin) that intrude into human spaces or which attack humans. These are utilitarian killings.

20. Ortega y Gasset, *La Caza y Los Toros,* 93–94. All translations of Ortega y Gasset are mine. There is an English translation of the long hunting essay in this book that might be more accessible for some readers. See Ortega y Gasset, *Meditations on Hunting,* trans. Howard B. Wescott (Belgrade, Mont.: Wilderness Adventures Press, by arrangement with New York: Scribner, 1995).

21. Cartmill, *View to a Death,* 29, emphasis added.

22. Cartmill's definition here is that, "for the hunter's purposes, a wild animal is one that is not *docile*—that is, not friendly towards people or submissive to their authority. No other criterion of wildness counts in hunting" (*View to a Death,* 29, emphasis in the original), and "we define hunting, then, as the deliberate, direct, violent killing of unrestrained wild animals; and we define wild animals in this contest as those that shun or attack people" (30).

23. Ibid., 410.

24. See ibid., 29, for the development of his examples.

25. Curnutt, "How to Argue for and against Sport Hunting," 65.

26. Jim Posewitz, a pro-hunting writer, also suggests that "fundamental to ethical hunting is the idea of fair chase. This concept addresses the balance between the hunter and the hunted. It is a balance that allows hunters to occasionally succeed while animals generally avoid being taken." Posewitz, *Beyond Fair Chase: The Ethic and Tradition of Hunting* (Helena, Mont.: Falcon Publishers, Inc., 1994), 57.

27. Ortega y Gasset, *La Caza y Los Toros,* 46.

28. I am indebted to Nigel Rothfels and Mark Woods (personal communication) for suggesting that my point about entering the countryside or the wilderness needs a more nuanced approach. This is because a considerable amount of hunting in the United States takes place on huge enclosed ranches that are stocked with native American game species as well as exotic species specifically for the purpose of being shot by hunters. Such hunting is referred to as "canned hunting," and an analysis of such events would need to be set against the sorts of hunting I am referring to here.

29. David Mamet, *The Village* (London: Faber and Faber, 1994), 194.

30. "Allowably" here refers to the rules about the open/closed season dictating when a hunter may kill certain animals and the rules concerning the acceptable age, gender, and species of hunted animals. "Acceptable" refers to taking a shot only when the hunter is reasonably certain of killing the animal rather than a risky shot by which the animal might only be wounded.

31. A fuller exploration of these issues would need to engage with a distinction that is often made by hunters between "ethical hunters" and "slob hunters." The latter term is used to refer to those hunters who, it is claimed, take no real interest in the art and science of hunting, who are interested only in shooting and killing, and who, inappropriately, use animals as living targets.

32. Not all forms of hunting with packs of hounds involve participants on horseback. For example, in some forms of foxhunting and hare hunting in the United Kingdom, all participants are on foot, as is the case with all mink hunting.

33. For a more detailed examination of a particular form of hunting with hounds, foxhunting, see Garry Marvin, "Natural Instincts and Cultural Passions: Transformations and Performances in Foxhunting," *Performance Research* 5, no. 2 (2001): 108, 115; and Garry Marvin, "Unspeakability, Inedibility, and the Structures of Pursuit," in *Representing Animals,* ed. Nigel Rothfels (Bloomington: University of Indiana Press, 2002).

34. Ortega y Gasset, *La Caza y Los Toros,* 104. I have taken this term from the translation of Ortega y Gasset by Howard B. Wescott.

35. Nigel Rothfels (personal communication) has also pointed out to me that hunters in North America are also able to purchase substances that are applied to their skin to disguise human scent.

36. For an evocative literary description of this process, see Mamet, *The Village,* especially 191ff.

37. Ortega y Gasset, *La Caza y Los Toros,* 47.

38. In suggesting the "absolute" freedom of wild animals, I realize that I have overstated some "essential" quality of their lives. In a fuller engagement with this issue, the notion of "wildness" would need to be considered in a more complex and nuanced manner—especially with regard to contested notions of wildness. For example, how and to what extent are, say, game birds raised for shooting "wild"; how and to what extent are animals that live within national parks or other reserves "wild" animals? Wildness will be differently perceived and differently configured in different societies and in different cultural contexts. I am grateful to Chris Wilbert for suggesting some rethinking along these lines.

2 What Is Doing the Killing? Animal Attacks, Man-Eaters, and Shifting Boundaries and Flows of Human-Animal Relations

CHRIS WILBERT

Inside the Smithsonian Institution's Museum of Natural History in Washington, D.C., there is a large taxidermic specimen of a Bengal tiger some eleven feet long, shot in India in 1967, which is reputed to have been a man-eater. This tiger is presented in the act of leaping upon a victim, perhaps a person, a deliberate and theatrical ploy to give a sense of movement and power, as well as shock, to what is of course principally a very static exhibition of "the natural world."

A few hundred miles east of the Smithsonian museum is the Chicago Field Museum, where two taxidermic specimens of lions, made up from the skins of the infamous "man-eaters of Tsavo," are on display. The skins of these lions were sold to the museum in 1925 for the then considerable sum of $5,000 by Lieutenant-Colonel J. H. Patterson—the man who shot them—and through skilled taxidermy were made into a rather more subdued exhibit, compared to the Smithsonian tiger.[1]

In many ways, these public displays of killer animals are not unlike waxwork displays and dioramas of notorious murderers found in other places of entertainment, such as Madame Tussauds Chamber of Horrors. Yet there is a difference in that these tigers and lions are represented as "real" killers, though of course they are highly stylized and designed through taxidermy and its close relations with photography.[2] Indeed, early-twentieth-century practices of taxidermy and photography involved particular spatial encounters, depending for their affectivity (in terms of their ability to emotionally and physically move people) upon a perception of physical closeness of humans and animals, which eroded a sense of distance with the animals and their habitat and the hunter and "his" homelands.[3] Such animal displays

Bengal tiger exhibit at the
Smithsonian Museum of
Natural History (2004).
Photo by Caroline Bassett.

arguably show both public fascination for animals that attack people—as
monstrous creatures—and also a perceived right to kill aberrant animals, as
well as an ability to domesticate and "house" animality through scientific-
technological powers.

In this essay, I am going to give another interpretation of the theme of this
book by focusing on animals that kill or attack people and their properties.
In taking animal attacks as my focus, I am going to reflect upon a series of
examples of stories of animals attacking people and how they seem to hold
a fascination in modern societies where human-animal relations are spa-
tially produced in increasingly complex and contested ways. In examining
recent reportings of animal attacks, I want to look at some of the media
forms these reports take and ask what they might tell us about aspects of
changing human-animal relations. As such, I want partly to focus on how
the imputed powers, or agency, of animals are discussed in and around sto-

ries of animal attacks, particularly about whom or what is to blame in such attacks. Therefore, I am interested in the ways these stories point to ways that agency is less internal to an organism (as might be found in many animal rights discourses that seek to extend agency to animals) and more a relational effect of *intra-actions* between people, animals, and other phenomena.[4] The term "intra-action" is used by philosopher Karen Barad to differentiate relations from the term "interaction," a term that seems to presuppose a boundary between two well-defined but independent entities, such as nature and culture.[5] Rather than seeing that two categories of things such as nature and culture *become* mixed in particular scenarios, it is argued here that, actually, things are always mixed (are always intra-acting) and that the categories of nature and culture are outcomes and purifications of processes of ordering.[6] As such, the notion of intra-actions draws attention to the promiscuous mixings of our worlds.

Moreover, agency has, at a general analytical level in the social sciences, been seen anthropocentrically as a purely human property. Yet, dividing lines between people, animals, and machines are actually more subject to negotiation and change across (and within) time-spaces. As such, in differing ordering processes, animals or machines can be seen to gain and lose attributes, and conversely, people take on and lose attributes of machines and animals over time, across territories, and in different spatial contexts, as is illustrated in the various other essays in this book.[7]

In setting out these themes, I take a geographical approach, one that emphasizes the varied spatialities of human-animal intra-actions, while moving "between" oppositions of nature and culture, recognizing the differing ways that the material and social are entangled in all manner of promiscuous combinations involving the co-production of things and people.[8] Such an acknowledgment of the affectivity of the nonhuman (whether animals, machines, texts, and so on) noticeably comes at a time when disciplining of animal life and death seems ever more pervasive and set to intensify through genetic modification, cloning, and transgenic practices, as well as through general and expanding degradation of ecosystems.

Circulations: From Tsavo to Chicago and Back Again

Lieutenant-Colonel J. H. Patterson's account of the killing of the Tsavo lions is told in his book *The Man-Eaters of Tsavo and Other East African Adventures* of 1907. In this story, he characterizes himself as the hero coming to the rescue of railway workers being preyed upon by local lions in the East African area of Tsavo in 1898. However, as the engineer employed by the railway and the senior white official in the area, his role as hunter of man-eaters was more a responsibility he shouldered as colonial officer and the only man legitimately armed with a rifle. The two Tsavo lions killed more than twenty-eight Indian laborers who were building the Mombasa to Nairobi railway (though a much larger, noticeably undocumented, number of local Africans were also killed). The lion attacks caused work to stop for several weeks with almost all workers abandoning the site in fear of their lives. According to Patterson, workers and local people began to see the lions as "devils" rather than as animals.[9] Patterson himself appears to have begun at some point to view them as having "charmed lives"; indeed, this may be some reflection of such colonialists' inability to frame the man-eater as animal, that the man-eater threatens the distinction of "the animal," becoming diabolical, more active, calculating, in ways that suggest qualities reserved for "the human."[10] Similarly, in his study of hunting, conservation, and British imperialism in India, John MacKenzie also notes how the man-eating tiger approached the status of the werewolf of European lore, with superstitions rife among European colonialists and Indian people alike.[11]

At Tsavo in 1898, Patterson eventually prevailed over the lions, and they were shot, giving him great notoriety in Britain and Africa. The fascination with this story, or what the narrative offered to writers, filmmakers, and others, has never really abated. The Tsavo story was loosely adapted for the first commercially released 3–D movie, *Bwana Devil* (dir. A. Oboler, 1952), affording the affective ability to scare and startle audiences with scenes of lions seemingly leaping out of the screen. The film's publicity poster offered: "A Lion in your lap, a lover in your arms." More recently Patterson's story was retold in the film *The Ghost and the Darkness* (dir. S. Hopkins, 1996), which reproduced the narrative of the white military man being outmaneuvered by the lions but ultimately rescuing workers and local people.

The Chicago Field Museum, where the Tsavo lions are represented as exhibits, has begun to undertake research around them in the last few years, allegedly finding the den of the lions, which Patterson mentions in his memoirs as a terrible place littered with human bones and body jewelry. Another lion, the "Man-eater of Mfuwe"—termed "the largest man-eating lion on record"—has since been added to the museum exhibition. In recent years, the Tsavo lions have moved into another form of consumption, with the Field Museum increasingly using the man-eaters as a brand in souvenirs such as T-shirts, caps, and mugs. Plans have also been announced to set up a joint museum with Kenyan authorities in what is now the Tsavo National Park, the thinking here apparently being that the fascination with man-eaters can function as an identifiable connection between wealthy North Amer-

ican or European tourists and an underdeveloped tourist resource and wildlife service beset by financial collapse.[12] The Field Museum has also run
safari tours to Kenya in recent years to view the current lions of Tsavo.

What this outline of a story begins, at least broadly, to point toward is the
seemingly complex mixings of what conventionally would be termed social,
natural, and technological entities and how entities circulate in differing
forms and are made and remade in exchanges with other things. Even in bare
outline, it can be seen that people, myriad technologies (especially media
technologies), exhibits, images, discourses, animals, and animal parts circulate in complex ways. That is to say, there are continuous exchanges of properties between "things"—human and nonhuman—which can also be seen
to be effects of these exchanges. This focus upon mixing of the social, technological, and natural is an approach that centers more upon process than
structure and upon how worlds are made and remade out of heterogeneous
things. As such, Sarah Whatmore's argument—that complex circulations
and linkages between "bodies, instruments and artifacts means that the distinction between being present and being represented no longer exhausts,
or makes sense of, the compass of possibility of social conduct"—seems
apposite for this approach to these man-eaters.[13]

Spatialities against Modernization?

So, some questions that seemingly need to be asked are: What is happening
in and around reportings of animal attacks? What kinds of things do these
stories point to regarding people's relations with animals? These stories seem
on the face of it to often imply monstrous practices—the monstrous here
being a description of hybrid forms—and, as Derrida remarks, the notion
of the monster is rather difficult to deal with, to get a hold on, to stabilize.[14]
One thing we can say is that if the popularity of the heroic narratives of
British colonialists like J. H. Patterson and others such as Jim Corbett in
India in the mid-twentieth century are anything to go by, it would seem that
public fascination with man-eaters, or animal attacks on people, has some
vintage.[15] Indeed, such narratives can be seen to be aspects of the cult of
trophy hunting—so widespread in the late nineteenth and early to mid-
twentieth centuries. These older narratives take place on the margins of
empire and may be seen to be about subduing and controlling nature, of
seeking to order spaces and environments according to dominant Western
views—which implicitly meant spaces that could not be shared with large
carnivores. Such spatial orderings were also reproduced in many early conservation programs initiated in Africa (or indeed India) in the twentieth

century where native peoples and (less often) white hunters were forcibly excluded from what became purely animal places (though increasingly with added tourists).[16] Implied here was a pernicious view that people could not live alongside animals, despite thousands of years of contrary evidence.[17]

Processes of what can (not unproblematically), as a shorthand, be termed "modernities" have brought with them concomitant geographies, orderings, of human-nonhuman spatial interactions. Spatial aspects of modernity, though not uniform, can generally be seen to function to order social life and to assume that an identifiable thing called the "social" exists separately from nature (a process mirrored in the separation of the social and natural sciences). Yet, looking further into how orderings are produced, we can argue that classifications of any kind acquire significance only within specific material settings. As Joseph Rouse argues, "Their meaning is as much in the reconfiguration of bodies and their surroundings as in shifting patterns of talk."[18] Typically, modernist spatial ordering processes have been viewed anthropocentrically as purely the result of human intentional actions. However, examinations of particular ordering processes reveal that this is not so. Any ordering, whether an attempt to grow organic food or to develop vaccines, is materially heterogeneous, involving combinations of humans, animals, and technologies in differing places and times. All kinds of "delegates," whether machines, laws, guns, words, computer programs, people, or other fleshy beings, enable the passage of properties between human and nonhuman subjects. It is this passage of properties and not the force of words alone that holds societies, orders, together.[19]

So, as Bruno Latour argues, modernist orderings seem to have been focused on *disentangling* us from other beings, from what we conventionally know as nature, but also from technologies. Yet paradoxically we find ourselves today having become *more* entangled with other nonhuman entities partly through unintended side effects of actions reverberating throughout the whole of society, such as global climate change or mass outbreaks of avian flu or BSE in cattle.[20] In practice, the spatial orderings of modernization as ideal forms were always "leaky," incomplete, producing marginal or liminal spaces, and were impossible to effectively police, even, or perhaps especially, in cities. For example, birds—such as seagulls, magpies, pigeons, even birds of prey—have long since adopted parts of London as a home, as have foxes, mink, squirrels, and a host of other animals such as ants or cockroaches, not to mention the many plants that have opportunistically colonized the myriad spaces of the constantly disturbed ecological zones of cities.[21] As such, we need to see our environments, especially cities, as more dynamic than modernist orderings proposed.

But, added to these more fleshy examples of nonhuman movements across boundaries, we may also mention in passing the influences of the many microorganisms around us and within us, which have long passed between species and move across spatial and species taxonomies. Yvonne Baskin, writing about invasive species from a North American perspective, argues that about three-quarters of the 156 emerging infectious diseases affecting people today are "zoonoses," that is, animal-borne diseases that can transfer to people. Moreover, diseases of domestic animals also increasingly move through wild animal populations. As such, as Nigel Clark has noted, we find that in the very heartland of the social there are all kinds of noticeable "re-surgences of natures."[22]

So, it might be argued that currently there is a consciousness of the in-tractability of risk and uncertainty in modern life, that as Latour argues, we have a "heightened awareness that mastery is impossible and that control over actions is now seen as a complete modernist fiction."[23] For example, there may be a reflection that human interventions into wilder spaces, or the irruptions of animals in urban spaces, require different responses from those of the past, which emphasized exclusions. As such, differing ways of theoriz-ing and producing spatial practices of human-animal encounters are very much needed now.

Yet it might also be argued that concurrent with such risk consciousness are processes of re-modernizations, re-orderings of human-animal interac-tions in deeper, more complex, and insidious forms than ever before. This can be seen in developments of technologies such as genetic modification, cloning of animals for drug production or xeno-transplantation, and other ways where threatening and aggressive potentialities are yet to be fully seen but which seek to remodel plants and animals from the inside out to suit the dubious "needs" of agribusiness. So, what can be seen to be occurring today are complex changes in human-animal relations, changes that seem to imply much potential conflict. Inserted in these changing spatial orderings of in-teractions we find media reports of animal attacks that also draw attention to the spaces and qualities of our intra-actions with other entities.

Monstrous Practices, or Please Don't Blame the Animals?

In this section, I want to discuss some recent reports of animal attacks on people in more developed world societies. Whereas in the recent past, animal attacks on people tended on the whole to be viewed as illegitimate, as aber-rations to be punished by the death of the animal, there is something in current reports of animal attacks that appears potentially to be more ambiguous. For example, it seems that, in some cases, animal attacks may be viewed as not necessarily the fault of animals, though this does depend on the particular case and its spatial context. What can become important here is more of a questioning of why animals attack people and of whom it is that can speak as translators of these occurrences. But we also find here a sense of what these attacks then mean in wider society, which extends to what human interactions with animals could or should be.

In focusing on recent reports of animal attacks, I acknowledge there is a risk of exoticizing such animal attacks on people in viewing them from an urban-centered and privileged, developed world position. It is firmly acknowledged that many people in the world have a very different engagement with the reality or risk of animal attacks—not to say the dangers posed from potentially encephalitic water snails, malarial mosquitoes, poisonous snakes, or the many other hazards faced by the very poor, especially in their everyday environments. Moreover, it has been vigorously argued that rural people in areas of developing worlds do experience everyday dangers from animals that are protected by conservation policies such as in national parks, where for example animals become a resource for tourists mainly from wealthier, more developed regions of the world. As already mentioned, many postcolonial nations continued conservation practices from colonial models that tended to exclude local peoples from large swathes of protected land.[24] In such places there is a perception, no doubt often very real, that animal attacks on local people are viewed as less newsworthy or important than attacks on tourists, which echoes earlier accounting of victims of attacks as discussed in the Tsavo lions example. Indeed, the everyday problems of those such as the Tonga people living on the shores of Lake Kariba in Zimbabwe, where several fishers are killed each year by crocodiles, or of leopard attacks on peasant farmers in the Utteranchal region of India are not the kinds of stories of animal attacks so beloved of Western media. Rather, media of advanced postindustrial countries tend toward cultural specificity in which the subjects of stories of animal attacks follow a wider developed world bias against the poor of the developing world.

However, my point in looking at the current fascination in stories of animal attacks as they appear in mass media in developed world contexts is deliberately situated from this perspective as this is where most reports found in the research undertaken here have been posted.[25] Not having much contact with nondomestic animals may of course play a role in people's experiences here, in that it may well be something of a shock for many people to find animals sometimes *acting* in forceful and threatening ways toward people in wilder places but also in their own cities. But this sense of shock may not necessarily be a negative one. It may be one that, as Jane Bennett argues, brings about a sense of surprising encounter, an uncanny sense of being disrupted out of our everyday dispositions, though in a sense that has a certain excitement.[26]

So let us critically view some stories of animal attacks that have recently appeared in the media. In 2000, a zookeeper was tragically killed by a twenty-year-old Burmese elephant in London Zoo. An inquest held at Westminster's coroner's court in 2001 came to the verdict that this was an "accidental death," with accusations being made that more than one keeper should have been on duty at the time. Yet evidence given to the inquiry by witnesses revealed that the elephant had seemingly "deliberately" sought to kill the keeper by holding him down with her trunk and purposefully standing down on his head. Of course, in current U.K. law, an animal cannot be found guilty of intentionally killing its keeper. Rather, it is the owners and institutions and their human members whom the law seeks to blame for these kinds of "accidents." But the extensive reporting of this episode of an elephant killing a keeper, one that led to calls for zoos to end the keeping of megafauna, also betrays a certain public and media fascination for stories of animal attacks.

An example where animals *are* blamed for attacks and attributed with agency of an aberrant kind in other tourist spaces is that of wild dingoes. Research by Adrian Peace documents how dingoes on Fraser Island, Australia, were transformed from indigenous "natural" inhabitants of a "wilderness" area into "natural born killers" in popular media and conservation discourses. This resulted from an attack on a mother and her children that culminated in the death of a nine-year-old boy. These dingoes, once protected and venerated as a last colony of a "pure breed" and solitary species fearful of human contact, became increasingly demonized as a result of this attack and wider forays into tourist spaces to search for food. Instead, Peace shows how all dingoes (not just those that attacked the children) were reperceived as vengeful animals organizing in packs to invade human spaces, attack people, and steal their food and belongings.[27] As a result, the dingoes of Fraser Island were to be cajoled with high frequency sound devices or sling shots or shot in a bid to return the population to their "natural" hierarchical and solitary behavior and "proper" spaces from which they had strayed.[28] Boundaries had to be policed, reasserted, cleansed of the "criminal" behavior of these animals, and in this furor animals were anthropomorphized, attributed with humanlike aberrant qualities. In such processes of explanation and justification for actions, we see numerous transferences of powers between "the human" and "the animal." Yet this process of ordering people-wildlife spaces was not without other interpretations. Further research in 2001 also noted that a number of tourists interviewed at Fraser Island blamed the aberrant behavior of dingoes on backpackers and other tourists who fed them rather than on the animals.[29] It would seem from this that practices of reasserting exclusive boundaries of people-dingo spaces have not gone uncontested.

So we move on. In the late spring and early summer of recent years, British news media have tended to contain reports of attacks on people by seagulls. In 2002, it was reported that an eighty-year-old Welsh man died of a heart attack while being attacked by gulls. In other cases, a dog was set on by gulls and killed.[30] Many reports describe people being chased by gulls as they have sought to leave or return to their houses. Underlying these reports are concerns that "urban" gulls are not inhabiting their "proper places" and are increasingly "out of control."[31] Unsurprisingly, such episodes bring to mind the scenes of Alfred Hitchcock's film *The Birds* of 1963, in which flocks of birds systematically turn on a small group of people in a remote fishing community. Ian Buchanan has stated that nearly all commentaries on *The Birds* focus around the question, "Why do the birds attack?"—and psychoanalytic answers to this question rather narrowly see the birds as purely symbolic actors in a narrative about a mother's loss of her son to another woman.[32] But, with regard to everyday news reports of seagulls and other animals attacking people, the question, "Why do the birds attack?" is a central, though oddly often an unasked, question.

Over the past decade there have also been many, often fearful, accounts of large cats roaming the English, Scottish, and Welsh countryside (and this too has been occurring in particular places of the United States where large cats have not been seen for some decades). Along with sightings there have been claims that large cats have killed dogs and livestock; there have been no reports, as yet, of serious attacks on people (though for many "cat-watchers" the implication is that this is only a matter of time). The British Big Cat Society, formed to monitor and research such sightings, cataloged 1,077 sightings in 2002 and 2,052 sightings between January 2003 and March 2004. Yet government studies have so far dismissed evidence produced by these groups—as far as they are concerned, British big cats do not as such exist.[33] On the other hand, activists have argued that many nonnative large cats have been released by owners of exotic pets and may have "hybridized" with other released cat species.[34] Moreover, activists have recently moved beyond camera technology to using DNA samples taken from sites of farm kills to try and prove that such large killer cats do indeed exist—though as yet without success. Debate has begun in nature conservation circles as to how to react to the burgeoning evidence of big cats, with some calling for them to be left alone and others pointing to the dangers to people and livestock that such animals pose.[35] As such, it might be argued that there remains a strong possibility that at some point in the future, we may think of these emergent nonhumans as "companion species" that accompany humans in their development in a slightly extended, wilder, though no less hybrid, form, which Donna Haraway has recently discussed as a means of moving beyond her earlier notion of the "cyborg."[36]

Hollywood cinema, especially since the 1970s, has of course had a fascination for "animals attack" movies, with a theme of a vengeful nature dominating narratives. *Jaws* (dir. Steven Spielberg, 1975) was the watermark, followed by numerous copies and variations, such as *Orca* (dir. Michael Anderson, 1977), featuring an avenging whale; *Congo* (dir. Frank Marshall, 1995), featuring killer "gray gorillas"; *Anaconda* (dir. Luis Llosa, 1997), with a killer giant snake; *Lake Placid* (dir. Steve Miner, 1999), having killer crocodiles; and *Deep Blue Sea* (dir. Renny Harlin, 1999), featuring killer genetically modified sharks, to name but a few.

Unsurprisingly, it is on television that animal attack stories have recently been most visible and also controversial in the urban developed world. CBS seemingly began things with *The World's Most Dangerous Animals,* shown in the United States in January 1996 and subsequently widely syndicated and imitated. Fox Network's hybrid reality TV/popular factual entertainment series *When Animals Attack* (first shown in 1996) and *When Good Pets Go Bad* (1998) are two of the more well known and popular examples of animal attack programs that have also been widely syndicated across the world. Like much popular factual programming, these series are presenter-led. Moreover, both programs adopt a "public service" narrative tone that seemingly advises on how to negotiate risks when animals become aberrant. The visual content of such animal attack programs is camcorder, surveillance, or repackaged local news video footage of rampaging animals in a variety of spaces such as circuses or wildlife parks. Programs also include eyewitness testimonies of attacks and dramatic reconstructions of events not captured on film. For example, one story from *When Animals Attack* features an interview with a witness to an attack by a crocodile at a wildlife park with still photographs of the attack. As in reality TV crime shows where detectives make expert statements, in animal attack programs expert scientists are interviewed to explain why the animal in question attacked, but this is the case only with wild animals. Witnesses or victims are left to speculate about why they think more domesticated animals attack people.

Presenters of these programs also make authoritative statements. For ex-

ample, in *When Good Pets Go Bad*, it is people who are blamed for the behavior of rampaging animals by not training and managing them properly.
When Good Pets Go Bad 2 ends with this grave statement: "Remember, there
is no such thing as a bad animal. It is the thoughtless acts of humans that
make good pets go bad." In *When Animals Attack 4*, the presenter (Louis
Gossett Jr., an actor who appeared in *Jaws 3D* [dir. Joe Alves, 1983]) repeatedly remarks that people who are attacked by animals say they do not blame
the animals. In the *When Animals Attack* programs, we are also treated to
faux-environmentalist sermonizing about "the need to coexist" and about
how "civilization" is encroaching upon wildlife. More often we are simply
told such things as: "When we put ourselves in a wild animal's habitat we
put ourselves at risk."[37] In such authoritative statements, we get a sense not
of wider contexts and causes of ecological degradation but rather a sense
that humans and wildlife should live in different spaces, a view that has for
too long been prevalent in conservation and wider society.

Yet, the focusing of blame in such television programs away from the
animals that attack people is interesting. For example, on the one hand, it
may seem as if animals are being seen as powerful, active beings that are
often at the brunt of capitalist economic developments, suburban sprawl,
cruelty, and so on, implying a need for change of some kind. However, on
the other hand, imputations of powers to animals may be much more limited, with animals viewed in behaviorist ways that imply that animals were
only doing what they were programmed to do. In the latter case, agency
seemingly remains tied to people, and animals are viewed as more or less
childlike, requiring better help and care from people or conservation organizations.

As with reality TV, generally these animal attack programs are low-cost
productions that are economically attractive to cable and television networks
in times of heightened competitiveness between broadcasters, fragmenting
audiences, deregulation, and internationalization of markets.[38] New portable
digital-video technologies have also been inserted within these economic
processes that afford further transformations in program styles, content, and
costs. Moreover, animal attack programs have also proved very popular with
viewers, though like much reality TV they have drawn extensive criticism
from commentators in the United States for being in bad taste. Yet, the *When
Animals Attack* programs that I have seen do not involve anyone actually
being killed. Instead, such programs may be better viewed as survivor stories
rendered as spectacle.

Natural history television programs have also recently been switching over
to presenter-led programs with emotional story lines that focus on large

predators, as well as dramatic human-animal encounters, in what Simon Cottle has termed changing "production ecologies of natural history programmes." Here again, programs on "man-eaters" and large predators attacking prey abound, a contemporary favorite being sharks—with, for example, *Maneaters: Sharks* and *Killers in the Water* (amongst others) by Tigress Productions or *Ultimate Killers* by the BBC Natural History Unit. Again, natural history programming has undergone changes in recent years, partly due to increased competition in the field of global natural history television production, falling commissions for older style "blue chip" wildlife programming, and pressure to reduce costs of production. But there have also been falling audiences and critical dissatisfaction with older production styles focusing on pristine habitats and more of a focus on human-animal encounters, as well as new possibilities opened by new digital-video technologies. Such processes have meant that there are increasing similarities between many recent natural history programs' content or form and programs such as *When Animals Attack*. By this I am not saying that the success of the latter programs have led to a reformulation of genres of natural history television but that such natural history programs increasingly draw on dramatic devices and narratives of soap operas or reality crime TV.[39]

Such popular stories and video-footage programs of animal attacks can of course simply be ignored, dismissed as morally unpalatable "snuff movies," or as irrational reactions to societies obsessed by minimizing risk. Yet I think more can be made of this long-term fascination for stories of animal attacks on people. As Val Plumwood argues, there is also a deep-seated unease about animal attacks as they threaten anthropocentric views of the world and mastery narratives that position a "nature" as external and as object to be manipulated. Plumwood, in telling her story of being attacked by a crocodile in the Kakadu National Park of Australia's Northern Territories in 1985, points to some directions for understanding aspects of the fascination of animal attacks. On this she is worth quoting at length:

> It seems to me that in the human supremacist culture of the West there is a strong effort to deny that we humans are also animals positioned in the food chain. This denial that we ourselves are food for others is reflected in many aspects of our death and burial practices of the strong coffin, conventionally buried well below the level of soil fauna activity, and the slab over the grave to prevent any other thing from digging us up, keeps the Western human body from becoming food for other species. Horror movies and stories also reflect this deep-seated dread of becoming food for other forms of life: Horror is the wormy corpse, vampires sucking blood, and alien monsters eating humans. Horror and outrage usually greet stories of other species eating humans.

This concept of human identity positions humans outside and above the food chain, not as part of the feast in a chain of reciprocity but as external manipulators and masters of it: Animals can be our food, but we can never be their food. The outrage we experience at the idea of a human being eaten is certainly not what we experience at the idea of animals as food. The idea of human prey threatens the dualistic vision of human mastery in which we humans manipulate nature from outside, as predators but never prey.[40]

This sense of humans as potential prey for animals thus has the possibility of shocking us into seeing that we are part of nature, as fleshy, meaty bodies that other bodies may sometimes view much as they do other bodies of prey in their environments. Plumwood also argues that this possibility of becoming prey is a haunting, a dread, that is played out within cultural forms such as horror films and stories. Reflecting upon her near-death encounter, she calls for a need to reconnect, to see ourselves as part of nature, rather than always scrambling to be outside, manipulating, and seeking to master that which we call nature. Furthermore, she bears no bad will toward the crocodile, no sense that it should be killed. Moreover, she fervently hopes that it does not take a similar near-death experience to instruct us all about our own ecological vulnerability.

Plumwood also writes of her reticence to face the media that quickly heard of her story and sought interviews. For, although there is substantial media fascination with attacks by large animals, she criticizes the stereotyping and sensationalizing of mass-media reports of such attacks. She objects to what she sees as the ways the media sexualizes the struggle, how the size of the crocodile is exaggerated. But I would also argue that Plumwood objects to what Ariella Azoulay terms the desire to have the survivor transform the "being there" into spectacle (a process that, as I have mentioned, is a feature of "animal attacks" television programs).[41] However, rather than viewing this interpretation of media accounts as an opposition between bodies and their representation, with the latter seeming to imply a "loss of body to spectacle," we could argue that Plumwood draws our attention to what Mark Seltzer terms "less an opposition between bodies and representations than their radical involution," that is, a "basic entanglement of bodily processes and technologies of reproduction and visualization, reproduction and mimesis, which is not simply reducible to, or contained by, the order of representation."[42]

As such, in saying all these things about possible reconciliations with "nature" that she felt after this attack (and despite what I would argue can be made from her reflections through Mark Seltzer's work above), Val Plumwood still appears, in this narrative, to hold to an ontological position that is problematic. Yes, we can agree, people are part of nature, but so too are these "natures" caught up in social, technological realms at the same time. That is, when she says we are part of nature, this is only a first stage of how we rethink our worlds. Nevertheless, Plumwood seems also to be onto something: that animal attacks have wider meanings, wider affects, wider possibilities of being thought about and of opening up other possibilities of engagement between people and animals.

The Welcoming of the Wild?

In summary, what is being worked through here is what appears to be a long-running fascination in more developed worlds with animal attacks on people, especially in the form of the man-eater, but also in the kinds of cases of attacks and media stories illustrated above. In recent times, there appear to be emerging contradictory and contested ways in which animal attacks are being viewed. On the one hand, we are experiencing changing ethical and practical views about human-nonhuman intra-actions that are moving from a concentration upon what can be termed domination to a more complex view.[43] This more complex view shows that in many situations, the animals are not necessarily blamed for such attacks. Rather, many attacks are seen as the fault of people, as both Plumwood and the *When Animals Attack* television programs argue, though with different implications as to what this means. Though fear may be one response of (some) people coming into contact with animals in the spaces in which they live or in stories they read about or see on television, we can find other modes of being: an urge for experiential encounters with animals, though not of course in the sense of actually being harmed. This seeking of encounters of "wildness" or "otherness" can arguably be found in the increasing popularity of such practices as trekking in wilder lands, visiting wildlife parks and zoos, and safari and (some) hunting tourism. Such encounters with a sense of the wild may also be found in kinesthetic practices such as forms of adventure tourism, whale- and dolphin-watching, bird-watching, wildlife gardening, and a multitude of differing commercialized practices of the tourism and leisure industries.[44]

Yet, the commercialization of many such encounters with wild animals inevitably leads to demands for more rigorous policing of these encounters as tourist companies obviously do not seek to endanger people. More problematically, many tour companies *guarantee* the experience of viewing the animals that they are selling to tourists. Such commercialized concerns, and unrealistic views of the powers of animals, can lead to very domesticated and highly managed forms of supposed "wildness" and of tourist encounters with animals that may be leading to detrimental changes in animal behavior.[45] As such, we can see that wildness is not "outside the compass of human society," as some place where people are not to be found. Rather, animals, plants, people, or landscapes designated as wild continue to be "routinely caught up within multiple networks of human social life" in complex ways, being found in and through cities, homes, gardens, food, natural history museums, and television as well as in more distant, less peopled spaces.[46]

But of course, views are still extant that animals perceived as "dangerous," or as potential pests, should be excluded from spaces used by people, a move that can be seen in Florida regarding alligators or in urban areas of Britain regarding seagulls, among many other examples.[47] Such "peopled" spaces have been extended immeasurably in recent years through suburban developments, agricultural extension, and the many leisure practices mentioned above. Moreover, this fear of, and aversion to, what has become designated as "pests" can be seen in the ways many ecological restoration policies seeking reintroductions of wolves, beavers, and other animals to particular environments have often been highly contested by certain interests, particularly landowners and farmers.[48]

So in a sense, stories of animal attacks are used, appropriated, and contested in a variety of ways. As mentioned, groups or individuals may seek to use them in terms of calling for better management of animals and more effective spatial distinctions between people and animals, as the earlier case of dingoes in Australia shows. But there are also other senses of the appropriation of such events and stories of animal attacks. One, which I have discussed elsewhere, is in the way some eco-anarchist political groups have sought to politicize animal attacks in particular ways, arguing that such attacks work as a kind of return of the repressed, where certain animal attacks against hunters, or state and corporate institutions, are rather humorously celebrated as forms of "defence and resistance."[49]

Little attempt has, however, genuinely been made to try and understand animal attacks from the viewpoints of animals (though oddly the *When Animals Attack* television programs mentioned earlier might be seen to inadequately attempt this). One recent exception is the work by Andrea Gullo, Unna Lassiter, and Jennifer Wolch in which they point to possible approaches to tackle the increasing encounters between cougars and people around suburban developments in California, which often lead to the death of cougars but also to occasional injuries to people. As in the case of dingoes mentioned earlier, cougar sightings and the very rare attacks by them that do occur have led to an increasing demonization of these animals. But Gullo, Lassiter, and Wolch seek, rather experimentally, to try to think how cougars may be viewing people who increasingly encroach upon their territories. They advocate interventions in the city or suburbs that help to encourage people to learn to live with cougars and to modify their behavior so as not to attract them to rubbish or their domestic pets. Moreover, by arguing that cougars are adaptive animals, having agency and "culture," Gullo and her colleagues argue for the need to *educate* cougars to keep their distance from people. Such work begins to point to ways of rethinking spatial possibilities of the urban in directions that Wolch has termed the "zoöpolis," in terms of cities/suburbs that are designed for people *and* at least *some* wild animals (though limiting urban sprawl and suburban development must also be a central aspect of any accommodation between people and large mammals).[50]

Finally, as I have argued, in a variety of academic disciplines in recent years there have been growing moves toward treating the nonhuman realm of machines, buildings, animals, microbes, winds, currents, and "things" as potential actors, as affective entities in constant relational intra-actions with other entities, including, of course, different peoples. This sense of moving to see how nonhumans are active in the making of our worlds is a widespread change, though a nonlinear one, from more human-centered accounts of agency and practice. Such a change toward viewing the affectivity of the nonhuman is a recognition that people are not the sole creators of our worlds; that the social is never *just* the social but is always "shot through" (perhaps a rather unfortunate metaphor in terms of this book) with what we conventionally term nature, technologies, nonhumans, animals, and other *things*.

Yet this move to recognize a more affective world also finds many animals in danger of extinction and facing massively decreasing wild habitats, processes of what could be called (perhaps too simplistically) domination. So, we might ask, is it an accident that we see a renewed imputation of powers to nonhumans at a time when environments are more highly and vigorously managed, converted into capitalist-focused production regimes through agricultural interventions and the possibilities of genetic modification? Perhaps it is. But it does start to suggest that there is a move toward accepting that we live in complex worlds with other beings, worlds that could be remade to more resolutely include animals *with* people, not in some romantic sense, but realistically, knowing that this carries risks. The fascination for reporting and reading of animal attacks, rather than necessarily being a reflection of fears of the other, of the monstrous, should draw our attention to existing conflicts and potential opportunities of how encounters can be remade between people, and between people and animals.

Notes

1. See the Chicago Field Museum Web site: http://www.fieldmuseum.org.

2. The stuffed animals in these cases, in natural history museums, can be seen to be directly connected to the "real thing," whereas the waxwork dioramas of Jack the Ripper and other murderers in Madame Tussauds merely have the appearance of "the real." I thank Rikke Hansen for this point.

3. James Ryan, "'Hunting with the Camera': Photography, Wildlife and Colonialism in Africa," in *Animal Spaces, Beastly Places: New Geographies of Human-Animal Interactions,* ed. Chris Philo and Chris Wilbert (London and New York: Routledge, 2000), 203–21.

4. See Karen Barad, "Meeting the Universe Halfway: Realism and Social Constructivism without Contradiction," in *Feminism, Science, and the Philosophy of Science,* ed. Lynn Nelson and Jack Nelson (Dordrecht: D. Reidel, 1996), 161–94. See also Joseph Rouse, "Vampires: Social Constructivism, Realism, and Other Philosophical Undead," *History and Theory* 41 (2002): 60–78.

5. The term "hybridity," which is also popular in technoscience studies, also has the problem of implying two static entities coming together.

6. On purifications, see Bruno Latour, *We Have Never Been Modern* (Hemel Hempstead: Harvester Wheatsheaf, 1993), 10–11.

7. See John Law, "Notes on the Theory of the Actor-Network: Ordering, Strategy, and Heterogeneity," *Systems Practice* 5 (1992): 379–93.

8. Sarah Whatmore, *Hybrid Geographies: Natures Cultures Spaces* (London: Sage, 2002), 4.

9. J. H. Patterson, *The Man-Eaters of Tsavo and Other East African Adventures* (London: Macmillan, 1907); see also http://www.lionlmb.org/gandd.html for a summary of the Tsavo man-eaters story of 1898.

10. This point is also made in a more current context by Elizabeth Marshall-Thomas, *The Tribe of Tiger* (London: Weidenfield and Nicholson, 1994).

11. John M. MacKenzie, *The Empire of Nature: Hunting, Conservation and British Imperialism* (Manchester: Manchester University Press, 1988), 180.

12. Financial collapse of the wildlife service has been aided by decreasing tourist numbers due to the security situation in Kenya. But it is also due to debt and International Monetary Fund–inspired austerity and liberalization programs forcing government spending to be cut severely. Finally, there has been a long-running battle over policies and control of the Kenya Conservation Service regarding the role and place of local people.

13. Sarah Whatmore, "Hybrid Geographies: Rethinking the Human in Human Geography," in *Human Geography Today,* ed. Doreen Massey et al. (Cambridge: Polity Press, 1999), 30.

14. J. Derrida, E. Weber, and P. Kamuf, *Points—Interviews 1974–1994* (Stanford: Stanford University Press 1995), 385–87.

15. Corbett's stories of hunting man-eating tigers in the 1930s and 1940s were published by America's Book of the Month Club, with over a million books in English being sold by 1957 and translations into eighteen other languages. See Jim Corbett, *Man-Eaters of Kumaon* (New Delhi: Oxford University Press, 2001).

16. See the introduction to W. M. Adams, ed., *Decolonising Nature: Strategies for Conservation in a Postcolonial Era* (London: Earthscan, 2003). Greg Mitman, *Reel Nature* (Cambridge: Harvard University Press, 1999), 187ff., briefly documents some post-1945 conservationist views of Africa as being focused on the removal of all humans—white hunters and native peoples—from contact with wildlife. The World Parks Conference held in Durban, in South Africa, on the future of protected areas sponsored by the International Union for Conservation of Nature in September 2003 saw many representatives of indigenous peoples demanding access to national park lands they had been forcibly removed from.

17. See Marshall-Thomas, *The Tribe of Tiger,* part 2.

18. Rouse, "Vampires," 76.

19. Bruce Braun and Lisa Disch, "Radical Democracy's 'Modern Constitution,'" *Society and Space* 20 (2002): 507.

20. Bruno Latour, "Is Re-modernization Occurring—and If So, How to Prove It?" *Theory, Culture and Society* 20, no. 2 (2003): 35–48.

21. See R. S. R. Fitter, *London's Natural History* (London: Collins New Naturalist Series, 1945).

22. Yvonne Baskin, *A Plague of Rats and Rubbervines: The Growing Threat of Species Invasions* (Washington, D.C.: Island Press, 2002), 69; Nigel Clark, "Botanizing on the Asphalt? The Complex Life of Cosmopolitan Bodies," *Body and Society* 6, nos. 3–4 (2002): 12–33, 28.

23. Latour, "Is Re-modernization Occurring?," 36.

24. Adams, *Decolonising Nature;* John Knight, ed., *Natural Enemies: People—Wildlife Conflicts in an Anthropological Perspective* (London: Routledge, 2001).

25. Animal attack stories are extensively reported in the Indian press, though again it seems tourist attacks are more newsworthy than those on local people. The *Protective Areas Update,* a bimonthly digest of Indian newspaper stories produced by KALPAVRIKSH, often includes animal attack stories on tourists in national parks.

26. Jane Bennett, *The Enchantment of Modern Life: Attachments, Crossings, and Ethics* (New Jersey: Princeton University Press, 2001), 5.

27. Adrian Peace, "The Cull of the Wild: Dingoes, Development and Death in an Australian Tourist Location," *Anthropology Today* 18, no. 5 (2002): 18.

28. Ibid., 19.

29. G. L. Burns and P. Howard, "When Wildlife Tourism Goes Wrong: A Case Study of Stakeholder and Management Issues Regarding Dingoes on Fraser Island, Australia," *Tourism Management* 24 (2003): 699–712.

30. "The Return of the Seagulls," *BBC News On-line,* July 5, 2002; "Seagull Savagery Blamed on Breeding," *BBC News On-line,* July 12, 2001, http://news.bbc.co.uk/1/hi/uk/1435360.stm.

31. Laura Barton, "Gull Trouble," *The Guardian,* June 30, 2004, sec. 2; Peter Rock, "Birds of a Feather Flock Together," *Environmental Health Journal* (May 2003): 132–35.

32. Ian Buchanan, "Schizoanalysis and Hitchcock: Deleuze and the Birds," *Strategies* 15, no. 1 (2002): 110.

33. See "Big Cat Evidence Gets Stronger as Society Calls for Government Study," Brit-

ish Big Cat Society press release, April 20, 2004, http://www.100megsfree4.com/farshores/engcat.htm.

34. E-mail discussion groups interested in big cat sightings seem to be obsessed with cross-breeding between large cats, seemingly because of this basic argument they put forward.

35. See Peter Taylor, "Big Cats in Britain: Restoration Ecology or Imaginations Run Wild?" *Ecos* 23, nos. 3–4 (2002): 56–64.

36. Donna Haraway, *The Companion Species Manifesto: Dogs, People and Significant Others* (Chicago: Prickly Paradigm Press, 2003).

37. *When Animals Attack 4*, Fox Network 1999.

38. Simon Cottle, "Producing Nature(s): On the Changing Production Ecology of Natural History TV," *Media, Culture and Society* 26, no. 1 (2004): 82.

39. Ibid., 95.

40. Val Plumwood, "Being Prey," *Utne Reader*, July/August 2000.

41. See Ariella Azoulay, *Death's Showcase: The Power of the Image in Contemporary Democracy*, trans. R. Daniels (Cambridge: MIT Press, 2001), 78.

42. Mark Seltzer, "Serial Killers (II): The Pathological Public Sphere," *Critical Inquiry* 22 (Autumn 1995): 130.

43. To say nineteenth-century views toward wild animals were wholly based on a notion of domination, even toward those that attacked people, is of course too simple. European hunters and colonial officials had a considerable fascination for animals that were reputedly man-eaters, and it could be argued that certain rituals grew up among them, including the need for these animals to be killed by skilled white hunters.

44. Nigel Thrift, "Still Life in Nearly Present Time: The Object of Nature," *Body and Society* 6, nos. 3–4 (2000): 49–50. Thrift sees such activities as an aspect of an emergent "experiential economy."

45. Anil Ananthaswamy, "Massive Growth of Ecotourism Worries Biologists," *New Scientist*, March 4, 2004, http://www.newscientist.com/news/news.jsp?id=ns99994733.

46. See Whatmore, *Hybrid Geographies*, 9.

47. The Florida Fish and Wildlife Conservation Commission annually deals with 15,000 "nuisance" complaints about alligators turning up in back gardens and swimming pools or being otherwise "out of place." See http://www.wildflorida.org/gators/default.htm (accessed June 5, 2004).

48. See, for example, Alec Brownlow, "A Wolf in the Garden: Ideology and Change in the Adirondack Landscape," in Philo and Wilbert, *Animal Spaces, Beastly Places*, 141–58.

49. See Chris Wilbert, "Anti-This-Against-That: Resistances along a Human-Nonhuman Axis," in *Entanglements of Power*, ed. Joanne P. Sharp et al. (London and New York: Routledge, 2000), 238–55.

50. Andrea Gullo, Unna Lassiter, and Jennifer Wolch, "The Cougar's Tale," and Jennifer Wolch, "Zoöpolis," in *Animal Geographies: Place, Politics, and Identity in the Nature-Culture Borderlands*, ed. Jennifer Wolch and Jody Emel (London: Verso), 139–61, 119–38.

3 Pangs Watched in Perpetuity: Sir Edwin Landseer's Pictures of Dying Deer and the Ethos of Victorian Sportsmanship

DIANA DONALD

Human attitudes to animals are, in every age, characterized by strange inconsistencies. The purposes and emotions involved in their killing are no less contradictory. At one extreme is the assumption that animals are merely expendable commodities, routinely killed for meat or in the course of scientific experiments. At the other extreme are the violent passions involved in blood sports. Those passions have ensured the continuance of hunting from ancient times down to the twenty-first century, as practices once devised to obtain food and furs or to exterminate "vermin" and dangerous predators have become increasingly ritualized and gratuitous.

The "sporting instinct" itself is, however, a strange compound of conflicting emotions. "Blood lust" and the joy of the hunt coexist with love and veneration for the hunted animal. Many writers have, indeed, discerned a connection between hunting and erotic urges: the pursuit, conquest, and possession of the desired animal equates to that of a woman.[1] It is certainly true, as this essay will show, that the imagery of the hunt is strongly sexualized. However, sexuality may be expressed in complex and various ways. Sportsmen often attach superior value to a male quarry and to the specifically masculine trophies of horns and antlers and often lay an embargo on killing females, an inhibition which is embedded in the "sporting code" of Western cultures.[2] At a deeper level, the parallel between hunting and rape fails to comprehend the agonized sympathy, even self-identification, with the sufferings of the prey that many hunters experience. Such intense feelings are not confined to earlier and more superstitious times. As recently as 1999, Roger Scruton, a latter-day apologist for hunting, wrote in quasi-mystical terms about the thrilling sense of release and catharsis it engenders. It supposedly connects the rider with the ancient rhythms of nature, the "dance of death and regeneration." Nevertheless, "there is scarcely a mounted follower who is glad of the death or unmoved to sympathy with the creature whose arduous course he has himself so arduously followed."[3]

Now that attitudes to hunting tend to be polarized along political lines, such effusions are easy to dismiss as a disingenuous defense of the indefensible. According to opponents, Scruton and his kind seek to embed in nature what is, in truth, a perverse, artificially contrived, and above all blatantly cruel practice. In fact, opposition to hunting can be traced back through the centuries, and many of the arguments of those who attack it in the twenty-first century were anticipated by writers of earlier times. In 1713 the poet and essayist Alexander Pope, writing in the *Guardian,* anathematized the "Sanguinary Sports" of his contemporaries. Only the force of custom, together with the group dynamic and excitement of the chase, could, he thought, explain their lack of compassion for the "helpless, trembling and weeping" stag at bay. Some people believed that hunting was merely a "remain of the Gothic barbarity," but Pope correctly discerned the pertinacity of the custom among the dominant and privileged groups in British society.[4]

During the eighteenth and nineteenth centuries, hunting and shooting, so far from retreating to the backwoods, actually developed in parallel with technological advances like selective breeding of horses and dogs, land management, the improved accuracy of firearms, and so on. Love of hunting should therefore be viewed, not as an instance of atavism, but as a problematic accompaniment to the development of the modern industrial world. Indeed, the aggressive competitiveness of nineteenth-century capitalism was often compared with the "manly" contest of wits and strength that blood sports entailed. Hunting was also, both in theory and practice, very closely associated with the expansion of the British empire: the penetration of virgin habitats and the subjugation of "inferior races."[5] The "survival of the fittest," which was increasingly understood as the basic law of nature, appeared to legitimate the violence of the human animal toward other species. Thus Sir Charles Lyell, in his epochal *Principles of Geology,* published in the 1830s, asserted that "if we wield the sword of extermination as we advance, we have no reason to repine at the havoc committed, nor to fancy, with the Scotch poet, that 'we violate the social union of nature;' or complain, with the melancholy Jaques, that we 'Are mere usurpers, tyrants, and what's worse, / To fight the animals and to kill them up / In their assign'd and native dwelling-place.'" Every advancing species must "maintain its ground by a successful struggle against the encroachments" of other kinds of animals, and hunting was just one expression of this urge to conquer the earth by force.[6]

Yet Lyell's poetic quotations resist his argument. Robert Burns, in *To a Mouse* of 1785, and Shakespeare, in the pathetic description of a stricken deer in *As You Like It* (act 2, scene 1), had both deplored the injustice of man's forcible dominion over other species. Even as he defends hunting as part of the system of nature, red in tooth and claw, Lyell is conscious of the anguished sympathy for oppressed animals to be found in imaginative literature through the centuries. The educated upper-class men who went hunting and shooting in the Victorian age were likewise familiar with this tradition, so that even books for sportsmen were full of allusions to descriptions of the cruelties of the chase in the works of Thomson, Cowper, and Wordsworth.[7] The hunting man could think of himself as a natural predator, obedient, like animal carnivores, to his killer instincts. But he could also stand outside his own actions and view them in a tragic light as part of what Lyell called the "incessant vicissitudes" in the history of nature: vicissitudes that doomed man himself to constant struggle, reversals of fortune, and eventual extinction.[8]

The imagery of the hunt in the Victorian era is full of such conflicts and paradoxes. It ranges from epic paintings of hunted stags by Richard Ansdell and Edwin Landseer to the cheery pictures and colored prints of foxhunts by artists such as Henry Alken and John Ferneley. Images of stags being run down by the hounds, or of game birds snatched by spaniels, are also ubiquitous in the decorative arts of the period, complementing the antler and horn trophies and skins and stuffed heads of animals that filled the houses of the wealthy and landed classes.[9] This essay therefore deals with two closely related themes: first, the divided emotions of the sportsman and the elaborate codes of behavior through which his mentality was expressed; and second, the central role of visual images in sustaining the "hunting myth" or in exposing its frailties.

A convincing and accurate description of events was the first requirement that patrons imposed on the "sporting artists" they employed. However, the representation of a hunt can never bear a direct relationship to the experience it commemorates: it embodies a *concept* rather than a record of the chase. There is often a process of idealization, which allows the buyer of the picture to contemplate it as a perfect wish-fulfillment. It is in the nature of a static image, moreover, that happenings which occur rapidly and chaotically in the field are distilled and frozen before our eyes. It is then impossible not to confront the fact of the kill. John Ruskin, a vehement opponent of blood sports, was disgusted that "magnificent art-power" should be degraded by "giving semblance of perpetuity to those bodily pangs which Nature has mercifully ordained to be transient . . . forcing us . . . to dwell on that from which eyes of merciful men should instinctively turn away." Worse, the "fascination of its stormy skill" might create joy rather than horror in the viewer. As Jonathan Burt has also demonstrated in the context of film, *visual* representation of the suffering and death of animals has a unique potency, which words could never attain.[10] But it is also uniquely capable of ambivalence. In these dramatic tableaux, the hunted animal might appear heroic or seductively desirable, but its plight might simultaneously prompt outrage or passionate sympathy. Many of the pictures in question were exhibited, engraved in numerous formats, and later acquired by art galleries and museums, which opened them to a great diversity of interpretations. The public's response to them, as contemporary accounts reveal, was troubled and contradictory. Often dismissed nowadays as merely sensational or sentimental, they are in fact fascinating historical documents that allow us to explore the psychological complexities of the hunt and the stratagems through which it was legitimated.

This was the era when wealthy industrialists as well as landed aristocrats could enjoy the pleasures of field sports through the renting of Scottish Highland estates, streaming northward by steamship or the new railway network. The areas where they shot red deer, grouse, or ptarmigan had once been farmed by crofters. The Highland clearances, and the subsequent reversion of the land to a "wild" state as sporting reserves, proved extremely profitable to the landowners.[11]

However, the commercial framework of field sports and the extensive modern apparatus of rifles, telescopes, protective clothing, and the like required by these hunting tourists played no part in the imagery through which Highland sports were popularized. Indeed, the "hunting myth" embodied in the paintings of Ansdell and Landseer represented a *denial* of the artificial means through which sportsmen gained their ends. Macpherson's *Ossian* and the novels and poems of Sir Walter Scott had evoked the romance of feudal society in medieval Scotland. This "primitive" aura was sustained by best-selling works like William Scrope's *The Art of Deer-Stalking,* first published in 1838 and illustrated by Landseer and his brothers, which glamorized the daring and skillful pursuit of stags across wild country and in wild weather. Scrope emphasized both the magnificence of the supposedly untouched mountain terrain inhabited by the deer and the arduousness and difficulty of creeping up on them unseen. Only when the stag was in clear view should it be shot; and those that did not die immediately were "brought to bay" by the dogs before being dispatched by the sportsman.

Scrope conjured up an ideal of sport, in which the prowess of the lone hunter was matched by the "courage," "sagacity," alertness, strength, and speed of the deer. The deer were allegedly given a sporting chance of escape, a leveling of the odds between the hunter and the hunted. Thus the illusion of an exciting, elemental battle "in nature" was maintained. It fostered a sense of adventure lacking in the tame, over-conventionalized foxhunting of the English shires, which Scrope dismissed as a pacing "over geometrical enclosures in pursuit of pigmy game." In reality, however, the weighting of advantage conferred by the gun could not be denied. In fact, the stalker's sense of unbounded freedom and the exhilaration of the kill arose from consciousness of human mastery over other species. "See what a boundless field of action is here, and what a sense of power these rifles give you, which are fatal at such an immense distance?"[12]

Richard Ansdell, who had a large clientele among the moneyed sportsmen of Lancashire, painted many life-size scenes of such triumphs; *Stag at Bay* was shown at the Royal Academy exhibition of 1846.[13] The wounded and exhausted animal has finally been cornered by the hounds, and the stalker now appears from behind a rock to administer the coup de grâce. A reviewer in the *Art-Union* admired the artist's "accurately drawn" depiction of the scene, especially the "extraordinary vivacity and spirit" of the dogs and the "great power and truth" of the stag.[14] The proximity of the man and the animals to each other and to the spectator gives the latter the illusion of being a privileged witness to this climactic episode, which Ansdell visual-

Richard Ansdell, *Stag at Bay* (1846), oil on canvas. National Museums Liverpool (Walker Art Gallery).

izes with the greatest possible realism. He imagines the split second when
the rifle goes off and the stag rears up under the impact of the shot, the
flowing diagonals of his body echoing the harsh forms of the rocks and
contrasting with the pent-up, concentrated form of the hunter. The struggle
of "natural" enemies, the stag and the dogs, yields to the greater power of
the human will and human intelligence in a raw image of man's now absolute dominion over nature.

Edwin Landseer's *The Stag at Bay* was shown at the same exhibition in
1846, and the coincidence of date and subject indicates the huge popularity
of such scenes of Scottish field sports, which Landseer himself had initiated.[15]
The public must have made direct comparisons between the two pictures. In
Landseer's, the sensation of immediacy is even more forceful. The stricken
stag has "gone to soil": that is, he has plunged into the loch in a vain attempt
to escape the dogs. In the ensuing courageous struggle, he has fatally gored
one of them and threatens the other. In contrast to Ansdell's rather literal and
brutal depiction of the stalker taking aim, Landseer's hunter is invisible. So
far from implying emotional distance, however, this device puts the *spectator*
in the place of the hunter, with his telescope and gun trained on the stag.
Indeed, Landseer produced a series of drawings of deer, *The Forest,* in which
some of the designs are circular, in direct reference to this kind of predatory
telescopic scrutiny.[16] We are brought so close to the animals' combat that the
deer's body looms up in the foreground and fills the picture space, and the
bodies of the dogs are actually cut off at the bottom edge of the design, as
though just beyond the zone of optical focus. The low horizon puts us literally on the level of the animals, augmenting the sense of intimate engagement
with their passions and their fate. The perspective is, however, strangely
warped: we look down on the animals' backs, yet the stag's head and antlers
are seen from below and silhouetted against the stormy sky. This dramatic
condensation of space and vision corresponds to the extreme naturalism with
which the animals are painted: the shaggy coat, dripping mouth, and frantic
eye of the stag; the dog's raised hackles and snarling teeth. The emphasis on
tactile sensation, making the spectator feel present at the event, has a counterpart in modern wildlife films, which often show savage encounters between
species. In the context of nineteenth-century aesthetics, Landseer's vivid depiction of textures, although broadly brushed, could have stamped him as a
merely descriptive painter, obsessed with surface appearances. But it was
clearly contributory, as the public realized, to a sense of painful actuality that
enhances the dramatic power and grandeur of the image.

The carefully contrived, frieze-like composition of *The Stag at Bay* is sta-
bilized by the horizontal of the water, creating an impression of equilibrium
and control. This is set against the curving rhythms of the animals, which

Sir Edwin Landseer, *The Stag at Bay* (1846), engraved by Charles Mottram without date, mixed media. © The British Museum.

interrupt the horizon, building up to the apex of the stag's magnificent head and carried on in the turbulent sweep of the storm clouds. As the *Times* critic noted, "The dark watery sky, all pregnant with rain, hangs in gloomy accompaniment to the expression of animal grief. One may almost hear the drops begin to patter upon the water . . . so lowly, blackly, and intensely does the weight of vapour press down upon it."[17] The fitful shafts of light, the wind whipping up the water of the lake into spray, the jagged shoreline, all heighten the pathos of the animals' plight. This effect could be construed as a piece of romanticism, making the wild passions of the deer and the dogs seem like emanations of the landscape itself. However, it is better understood as a response to Lyell's scientific concept, later developed by Darwin, of nature as the locus of perpetual struggle in which animals are destined to fight not only against each other but also against the hostility of their environment.[18] In the background of Landseer's painting, the eagle hovering in the clouds in the hope of carrion is a reminder of the inexorable cycle of killing in which only the strongest or the luckiest survive.

Through this emphasis on animal predation and on the power of the elements, Landseer subtly *naturalizes* his subject. The unseen hunter is no longer perceived as the initiator of the contest, who aimed the gun and set on the dogs. Instead we witness a tragedy that is endemic to the natural order: an order that determines the fate of man and other species alike. In this light, man can, paradoxically, be identified with his victim. As is so often the case in literature, from Shakespeare's description in *As You Like It* onward, the sequestered stag symbolizes the persecuted and abandoned human being, and at least one nineteenth-century writer thought that such pictures symbolized Landseer's own defeat by mental illness.[19] His depiction is in fact strikingly anthropomorphic. The stag seems aware of his own fate, his facial expression conveying both defiance and despair. The way he lifts his head to heaven would have reminded cultured Victorians of the dying heroes in traditional history painting, and the balanced, classic perfection of the design confirms the seriousness and dignity of the artist's conception of his subject.

The responses of journalists who reviewed the Royal Academy exhibition in 1846 reveal the divided feelings of the public about this subject: a conflict that Landseer—himself torn between opposing impulses—must have anticipated and even fomented. It was as though the public had ringside seats at an actual animal combat, the outcome of which still hung in the balance. The *Art-Union*'s writer observed that the picture was painted with "such truth and spirit . . . that we cannot help (although not of the laird's hunting party) entering warmly into the interest of the chase—but upon the side of the noble stag, upon whose escape we offer any odds, if the laird and his gillies are not at hand."[20] The taking of sides may sometimes have coincided with the gender division among exhibition visitors. A friend of Landseer's, William Russell, wrote to him in 1842 about another painting of a hunted stag, *The Sanctuary*, where the animal is visualized as finding temporary refuge on an island in a loch. Russell jokingly surmised that "a gentleman will come early next morning with his double-barrelled Purdy, & a very good deer-hound, & so finish the *Stag*—but that may be left to the imagination, and whilst you or I may be all for getting the beast, the ladies at the Exhibition may be all for his recovering."[21] The poem that Russell wrote to accompany the painting actually deferred to the presumed sensibilities of "the ladies," beginning "See! the proud Monarch of the hill and glen, / But just escaped the cruel sport of men." In view of Russell's privately expressed sentiments, the tone he adopted in these verses might be interpreted as hypocritical. Yet it was recognized that even those who hunted deer experienced contending emotions when confronted with images of this kind. The *Times* critic, writing about *The Stag at Bay*, exclaimed, "What a tale of sorrow is written in the countenance. . . ! It is the perfection of brute-eloquence, which calls on the most unfeeling of hunters to sympathize."[22] Cosmo Monkhouse, who wrote one of the early monographs on Landseer's work, discerned that "if we cannot bear to gaze long on the canvas, it is because our feelings of pity will not permit us to contemplate unmoved a scene of intense animal suffering depicted by so masterly a hand. The case might be different did the reality come before us in the full excitement of the chase."[23]

Monkhouse's comments involve a recognition that response to the depiction of an animal's death is wholly different from feelings about an actual death, particularly if it occurs in the heat of a pursuit. *Visual* representation of physical suffering has a unique potency, and for this reason has often, in recent history, been subjected to exceptional restraints. Nevertheless, the Victorian public did gaze long on Landseer's image, which was reproduced in several engravings and even in silver statuettes.[24] The invitation to "feelings of pity" validated the artist's high-minded intentions, and perhaps even the practice of hunting itself, just as the public's conscious exercise of such feelings was a kind of self-vindication. Monkhouse's comments thus bring us back to a consideration of the peculiar properties and functions of *representations* of the killing of animals. Does a "masterly" picture by Landseer disturb the spectator by presenting him or her with the cold fact of an intolerable reality, like photographs of concentration camps in 1945? Or does it seek to exculpate the perpetrators of a morally obnoxious practice by dignifying it as high art, which moves the spectator and makes him or her forget the chain of causation behind the grand catastrophe? Does it, alternatively, involve manipulation of the spectator's emotions through a contrived anthropomorphism, alien to the animal's real subjectivity and experience?

The critics wrestled with Landseer's motives in producing a succession of such depictions and with their own half-fascinated, half-nauseated reactions to them. A writer in the *Art-Journal* in 1851, describing Landseer's *Deer and Deerhounds in a Mountain Torrent* of 1833, thought that it was wrong to suppose "that mankind in general are accustomed to take delight in witnessing representations of mental or bodily suffering, whether endured by their own species or by the brute creation." In fact, "no noble or wise lesson" could be learned from them: "The tender-hearted turn aside from such pictures . . . and the more truthful and natural they are, the stronger is the impression made; while they serve only to confirm the callous in those feelings which render them insensible to the distresses of others." Despite these Ruskinian sentiments, however, the *Art-Journal* illustrated its article with a fine, full-page plate of Landseer's *Deer and Deerhounds* engraved by J. Cousen.[25] The uncomfortable truth was that sadistic pleasure or mere voyeurism could not so easily be separated from moral and physical repugnance. John MacKenzie has suggested that Landseer's paintings of deer hunting "successfully conveyed the sensuality of killing."[26] The stark physicality of his images could, as the *Art-Journal* claimed, aggravate the distress of the sensitive viewer, but it could equally stimulate excitement and a vicarious participation in the killing.

It has already been noted that Landseer's ability to conjure up such tortured images derived in part from his own mental struggles: he became steadily more fatalistic, more pessimistic, and more ambivalent about man's relationship to the natural order. Thus his images of field sports ranged from game cards for the Duke of Bedford, with astonishingly graphic and apparently exulting depictions of hares and birds at the very moment of being shot, to the meditative works of his later years, which represented stags and other hunted animals with passionate, some would say morbid, sympathy.[27] In a letter to Lord Ellesmere written in 1837, the artist pondered the fact (already pointed out by Pope over a century earlier) that the ardor of hunting "makes butchers of us all. Who does not glory in the death of a fine stag? on the spot—when in truth he ought to be ashamed of the assassination?" Despite all this, Landseer found that his love for the stag "*as a subject for the pencil* gets the better of such tenderness."[28] Apologists tried to distinguish between his allegedly half-hearted and ham-fisted efforts as a sportsman and his triumphs as a sensitive painter. He "often carried the gun," F. G. Stephens explained, "as an introduction to the sketch-book."[29]

In reality, however, seeing, representing, and killing were closely associated. Landseer, in conversation with his friend Frederick Keyl, remembered and reenacted the experience of stalking with extraordinary vividness, even mimicking the "voice & gesture & expression of the very Animals, the Deer head and neck up—eye faintly rolling in Corner—the very ears seemed to go back."[30] Such acute observation could be preparatory to either shooting or drawing; but, as Monkhouse recognized, a sketch was simply a "shot of a different fashion."[31] Landseer's images of deer and other hunted animals spied on their intimate life in the wild, in a manner that paralleled that of the hunter. Matthew Brower has, indeed, recently shown how early wildlife photography in America was called "camera hunting": a practice "shaped by the discourses of hunting," whose products were spoken of as both "trophy and kill."[32] W. J. T. Mitchell has even suggested that the realist conventions of Western postmedieval art are implicated in a striving for mastery, not unlike that of the hunter. The "problem of illusion" is "deeply interwoven with structures of power and social otherness"; and the "centrality of animals" to its aesthetic discourse "suggests just how radical this otherness may be, how deeply linked with motivations of domination, enslavement, and violence, as indicated by the frequent metaphors of illusionistic 'capture' and 'taking in.'"[33]

It was not only the artist and his public who experienced a conflict between simultaneous attraction to the living animal and a desire to kill and possess its body. Sportsmen themselves felt it—but was this frisson indeed part of the pleasure of the hunt? In Victorian hunters' and explorers' yarns of the chase, the quarry's efforts to escape and its prolonged death throes were often narrated in pathetic but apparently gloating detail, narrations often heightened by descriptions of the animal's physical allure. In Scrope's *Art of Deer-Stalking,* one of its fictionalized protagonists, a young tyro called Harry Lightfoot, is temporarily overcome by remorse when a stag he has shot dies slowly before him. He vows to abandon the "barbarous and inhuman practice" of stalking; but this resolve is short-lived. Later, "one of the wonderful harts . . . a stupendous animal, very sleek in his coat, and had royal antlers" is mortally wounded. "The pangs of death were brief, but very painful to witness. . . . Lightfoot could not be torn away from the dun beauty."[34]

The indulgence of such morally dubious emotions was restrained by notions of a "sporting code": a self-denying ordinance devised by sportsmen themselves that, in their own view, operated like the rules of a game, legitimating their "fair" kills. In Britain, there was, for example, general distaste for the battues or organized drives of game animals still prevalent in parts of mainland Europe; and the existence of a counterpart to these practices on some of the Scottish estates was largely unacknowledged in the literature. The organization of an army of retainers to funnel the terrified animals into an enclosure, where large numbers were shot as sitting targets from a safe vantage point, was repellent in its artificiality. It demolished the cherished myth of hunting as a natural activity, in which man entered into the rhythms of the wild—the perennial struggle, death, or survival of animals decreed by fate. Of course, the code of abstinence from mass slaughter was also, at bottom, a measure for conserving the breeding stock of a species. Thus sportsmen were supposed to refrain from killing female deer, a rule that was represented as a sort of gallantry. However, as the females—the civilians in this war between species—often led the flight of the herd and ran between the stags, killings were inevitable. As Scrope explained, a "good sportsman" would never fire at hinds and calves: "Indeed, it is reckoned a disgrace to do so; and a most wanton act of cruelty it certainly is. The best shots, however, will occasionally kill them accidentally; for they . . . often, like Polonius, get that which was meant for their betters."[35]

In Landseer's *A Random Shot,* exhibited in 1848, a sporting "accident" of this kind is raised to the level of sublime tragedy.[36] The histrionics of *The Stag at Bay* have given way to bleak simplicity and quiescence. A fatally wounded hind has evaded the shooters and struggled to a mountaintop to quench her thirst at a spring that still runs, unfrozen, through the snow. The confused hoof marks, showing where she has threshed around in her dying agony; the blood oozing from her mouth and staining her footprints; her

Sir Edwin Landseer, *A Random Shot* (1848), oil on canvas. Bury Art Gallery and Museum.

glazed eye and outstretched, stiffening limbs: all confront the spectator with the dreadful *actuality* of what has happened. Such intensely observed physical details in Landseer's paintings—what one contemporary critic called "truth . . . exaggerated into painfulness"—could, in some cases, enhance the sensuality of killing.[37] Here, however, the sexuality of the image is less seductive than pathetic. The blood that stains the whiteness of the snow is a staining of virgin nature's bedsheets. Man, whose guilty presence is hinted at by the blue shadow on the snow at the bottom left of the picture, is, by implication, a brutal violator of the wild, alien to its ways, destructive of its fecundity. A fawn, itself now doomed, tries to suckle from its dead mother, its ungainly infant legs silhouetted against the snow. We know from Landseer's conversations with Keyl that the effect of winter weather was introduced at a late stage in the picture's genesis.[38] The bleak mountains, the lonely waste of snow, and the dying glow of sunset reflected from its surface immeasurably intensify the power of the image. A writer in the *London Quarterly Review* later commented: "All nature seems to mock the sufferings of these two hapless innocent creatures . . . and smiles on heedless of their fate" in "unfeeling splendour."[39] The poignancy of Landseer's imaginative vision was too much for some viewers. The *Art-Union*'s writer protested, in a variation of Ruskin's argument, that "real life has sorrows enough in store . . . without giving to us those which arise from fiction. It is not in painting as it is in books; the sufferings we endure from the one are transient, while those which result from the other must be continuous; for a picture will be frequently in sight."[40]

The hind's suffering was only bearable if it became the object of conscious and conscientious pity. In a strange reversal of the pattern of agency, human empathy was felt to compensate for the "heedless" insensibility of the elements. The latter was, once again, a reminder of the inexorability of natural law, the rule of endless struggle that governed the fate of human beings as well as other animals. In *A Random Shot,* even more than in *The Stag at Bay,* the spectator is encouraged to identify with the animals. As the *Athenaeum*'s critic perceptively noticed, the motif of the orphaned babe, vainly seeking its dead mother's milk, had a *human* prototype in some of the Old Masters' paintings of scenes of disaster, plague, and massacre.[41] While eschewing obvious anthropomorphism, Landseer has universalized the deer's experience and thereby subtly mitigated our impression of the direct culpability of the random shooter.

The moving effect of this large painting, particularly when seen in the original, is such as to absolve Landseer from any suspicion of mere maudlin sentiment or contrivance. It remains true, however, that Victorian sportsmen condemned the cruel shooting of hinds only to vindicate the killing of stags, the "monarchs of the glen," as somehow *not* cruel. Moreover, the rules of sportsmanship were more arbitrary, more easily set aside, or at least more frequently infringed than would have been openly admitted. They broke down altogether in the conditions of big game hunting in the colonies, often carried on in the mid-nineteenth century by buccaneering trophy-collectors for whom the caste-based conventions of British sporting behavior had little meaning. Roualeyn Gordon Cumming's *Five Years of a Hunter's Life in the Far Interior of South Africa* was first published in 1850 and much reprinted.[42] Here a *Boy's Own* kind of enthusiasm for the life of the lone tracker and shooter in the wild, such as is found in Scrope's *Art of Deer-Stalking,* transmutes into freebooting recklessness. The gentlemanly scruples of sportsmen in the Scottish Highlands about the killing of female deer, or about culpable failures to trace and dispatch painfully wounded animals, are entirely absent from Cumming's narrative. It exposes in embarrassing nakedness the lust to kill that lay at the root of the hunter's activities. Cumming was unashamedly thrilled by breakneck pursuit, marksmanship, and the slow infliction of death, which were all dwelt on in pathological detail in the text and illustrations of his book and were presumably relished by his many readers.

CAMELOPARD HUNTING AT MASSOUEY.

Camelopard Hunting at Massouey, wood-engraved illustration from Roualeyn Gordon Cumming's *The Lion Hunter of South Africa* (1857).

The collection of tangible trophies such as horns and skins verified his exploits and brought him fame and fortune in Britain. The extraordinary scale and the indiscriminate nature of the carnage wreaked by Cumming and some other Victorian big game hunters shock the modern reader, as they shocked many people at the time. What is even more striking, however, is the paradoxical nature of Cumming's instincts as a hunter, which represent in an extreme form the hunting mentality explored in this essay. He watched the habits of wild animals intently; was hypnotized by their beauties of form, texture, color, and scent; killed them ruthlessly; and possessed them voluptuously. Once when he had brought down a gemsbok (large antelope), "a beautiful cow with a pair of uncommonly large horns . . . my thirst was intense, and, the gemsbok having a fine breast of milk, I milked her into my mouth, and obtained a drink of the sweetest beverage I ever tasted." On another occasion, he chased a herd of giraffe "like one entranced," and wounded a female. He dismounted from his horse and "gazed in wonder at her extreme beauty, while her soft dark eye, with its silky fringe, looked down imploringly at me: I really felt a pang of sorrow in this moment of triumph for the blood I was shedding; but the sporting feeling prevailed. . . . A thick stream of dark blood spouted far from the wound, her colossal limbs quivered for a moment, and she expired."[43]

The strange tension between a desire to kill and an agonized empathy with the quarry, which inspired Landseer's epic paintings of deer, is here crudely dissipated. In Cumming's recital, the murderousness of the hunter as well as the brutal mechanics by which the wild was conquered are overt and unmitigated. Thus the brilliant wildlife illustrator Joseph Wolf, a friend of Landseer, produced in 1875 a sketch that referred to Cumming's African exploits and called it, with bitter irony, *Sport*.[44]

A nursing lioness lies killed, no longer able to feed or defend her cubs. Her swollen teats are pitifully exposed, her sprawling body uncomfortably reminiscent of a playful domestic cat's. The hunter approaches cautiously, a crouching dark shape against the sky, his shaggy hair and Neanderthal gait contrasting with the erect, menacing form of the gun. Wolf's own studies of wild animals reveal an obsession, akin to Landseer's, with the pattern of predation in nature. Yet, according to his biographer, he believed that man's "insatiable desire to kill" was "a relic of a savage condition, out of keeping with the exalted culture and civilization we claim." In Wolf's opinion, even lions and tigers could never rival man in gratuitous ferocity.[45] So far from representing a fair, free, and "natural" combat between man and other species, as the promulgators of the hunting myth maintained, the killing of animals with firearms was a perverse application of those very technological

Joseph Wolf, *Sport* (1875), untraced charcoal sketch reproduced in A. H. Palmer's *Life of Joseph Wolf* (1895).

advances that underpinned the "exalted culture" of modern Britain and its growing imperial power across the globe.

The paradoxes did not end there. Landseer's *A Random Shot,* an image of unrelieved tragedy, stirred the consciences of sportsmen and brought becoming expressions of pity from the Victorian public. But the kind of incident it showed was replicated many hundreds of times in the course of stocking the new zoological collections of the European nations. Only through first shooting females could their young, which were more tractable and easier to transport, be captured and shipped to the West.[46] In 1834, the Zoological Society of London obtained its first giraffes in this way, through a commission to a French trader, Thibaut. An article in the *Quarterly Review* reassured its readers that the young captive giraffes "became gradually reconciled to their condition" and were now "extremely fond of society . . . very sensible. I have observed one of them shed tears when it no longer saw its companions."[47] The anodyne, tastefully colored prints of the Zoological Gardens in Regent's Park, produced at this time by George Scharf, emphasized not only the tameness and humorous appeal of the animals but also the refined sensibility and civility of the visitors.[48] These decorous men and women evince a familial concern for the animals almost as tender as that for their own children, and the violent means by which the captive specimens reached London is effectively obscured. As we have seen, the public's expression of pity for Landseer's pictured stags could be interpreted as a kind of ritual wringing of hands, which had no effect, and was not expected or intended to have any effect on the practices it ostensibly deplored. So also, the humane demeanor of those who visited Regent's Park was in the strongest contrast to the brutality and lawlessness of conquest—conquest of both men and animals—which was tacitly sanctioned by metropolitan opinion on the frontiers of empire. Moreover, the power of representation to *construct* a view of man's interactions with the natural world is as apparent in the early views of the Zoological Gardens as it is in Landseer's pictures of dying deer. We must find effective ways to deconstruct these images: to interpret their rhetoric in the unflattering light of history and to hear their silences.

Notes

1. Matt Cartmill, *A View to a Death in the Morning: Hunting and Nature through History* (Cambridge: Harvard University Press, 1993), 80–81, 238–40.

2. Maureen Duffy, "Beasts for Pleasure," in *Animals, Men and Morals: An Enquiry into the Maltreatment of Non-Humans,* ed. Stanley and Roslind Godlovich and John Harris (London: Gollancz, 1971), 111–24, especially 116.

3. Roger Scruton, *On Hunting* (London: Yellow Jersey Press, 1999), 31, 94. Scruton is

here contrasting the sensibilities of gentlemanly hunt followers with the wild instincts of the hired huntsman.

4. *Guardian*, no. 61, May 21, 1713; Norman Ault, ed., *The Prose Works of Alexander Pope* (Oxford: Basil Blackwell, 1936), 1: 109–10.

5. John M. MacKenzie, *The Empire of Nature: Hunting, Conservation and British Imperialism* (Manchester: Manchester University Press, 1988).

6. Charles Lyell, *Principles of Geology: Being an Inquiry How Far the Former Changes of the Earth's Surface Are Referable to Causes Now in Operation*, 3rd ed., four vols. (London: John Murray, 1834), vol. 3, book 3, 67. The first edition of Lyell's great work had begun to appear in 1830.

7. For example, William Henry Scott (a pseudonym of John Lawrence), *British Field Sports: Embracing Practical Instructions in Shooting—Hunting—Coursing . . .* (London: Sherwood, Neely, and Jones, 1818), 294–96, 421–23.

8. Lyell, *Principles of Geology,* vol. 3, book 3, 48–49.

9. Stella A. Walker, *Sporting Art, England 1700–1900* (London: Studio Vista, 1972); Dudley Snelgrove, *British Sporting and Animal Prints 1658–1874 (The Paul Mellon Collection)* (London: Tate Gallery Publications for the Yale Center for British Art, 1981). On trophy collecting, see MacKenzie, *Empire of Nature,* 28–31.

10. John Ruskin, *Modern Painters,* vol. 5, 1860, part 9, chap. 6, in *The Works of John Ruskin,* ed. E. T. Cook and Alexander Wedderburn (London: George Allen, 1905), vol. 7, 337; Jonathan Burt, *Animals in Film* (London: Reaktion Books, 2002), esp. chap. 2.

11. Richard Ormond, *Sir Edwin Landseer* (Philadelphia: Philadelphia Museum of Art and London, Tate Gallery, 1981), 60; Trevor R. Pringle, "The Privation of History: Landseer, Victoria and the Highland Myth," in *The Iconography of Landscape: Essays on the Symbolic Representation, Design and Use of Past Environments,* ed. Denis Cosgrove and Stephen Daniels (Cambridge: Cambridge University Press, 1988), 142–61; T. C. Smout, "Landseer's Highlands," in *The Monarch of the Glen: Landseer in the Highlands,* ed. Richard Ormond (Edinburgh: National Galleries of Scotland, 2005), 13–17.

12. William Scrope, *The Art of Deer-Stalking, Illustrated by a Narrative of a Few Days' Sport in the Forest of Atholl . . . Illustrated by Engravings and Lithographs after Paintings by Edwin and Charles Landseer first published 1838* (London and New York: Edward Arnold, 1897), 43, 211.

13. James Dafforne, "British Artists: Their Style and Character . . . No. L.—Richard Ansdell," *Art-Journal,* n.s., 6 (1860): 233–35; Arthur Todd, *The Life of Richard Ansdell, R. A.* (Manchester: Sherratt and Hughes, 1919), 17; Walker Art Gallery, Liverpool, *Merseyside Painters, People, Places: Catalogue of Oil Paintings,* 2 vols. (Liverpool: Merseyside County Council, 1978), text vol. 26–27, plates vol. 161.

14. *Art-Union* (June 1846): 182.

15. James Dafforne, *Pictures by Sir Edwin Landseer . . . With Descriptions and a Biographical Sketch of the Painter* (London: Virtue and Co., n.d. [1873]), 62–63; F. G. Stephens, *Memoirs of Sir Edwin Landseer* (London: George Bell, 1874), 116. The painting is now at Dublin Castle, on loan from the Guinness family. Ormond, *Monarch of the Glen,* 114.

16. The twenty drawings date from 1845 onward; a folio of prints from them was published in 1868. W. Cosmo Monkhouse, *The Works of Sir Edwin Landseer, R. A.* (London: J. S. Virtue, 1879), 156; W. Cosmo Monkhouse, *The Studies of Sir Edwin Landseer, R. A.*

Illustrated by Sketches (London: Virtue and Co., n.d.), 118–21; Campbell Lennie, *Landseer: The Victorian Paragon* (London: Hamish Hamilton, 1976), 198–200.

17. *Times,* May 6, 1846.

18. Lyell's view of nature in *Principles of Geology* was developed by Herbert Spencer and Alfred Wallace and was conclusively theorized by Charles Darwin in *On the Origin of Species by Means of Natural Selection,* first published in 1859.

19. Anon. [Anne Thackeray, Lady Ritchie], "Sir Edwin Landseer," *Cornhill Magazine* 24 (January–June 1874): 81–100.

20. *Art-Union* (June 1846): 176.

21. Landseer manuscripts (Eng. MS, 86.RR) in the National Art Library, Victoria and Albert Museum, London, vol. 5 (MSL/ 1962/1316), nos. 283–85. *The Sanctuary* is discussed and reproduced in Ormond, *Landseer,* 170, and in Ormond, *Monarch of the Glen,* 111–12.

22. *Times,* May 6, 1846.

23. Monkhouse, *Works of Landseer,* unpaginated commentaries on plates, re. *The Stag at Bay.*

24. One of the Landseer manuscripts (see note 21), vol. 2, no. 72, reveals that the artist stood to make large sums from royalties on reproductions in silver and base metal of *The Stag at Bay.*

25. "The Vernon Gallery. The Death of the Stag," *Art-Journal* (1851): 4. The painting is now known as *Deer and Deerhounds in a Mountain Torrent;* Ormond, *Landseer,* 81; Ormond, *Monarch of the Glen,* 54–55.

26. MacKenzie, *Empire of Nature,* 33.

27. The game cards were included in *Engravings from Drawings by Landseer* (London: E. Gambart, 1848), as plates 2–3.

28. Quoted in Ormond, *Landseer,* 17.

29. Stephens, *Memoirs of Landseer,* 108.

30. Keyl papers in the Royal Archives, Windsor Castle, VIC/ ADD X 14/20/1, August 31, 1866.

31. Monkhouse, *Works of Landseer,* 150–51.

32. Matthew Brower's paper entitled "Hunting with a Camera: Gendering Early North American Wildlife Photography, 1890–1910," was delivered at the Millennial Animals conference at the University of Sheffield, July 2000. It is quoted by Steve Baker in his editor's introduction to a special issue of *Society and Animals* on "The Representation of Animals," 9, no. 3 (2001): 190. Cf. Burt, *Animals in Film,* 99.

33. W. J. T. Mitchell, "Illusion: Looking at Animals Looking," *Picture Theory: Essays on Verbal and Visual Representation* (Chicago: Chicago University Press, 1994), 333.

34. Scrope, *Art of Deer-Stalking,* 71, 210.

35. Ibid., 15.

36. Ormond, *Landseer,* 172–73; Ormond, *Monarch of the Glen,* 113–14.

37. *Athenaeum,* no. 1072 (May 13, 1848): 489.

38. Keyl papers, VIC/ ADD X 14/20/13, February 5, 1870.

39. *London Quarterly Review* 83 (April 1874): 59.

40. *Art-Union* (1848): 173.

41. *Athenaeum,* no. 1072 (May 13, 1848): 489.

42. Roualeyn Gordon Cumming, *Five Years of a Hunter's Life in the Far Interior of South*

Africa, 2 vols. (1850); republished in a shortened version as *The Lion Hunter of South Africa. Five Years' Adventures in the Far Interior of South Africa* (London: John Murray, 1857), with extracts from reviews. MacKenzie, *Empire of Nature,* 28–29, 96–100.

43. Cumming, *Lion Hunter,* 68, 161.

44. Reproduced in A. H. Palmer, *The Life of Joseph Wolf, Animal Painter* (London and New York: Longmans, Green and Co., 1895), opposite 135. On Wolf, see also Karl Schulze-Hagen and Armin Geus, ed., *Joseph Wolf (1820–1899), Animal Painter* (Marburg an der Lahn: Basilisken-Presse, 2000).

45. Palmer, *Life of Wolf,* 136–40.

46. Nigel Rothfels, "Catching Animals," in *Animals in Human Histories: The Mirror of Nature and Culture,* ed. Mary J. Henninger-Voss (Rochester, N.Y.: University of Rochester Press, 2002), 182–228.

47. Review of various Zoological Society publications in *Quarterly Review* 56 (April and July 1836): 325–26. Wilfrid Blunt, *The Ark in the Park: The Zoo in the Nineteenth Century* (London: Book Club Associates, 1976), 80–82.

48. Some of Scharf's lithographs, published in 1835, are reproduced in Blunt, *Ark in the Park,* between 48 and 49.

4 "You Kill Things to Look at Them": Animal Death in Contemporary Art

STEVE BAKER

"Only the wound, speaking wordlessly in the dark."
—William Gibson, *Pattern Recognition* (2003)

Here is the blunt, stubby outline of a head in profile, a rabbit-like or maybe dog-like thing that the artist, in conversation, in fact identifies as a snared rabbit. And immediately below the head, so close as unquestionably to be the animal's own blunt address to the viewer, are the words "I am dead." Nothing else about the death is clear, though the piece has the feel and the tone of an accusation. Roland Barthes, of course, had famously cautioned in a different pictorial context that "to reproduce death . . . tells us, literally, nothing,"[1] but that doesn't seem quite right in the case of David Mackintosh's drawing (see figure 4.1).

David Mackintosh, *I Am Dead* (2002), gouache on paper. Courtesy of the artist.

In its careful but botched-looking facture, the image undertakes or engages with a particular kind of work. It is this work—the work of animal imagery at the point of its engagement with violent or unnecessary death—that will be the subject of this essay.

Contemporary art, along with literature and nondocumentary film genres, is a field in which the killing of animals can undoubtedly figure as a subject but where it is not necessarily clear how the field can usefully contribute either to knowledge of the other-than-human or more-than-human world or to what might broadly be called the cause of animal advocacy. The direct concern of this essay is therefore with what contemporary art and contemporary artists might *productively* say about the question of killing animals. For this reason, the fact that artists (like film directors, but generally unlike poets and novelists) can themselves cause animals to be killed during the production of their own creative work will not itself be considered in any detail. The ignominious history of recent artists harming or killing animals as part of their work has begun to be documented, but because such work is clearly not in the interest of animals and—less obviously but more intriguingly—is not always the kind of work that causes most offense, that history will be touched on only tangentially here.[2]

Can contemporary art productively address the killing of animals? Expressed in this way, the question is indeed a blunt one, but it is an important one for a number of reasons. The art of recent decades has made increasing use of animal imagery (and indeed of animals themselves), and by no means only in a symbolic or sentimental context. This art has often been seen as both ethically and aesthetically disturbing, though it has equally often been accompanied by the artists' acknowledgment of their responsibility toward the animals presented or represented in their work. It is harder than might be expected to disentangle ethical and aesthetic questions in this context: the desire of some artists to address a subject such as the killing of animals may well be driven by ethical concerns, but the manner in which they try to do so will almost inevitably bring aesthetic concerns into play. The apparently simple question "Can contemporary art productively address the killing of animals?" therefore seems to raise far wider questions about the effectiveness of art (and, more generally, of visual representations) in a postmodern era.

In his book *Animal Rights and the Politics of Literary Representation,* John Simons includes discussion of a few examples of visual art, including a famous photograph by artist Cindy Sherman, *Untitled #140* (1985). Using the disguised and compromised image of her own body, as so much of her work does, this dark image from her *Fairy Tales* series shows her head in profile wearing a pig snout. Simons is critical of the image, not because he believes Sherman to be "wearing an actual pig's nose," but rather because this photograph's status as art diverts viewers from thinking about what the image actually shows. He proposes that viewers should look more attentively and more humanely. In order to make this image, he contends, "a pig has died (or it is to be imagined that a pig has died)"; and in it "a human is using the broken body of a pig in order to do something or become something." The image therefore depends "on the speciesist assumption that the pig's body is there for us to use." He speculates that if a pig could make anything at all of the photograph, "what it would see would be the death of a pig. Perhaps that is what we should see too."[3]

Elsewhere, and equally uncompromisingly, Simons has written of the controversial animal imagery found in much postmodern art: "When I see a work of 'botched taxidermy' . . . I do not see an epistemological problem. I see a dead animal (or a simulation of a dead animal)."[4] The complaint was prompted by a book by the present author, called *The Postmodern Animal,* which coined the term "botched taxidermy" to describe a range of recent artworks in which the image of the animal takes an unconventional and sometimes startling form. More specifically, the term was an attempt "to characterize those instances of recent art practice where things . . . appear to have *gone wrong* with the animal, as it were, but where it still *holds together.*"[5]

Both descriptive and provocative, the term was not intended to be taken too literally. Some of the examples offered did indeed use taxidermy, such as the battered and paint-spattered Angora goat that dominates Robert Rauschenberg's sculptural construction *Monogram* (1955–59). Others, such as the various butchered animals preserved in formaldehyde in Damien Hirst's *Natural History* series from the 1990s, present the imperfectly preserved animal body in different ways. The term was even stretched to include temporary and approximate cross-species hybrids and alliances, including both the 1982 photograph of William Wegman's living weimaraner dog, Man Ray, preposterously dressed up as a frog, and Cindy Sherman's willing identification with the animal in the "pig snout" photograph discussed by John Simons.

The Postmodern Animal proposes not only that these artworks "botched" the animal body, or got it wrong (in contrast to the illusion of life attempted by conventional taxidermy), but also that in doing so these works could collectively be regarded as "*questioning* entities"—a term that Jacques Derrida had in fact employed some years earlier to characterize humans.[6] And it is this idea that an artwork that may include an actual dead animal body could ever usefully constitute a questioning entity that Simons seems to doubt in saying that faced with such works, what he sees is not "an episte-mological problem" but simply "a dead animal." For him, it would seem, such art cannot therefore productively address the killing of animals: the presence of the animal body is too much of an obstacle.

This is a specific and rather telling instance of a more general difficulty concerning the effectiveness of the visual image. Can visual imagery itself ever really "address" issues? There are certainly those who have doubted it. In an essay called "The Visual Image," art historian Ernst Gombrich wrote: "Looking at communication from the vantage point of language, we . . . shall see that the visual image is supreme in its capacity for arousal, that its use for expressive purposes is problematic, and that unaided it altogether lacks the possibility of matching the statement function of language." Anthro-pologist Sol Worth concurs: "Pictures do not have these abilities to make true-false statements or to assert the negative: they can't say ain't, either." And to return to Barthes's words, in one of his earliest essays on photography he acknowledged the ability of the medium to represent aspects of common human experience such as birth and death but scathingly assessed its limita-tions: "The failure of photography seems to me to be flagrant in this con-nection: to reproduce death or birth tells us, literally, nothing." To become meaningful, Barthes suggested, such imagery had to gain access to a "true language" in which the historical specificity and particular circumstances of these "facts" could be addressed *and potentially transformed.*[7]

These observations (from three perceptive and sympathetic interpreters of the visual image) concerning the allegedly limited effectiveness of the image when it is unsupported by verbal clues to its context or purpose are highly pertinent to the concerns of the present essay. Mieke Bal recently described Louise Bourgeois's 1997 installation, *Spider,* as "astonishingly var-ied, dense in meaning, and exuberantly visual, yet difficult to 'read' and far from 'beautiful.'"[8] This seems an apt characterization of a good deal of contemporary animal art, but the very fact that this art can be so "difficult to 'read'" only exacerbates the problem of how effectively some of the artists who make it might address a subject such as the killing of animals.

Writing Rights and Picturing Wrongs

In the case of many artists, their explicit engagement with the relationship of animals, ethics, and killing has indeed come through their words. Mark Dion's "Some Notes towards a Manifesto for Artists Working with or about the Living World," reproduced in an exhibition catalog in 2000, is an earnest set of handwritten notes that eschews the irony (and the difficulty) found in much of his work and includes this uncompromising declaration: "Artists working with living organisms must know what they are doing. They must take responsibility for the plants' or animals' welfare. If an organism dies during an exhibition, the viewer should assume the death to be the intention of the artist."[9]

Similarly, as part of their collective and ongoing effort to "sensitize" the arts community to the fact that animals are "sentient beings, not ideas or inanimate materials with which to create a performance or an exhibit," the Minnesota-based artists who in 2000 had formed the Justice for Animals Arts Guild (JAAG) got involved in 2003 (along with PETA—People for the Ethical Treatment of Animals—and other non-arts organizations) in the lobbying for a thorough and open investigation of the case of an art student at Berkeley who had hacked off the head of a living chicken during a "new genres" art class. According to the chancellor's office at Berkeley, the action was undertaken by the student "in an apparent attempt to dramatize the connection between the food we eat and the killing of animals." Amid some fairly intemperate responses, JAAG attempted to situate the incident historically and urged the university "to establish guidelines to protect *ideas* but censor *acts* that cause direct harm or potential harm to others committed in the name of art."[10]

For the New York–based artist Sue Coe, it is not other artists' killing of animals but rather "illogical economic systems that put profit over any and all other considerations, especially life" that concern her (see figure 4.2). Since the mid-1980s, she has produced what is probably the best-known body of contemporary visual work that is explicitly opposed to the killing of animals and to other forms of animal abuse, whether in factory farms, research laboratories, or elsewhere in "the Wall Street branch of animal slaving." She describes herself as "primarily an artist for the printed page" and also as a "visual journalist," and her images (which range from the documentary to the satirical) are widely reproduced in newspapers and magazines. Her 1995 book, *Dead Meat,* in which her extensive research into conditions and practices in North American slaughterhouses is documented in both words and images, is typical of her approach and exemplifies her view that the graphic image can be "a powerful witnessing tool" with the potential to change things for the better.[11]

In all three of the cases mentioned above, it is clear that language plays a crucial role in how these artists address the killing of animals, and this appears to make their stances on the issues relatively easy to read. Their entirely proper concern to distinguish right (and animals' rights) from wrong in increasingly complex economic and aesthetic circumstances recalls Carol

Sue Coe, *The Ghosts of the Skinned Want Their Coats Back*
(1998), lithograph. Copyright © 1998 Sue Coe. Courtesy Galerie
St. Etienne, New York.

Adams's remark that it may be an increasing problem for the animal rights
movement that it is, in her words, "a 'modern' movement in a postmodern
time."[12] The concern of modernist practice straightforwardly to right wrongs
may be hard to reconcile with postmodern art's fascination with a sense of
the rightness of things going wrong.

But in all three cases, the artists' visual work inflects any reading of their
words. JAAG's credibility as a campaigning organization depends in significant part on the fact that it is made up of artists and that its criticisms of
some contemporary art are therefore much harder to dismiss as philistine
misunderstandings. Much of Dion's work undermines certainties by addressing the precariousness (or even the absence) of human knowledge of

the nonhuman world, often through the image of animals-gone-wrong. On more than one occasion, his multimedia installations have featured taxidermic animals that have been quite deliberately botched by the "very crazy taxidermist" he employs. In the best-known instance, he showed a polar bear that had in fact been covered in goat fur, though many viewers (the present author included) were unaware of this on first seeing the piece. And Sue Coe not only considers the success of her work to be largely dependent on the persuasive use of her graphic skills but also acknowledges that "the most political art is the art of ambiguity."[13]

Postmodern animal art is drenched in ambiguity, and this of course is the source of both its strength and its weakness. There is undoubtedly a case here for arguing that an artist's aesthetic practice may be more persuasive, less obvious, and ultimately more revealing than any ethical pronouncements he or she might make. This art—not least when it appears to take liberties with animal form—might usefully be thought of as constituting a kind of *fluid sub-ethical practice.*

The Aesthetic Dimension

The Cindy Sherman "pig snout" photograph criticized by John Simons was not intended by the artist to be a direct comment on either the lives or deaths of animals, but her own comments on the *Fairy Tales* series as a whole will help to clarify the manner in which conflicting readings of postmodern art may come into play. Characterizing the fascination with the morbid in fairy tales as "a way to prepare for the unthinkable," she has stated that "it's very important to me to show the artificiality of it all, because the real horrors of the world are unmatchable, and they're too profound. It's much easier to absorb . . . if it's done in a fake, humorous, artificial way."[14] The pig snout is one of many prostheses and theatrical props employed in this series of photographs. But the fact that a pig did not actually die in order that this image could be made is strictly irrelevant to Simons's attempt to read the piece against the grain of art criticism. His more general concern is that here, and in other examples of botched taxidermy, the "aesthetic dimension" seems "to act as a desensitising force." He allows that viewers may indeed be "ravished by Sherman's photograph" (his concern is not therefore directly to question its status as art) but argues that such a reaction "causes us to abandon our everyday humanity."[15] Both ethical judgment and attentive viewing are, it seems, too readily suspended in the face of aesthetic pleasure.

Simons is by no means alone in leveling these very serious charges against contemporary animal art. Art's particular provocation here lies in its presenting (or in the Sherman photograph, in its *appearing* to present) a bit of a real animal, as opposed to the mere imaginative representation of the animal in literature, painting, and so on. In Jonathan Burt's book *Animals in Film,* which is especially strong on the subject of the construction and artificiality of the animal image throughout the history of film, the case is made that "the conflict over acceptable and unacceptable animal imagery turns on the point at which . . . fiction and reality collapse into each other." This, Burt argues, is because throughout the history of film, viewers seem to have been unable "to read the animal image purely as an image." But Burt has his own rather different concerns about the reading of works of botched taxidermy in contemporary art. Noting a tone "of austerity and discipline" that is adopted in critical writing on modern animal imagery, including *The Postmodern Animal,* he speculates that it is based "on assumptions that most human-animal relations in modernity are in various ways wrongful" and suggests that the artworks under discussion typically reject "sentimentality, anthropomorphism and a literal depiction of animal beauty . . . in favour of bleak and figuratively transgressive versions of the animal."[16]

Here, uncharacteristically, Burt seems to come close to reading form *as content,* and in doing so he echoes many readings of the modernist art of the early twentieth century. In an interesting essay called "Beauty from Violence," Brandon Taylor quotes a British psychoanalyst describing the subject matter of Klee, Picasso, and Dali as "either grossly distorted or broken up into fragments, or subjected to both these mutilating processes." Taylor suggests that for psychoanalysis, as perhaps also for the bewildered general public, "one has the impression that modern art's lack of overt 'beauty' . . . took the form of a symptom that had to be dealt with and somehow 'cured.'"[17] The argument of the present essay is that this contemporary animal imagery—"bleak and figuratively transgressive," as Burt puts it—is not something to be cured or *put right.* Its botchedness or gone-wrongness is deliberate and has its own integrity.

The harshest critic of this kind of work is almost certainly Anthony Julius in his recent book *Transgressions: The Offences of Art.* In many ways this is a brilliant book, though it is decidedly idiosyncratic in parts. Its central concern is to explore the "transgressive aesthetic" that runs through what Julius calls the "taboo-breaking art" of recent times.[18] Rightly identifying the limitations of a formalist defense of this art, the book has its particular and distinctive strength in its insistence that both the form *and content* of this art should be taken seriously.

In his discussion of the role of animals in contemporary art, Julius notes in a withering but understated parenthesis: "(Animals are not safe in the art world; from time to time, they are exposed to harm in the interests of art.)" But his bitterest words are generally reserved for works that appear to incorporate dead animal bodies rather than living animals. He discusses a handful of works that had been called botched taxidermy in *The Postmodern Animal*. One is from Damien Hirst's *Natural History* series—the animals preserved in formaldehyde (which Hirst had himself characterized as a "zoo of dead animals")—and Julius reads "a certain heartlessness" into Hirst's "ignominious" display of these dead animals.[19] Another is from Thomas Grünfeld's *Misfits,* the series of alarming but visually convincing hybrid taxidermic creatures. And there is also John Isaacs's *Say It Isn't So*, in which the body of a mad scientist (wearing the obligatory white coat and clutching a test tube) is a modified tailor's dummy and whose odd farmyard-animal-like head is in fact the wax cast of a frozen chicken.

Julius seems to loathe these works and is at his least persuasive in his interpretation of them. In them, he laments, "That most fundamental of hierarchies, which places the human above the merely animal, is subverted." Of the pieces by Grünfeld and Isaacs in particular, he writes, "These works are not instances of that benevolent postmodern celebration of 'impurity, intermingling, the transformation that comes of new and unexpected combinations of human beings, cultures, ideas'" (he is quoting Salman Rushdie's words here). "On the contrary," says Julius. "They are counter-Enlightenment taunts. They present the monsters, the taxidermic aberrations, that a humanity unconstrained by moral scruple, basest when least confined, will produce. . . . These man-beasts, minatory or comic, deny the divinity of the human form that is the premise of Western art."[20]

So that, according to Julius, is botched taxidermy in a nutshell: base, unconstrained by moral scruple, and having the temerity to question the hierarchical superiority of the human over the merely animal. More than that, this kind of hybrid, taboo-breaking art is an assault on its audience because, he says, it "can force us into the presence of the ugly, the bestial, the vicious, the menacing. These are all kinds of cruelty."[21] It is worth noting that John Isaacs's own account of the "force" of the life-sized figure in *Say It Isn't So* is rather different. Its effect, he hoped, would be to "force the viewer[s] from their intelligence" and to take them unawares, prompting a moment of perplexity and nonrecognition, of genuine thinking. More generally, Isaacs has observed that much of his work "comes from trying to fit together different information sources—art, science, whatever—and allowing them to cohabit, coexist, to form more of a question than an answer."[22]

Leaving to one side, for the moment, both the evident tension here between artistic intention and critical interpretation—and the fact that Julius seems more acutely concerned by the "cruelty" to the sensibilities of art's human viewers than to the lives of its occasional animal victims—it seems that Simons, Burt, and Julius share an acknowledgment that dead animal bodies (or even images of dead animal bodies) carry a considerable symbolic weight. They do things to viewers, and they make it genuinely difficult to differentiate the ethical and the aesthetic strands of the arguments they raise. They do, it seems, "address" things, though the question of how coherently they can do so has yet to be considered.

The Symbolic Weight of the Dead Body

To speak of the dead animal bodies in recent art in terms of their "symbolic weight" is hardly ideal, especially as one of the defining characteristics of postmodern animal art is arguably its avoidance of symbolism. There is no single explanation for this avoidance, but Sue Coe perhaps speaks for a number of artists who are committed to animals' interests in objecting strongly to the idea of using animals as symbols, because by using an animal (or its image) as a symbol of or for something else, that animal is effectively robbed of its own identity, and its interests will thus almost inevitably be overlooked.[23] Nevertheless, the term "symbolic weight" will serve well enough as a shorthand for the considerable body of meanings, expectations, and questions of propriety and respect that continue to cluster around the dead body, regardless of whether that body is human or animal.

The dead body continues to be a highly charged object. It is, for very many people, more than mere inert material. It is due a certain respect in the manner in which it is treated, and in certain contexts—including that of art—this may be more usefully thought of as an aesthetic respect rather than an ethical respect. Here, the distinction between art and everyday life is of little importance, and Wendy Steiner's concise formulation—"Art occupies a different moral space from that presented in identity politics, because art is virtual"[24]—fails to convince in this context because of the presence and pressing reality of the dead body. Three brief examples will confirm the weight of this body in the context of contemporary cultures of display.

In November 2002, in a Victorian building in London's East End that had been converted to house his *Body Worlds* exhibition of preserved human corpses, Professor Gunther von Hagens conducted the first public autopsy in the United Kingdom in 170 years. The corpse of a seventy-two-year-old man was the subject of the autopsy, conducted in the presence of Channel 4 television cameras and several hundred people who had each paid a small fee to watch the spectacle; 2,000 others had failed to get tickets. Several members of the audience left as the professor cut through the man's skull with a hacksaw in order to remove the brain. At another point in the procedure, the man's sternum and ribcage was passed around on a stainless steel salver for the audience to inspect.[25]

Von Hagens contended that the medical profession should not have a monopoly on the secrets of the body after death, but comments in the more serious newspapers the following day were generally unsympathetic. A *Guardian* editorial noted: "Dr. von Hagens might have good intentions, but they are undone by the gawping voyeurism such a spectacle entails." In the *Independent,* a doctor argued: "Von Hagens champions a travesty of medical science," and asked, "What will be 'demystified' by viewing the performance that couldn't be achieved by . . . a trip to the butcher?"[26] More interesting was the explanation by the president of the Royal College of Pathologists of the serious decline in the use of postmortem examinations: "People don't like the idea of being messed about. A common response to the request for a post-mortem is, 'He or she has suffered enough.'" In the same paper, another writer noted that prior to the end of the eighteenth century, postmortem dissection "was occasionally tacked on to a death penalty as an extra punishment."[27] And at the event itself, it seems, von Hagens was asked why he had not removed "his trademark fedora" as a sign of respect to the body on which he was operating.

Some months later, an acknowledgment of the continuing resonance of the dead body as an art material came in an announcement from Damien Hirst. Despite his own restless shifts in subjects and materials (perhaps reflecting the contemporary art world's more general appetite for novelty) and the fact that he had used real animal carcasses—butchered or whole—in his work since the start of the 1990s, he revealed plans for his most technically ambitious project to date: "a sculpture of three preserved cows being crucified." The opened bodies of the cows would be strung from huge crosses made from steel girders and then lowered into formaldehyde-filled tanks. The title of one of the three was to be *I Blame the Parents.*[28]

The fashion industry's renewed enthusiasm for using the pelts of animals killed for that purpose was also given considerable press coverage at this time, including a ten-page "Fur-*y*" special issue in one paper that featured a profile of PETA's "headline-grabbing anti-fur demonstrations." Sean Gifford, PETA's European campaigns director, who had been personally involved in disrupting Paris fashion shows that prominently featured furs in the early months of 2003, was quoted as saying: "There is nothing creative about skinning an animal."[29]

Why might art be exempt from such judgments? How might it be possible to agree with Gifford about the fur industry but to argue that works of botched taxidermy in contemporary art, some of which prominently feature skinned animals, are indeed creative? The works to be discussed in some detail in the later stages of this essay are of this kind. They exhibit a certain visual playfulness in the liberties they take with animal form, despite their gory theme. Made by four artists working in different parts of the world, and with little awareness until recently of each other's work, these are pieces in which taxidermy and related techniques are used directly or indirectly to address and to reconfigure the idea of the dead animal head as a wall-mount-ed hunting trophy. Each artist uses real animal body parts in their work, and by referencing the hunting trophy—a genre in which the killing of the animal was central to its purpose and its display—they have at least a chance of reframing human thinking about that killing.

The fact that this strategy involves not the representation of the killed animal but the literal presentation of part of the killed body to the gallery visitor is significant for a couple of very different reasons. On the positive side, it is one example of how art can address the question of killing animals in a manner quite distinct from that of filmic and literary representations. More problematically, the "literalism" of the materials—the animal body parts—nevertheless has no apparent relation to the clarity of the works' meanings, either for their makers or their viewers. There is troublingly little physically to differentiate the animal skins used in a fur coat, a hunting trophy head, or an artwork that "reworks" the trophy theme. The remainder of this essay therefore tries to offer a preliminary assessment of this kind of art's political efficacy in questioning the anthropocentric values that con-tinue to tolerate the human killing of animals.

Art's Opened Animal Bodies

In Angela Singer's installation *deer-atize* (2002), the bodies of a trophy-kill taxidermy doe and fawn inhabit a claustrophobic space in front of a trophy shield painted with deer and goat skulls (see figure 4.3). The doe and fawn have been "tragically beheaded" by the artist. In Jordan Baseman's *Surrender* (1997), which was initially and more starkly entitled *Flat Cat,* a skinned cat with a modeled head seems to enact a travesty of a travesty, presenting it-self—real though the skin is—as a cartoon-like domestic parody of a tiger-skin rug (see figure 4.4). Both artists have on occasion been angrily criticized for their work. Baseman reports having been accused of being "morally bankrupt" and Singer of turning "gallery walls into open graves."[30]

Angela Singer, *deer-atize* (2002), recycled trophy-kill taxidermy doe and fawn, acrylic and oils on paper and board. Courtesy of the artist.

To understand something of the power of this imagery and the extent to which it can prompt what both artists would regard as serious misreadings of their intentions, it may be helpful to turn to Elaine Scarry's classic study, *The Body in Pain*. Contemplating opened human bodies in the context of wartime injuries and opened animal bodies in the context of sacrificial rituals, she tries to work out *how* they acquire meaning. "The wound is empty of reference," she insists, seeing this as a more extreme instance of "the referential instability of the body." It is that instability that allows the body, and more particularly the opened body, "to confer its reality" on to whatever ideas lie closest to hand. She writes: "When the referential direction is determined by proximity or juxtaposition, what is proximate, what is juxtaposed, can be changed: a different symbolic counterpart or cultural fragment can be placed beside the wound whose compelling reality may now work on behalf of the different constellation of beliefs clinging to that new fragment."[31]

This is very much about seeing and looking: "The visible and experienceable alteration of injury has a *compelling and vivid reality*" that enables it to "substantiate" or to "lend force and conviction" to anything with which "the

Jordan Baseman, *Surrender* (1997), skinned cat, modeled head.
Courtesy of the artist.

open bodies are juxtaposed." She argues, "The observer . . . sees and touches the hurt body of another person (or animal) juxtaposed to the disembodied idea, and having sensorially experienced the reality of the first, believes
he or she has experienced the reality of the second." That idea "may be believed, received as compelling truth, because the open body has lent it its
truth."[32] A recent example might be the "extraordinary step" taken by the
US administration in July 2003 (contrary to "the military tradition of respecting enemy dead") of publishing "grisly photographs" of the smashed and
bloodied heads of Saddam Hussein's sons Uday and Qusay, killed by the
occupying US forces in Iraq some months after the overthrow of Saddam's
regime.[33] The intention was to convince a doubting Iraqi public that his sons
were really dead, but the more important disembodied idea (to use Scarry's
phrase) to which the image of these opened bodies lent its reality was that
the old regime had indeed been defeated and replaced—entirely contrary to
the gruesomeness of the imagery—by something better and more just.

Scarry's argument continues: "It is as though the human mind, confronted by the open body itself (whether human or animal) does not have the
option of failing to perceive its reality that rushes unstoppably across his eyes
and into his mind, yet the mind so flees from what it sees that it will with
almost equal speed perform the countermovement of assigning that attribute
to something else, especially if there is something else at hand made ready
to receive the rejected attribute, ready to act as its referent."[34]

This last observation is particularly useful and may help to explain a number of the aesthetic judgments already encountered in the present essay. Writing of the effect of taboo-breaking art, Julius notes: "Violating bodies or picturing their violation puts our sense of our own bodily integrity into momentary jeopardy." And another critic, writing of Damien Hirst's work, similarly observes that "life-negating imagery or any image which has death as its referent resonates in ourselves on or near the self-preservation instinct."[35] The idea of the fleeing mind's attempt to evade this imagery and to reassign its significance may help to account for the extent to which Julius feels affronted by some of the taboo-breaking art he encounters, arguing that these works "address pain, death and dismemberment from a detached, speculative perspective" and that they "force" the viewer into the presence of "cruelty."[36] It may also explain why Burt, Simons, and others seem surprised and perplexed by what they read as the unremitting ugliness of much postmodern animal imagery, including botched taxidermy.

To designate this art as cruel or ugly, as irresponsible or perplexing, is a way of holding in place aesthetic criteria by which to assess this art's rightness or wrongness or to make sense of its wrongness. Something similar is apparent in Kitty Hauser's dismayed reading of traditional taxidermy as an art in which "the sign has swallowed up its referent," a making-meaningless of animal killing, and a rendering-invisible of the animal whose opened body retains a compelling visual reality but a reality that has nothing to do with, and says nothing about, the life lost.[37]

The utter wrongness (in an ethical rather than an aesthetic sense) of the injuring described by Scarry—the wrongness of opening up the living human or animal body in this manner—is vividly expressed in the words of Cayce Pollard, a fictional character in William Gibson's recent novel *Pattern Recognition,* who is describing something rather different. Writing of her memory of watching the destruction—the gutting—of the twin towers of the World Trade Center on 9/11, she characterizes it thus: "Some vast and deeply personal insult to any ordinary notion of interiority. An experience outside of culture."[38]

And yet, to shift focus once again, there may be something characteristically postmodern about this experience of visual intensity combined with conceptual instability. Susan Shaw Sailer's underrated essay on "reading postmodern images" describes postmodern works as those "whose points of view are unlocatable or unstable, and whose semantics defy efforts at a literal reading or viewing," and she endorses another critic's view that postmodern artworks gain what coherence they have from the fact that they "register themselves with intensity."[39] These ideas also call to mind Gilles

Deleuze and Félix Guattari's philosophical accounts of creative experience. This experience, they suggest, may involve "opening the body to . . . distributions of intensity," not least in the process they call becoming-animal: "To become animal is . . . to find a world of pure intensities where all forms come undone," as do all meanings, and "the becoming-animal . . . only lives and is comprehensible as an intensity."[40]

Looking and Killing: Three Perspectives

From here it is possible briefly to outline three experiences of looking—intense or otherwise—that relate to the killing of animals, in art and elsewhere. The first takes as its starting point humanity's familiar (and wholly unreasonable) anthropocentric expectation of animal propriety: that it is humans who are to do the looking and expect the animal to be there to be seen, to look like an animal, and not to look back. It then extends this cold human gaze to killing, as perhaps epitomized in Damien Hirst's disingenuously naive statement of the artist's priorities: "I like ideas of trying to understand the world by taking things out of the world. You kill things to look at them."[41] The comment may not have been wholly ironic, but it seems inconceivable that Hirst would not have realized that his words might equally well describe the motives of the animal trophy hunter.

The second experience, in which the looking flows in the same single direction, is that described by Scarry, where humans *cannot but look* at the opened body of the killed animal, such is its intense reality. Here the looker is not the killer, and some of the power in the relationship therefore lies with the looked-at thing, dead though it is.

The third starts from a recognition of the particular importance of the look of an animal's eyes, whether it is alive or dead. In John C. Metcalf's *Taxidermy: A Complete Manual,* the author writes: "Many are the times I have left my studio in angry frustration at the difficulty of getting the eyes to look natural." And referring again to the eyes in a section on "mounting trophy heads," he advises: "Special care should be exercised here as the eyes are the focal point of the whole job."[42] The living animal's eyes may pose a different difficulty for the looker who may also be a killer. Lynda Birke recounts a story of scientists who were working with laboratory rats and insisted that a technician put the rats in opaque cages. As they explained to her, they did not like having the rats in clear cages because the "animals could look at you."[43]

It is this third perspective, in which the troubling or even accusatory power of the animal's gaze is engaged, that Angela Singer explicitly explores in her attempts to turn the meanings of the hunting trophy, turning the killed animal's own glazed gaze back to meet and to confront that of the sometimes too complacent human viewer. This New Zealand–based artist has made a series of works since the mid-1990s that explore strategies for turning taxidermic meaning. Motivated by a commitment to animal rights ("The very idea of a trophy animal is sickening to me"), Singer talks of her work as "recycled taxidermy" and says of it: "I think using taxidermy is a way for me to honour the animals' life, because all the taxidermy I use was once a trophy kill."[44]

In a work entitled *sore (flay)* (2002)—sore, she explains, being the Victorian name for a fallow deer—she has stripped the skin from the trophy head of a deer, taking it back to the supporting taxidermic form, and created a new "flesh" for it "by coating and carving red wax, iron oxide pigments and varnishes" (see figure 4.5). Like many of her works, its look relates to the history of that particular individual animal. As the family that donated the trophy head to Singer had explained, both the hunter who shot it and the deer itself had been drenched in blood, because "the antlers act as a blood reservoir" and it spurts everywhere when, as happened here, they were sawn off.[45]

Seeking to challenge a culture in which hunting trophies "are so prevalent, so accepted and so ignored, like some kind of cosy furniture for the wall," she writes as follows of her intentions for this piece: "Mounted on the wall my trophy echoes the just-killed animal, antlers hacked off, blood pouring from its head, hung to be skinned, gutted and bled out. The glass eyes bulge, caught somewhere between life and death."[46] The bulging eyes are a deliberate contravention of proper taxidermic practice: as Metcalf's manual of taxidermy insists, "great care must be taken because the eyes are probably

Angela Singer, *sore (flay)* (2002), recycled trophy-kill taxidermy form, wax, pigments, varnish, glass eyes. Courtesy of the artist.

the most important feature of the mounted animal. . . . They must be pushed well into the skull; otherwise when the skin dries they will appear to bulge and stare."[47] For Singer, *sore (flay)* is a quite explicit attempt to reverse the direction of looking, and of power, in relation to trophies: "The emphasis of the taxidermy trophy is on the size of the animal head. With *sore* I wanted to bring the attention away from head size because that is about the viewer looking at the animal. I wanted to emphasize the animal looking at the viewer. With the skin stripped away the eye is prominent." In *deer-atize* (figure 4.3), referred to earlier, she suggests that the same idea was addressed from the opposite direction: "By removing the heads of the doe and fawn I wanted to place the emphasis on the viewer looking at the trophy animal and the animal not being able to look at the viewer."[48]

Turning Meaning

It is not only in contemporary art that attempts can be made to turn the meanings of the killed animal (or, as Scarry might prefer to express it, to put the reality-conferring effect of its opened body to work on behalf of a "different constellation of beliefs"). In December 2002, echoing a practice it had already tried in the United States, PETA engaged in its first British attempt to turn the meaning of the fur coat: to take the material of the killed animal's pelt and to reconfigure its meanings without significantly changing its appearance. According to its press release, "People for the Ethical Treatment of Animals have a somewhat unusual present for people living rough in Liverpool this Christmas: free furs. PETA will hand out dozens of furs—all kindly donated by those who've had a change of heart about killing animals for fashion—to some of the city's neediest people. . . . 'We can't bring these animals back, but we can send a message that only people truly struggling to survive have any excuse for wearing even donated furs,' says PETA director Ingrid Newkirk."[49]

The effectiveness of the strategy is undoubtedly open to question, but in its very precariousness the form of that strategy is perhaps surprisingly close to that of some contemporary art. PETA's Sean Gifford would only a few months later be quoted as saying that there is "nothing creative about skinning an animal," but here was PETA showing that *creative use* could certainly be made of a skinned animal. The strategy even depended on an artlike botching. As a local newspaper reported: "Each coat has a paint mark on one arm to show it is second-hand and has not been bought by the wearer."[50]

Turning meaning, or at least the successful turning of meaning, calls for more (or other) than what Julius dismisses as the mere "carnivalesque inversion" of the culture's hierarchy by discontented artists. Angela Singer's approach to turning the trophy's meanings, for example, is no *inversion* of what Julius calls the "most fundamental of hierarchies, which places the human above the merely animal."[51] Rather, it involves a turning away from that entire spectrum of meanings and a questioning of the viability and ethical adequacy of that spectrum.

It is not simply a matter, however, of substituting one set of ethical priorities for another. Julius's concern with botched taxidermy's lack of "moral scruple"—like Suzi Gablik's concern in the 1980s with what she called "art's moral centre"[52]—cannot conceive of the possibility that the integrity of artworks such as those discussed in this essay is not fashioned out of, and is not best expressed through, the language of morals and ethics. This integrity might be better thought of as a working method, as an intuitive way of operating, as the fluid sub-ethical practice referred to earlier, or perhaps as what Donna J. Haraway has called a "mode of attention" to the animal.[53] As often as not, that mode of attention may be focused on making, and on form, rather than on meaning.

Twists and Turns of the Trophy

When artists' statements about their own work are taken seriously, an answer to the question with which this essay opened—Can contemporary art productively address the killing of animals?—seems to become more elusive than ever. Even within the handful of recent artworks that appear directly to reference the hunting trophy, there is little consensus on the intentions informing and shaping these works. In raising the question of artists' intentions here, the point is not to privilege the interpretations offered by the artists themselves but rather to show that the kinds of formal experimentation or investigation in which contemporary artists habitually engage may have little direct bearing on or relation to the ethically controversial or ethically engaged "look" of some of their work.

"They're trophies, they're empty trophies," the British-based American artist Jordan Baseman has explained of the taxidermic sculptural pieces he made in the mid-1990s. None of the animals used were killed for the artist's purposes, and several were simply found as roadkill outside his London studio. Talking about the pair of animal skins with modeled heads that comprise his stunning *The Cat and the Dog* (1995), owned by the Saatchi Gallery, he has described the effect of these wall-mounted bodily remains as being "exactly like tiger skins, or bear skins or whatever."[54] The floor-based *Surrender* (figure 4.4) works to similar effect and employs similar basic taxidermy techniques, with the cat's skin stretched and pinned over the dried clay of its modeled head.

But *Bred* (1997)—a preserved rabbit's head with its eyes and mouth stitched closed—is rather different (see figure 4.6). Despite its wall-mounted position giving it something of the appearance of a trophy, the stitched eyelids are not intended as a Singer-like commentary on the blocking of a hunted animal's gaze. Baseman explains: "In *Bred* I researched and collected recipes for making shrunken heads. I then modified these recipes and used them to shrink animal heads (particularly rabbits)—hence the stitching on the rabbit's eyes and mouth." Pieces like this are driven not by an attempt to convey a single clear message but by something more like technical and visual curiosity. If viewers are put off by the work's appearance—if they imagine that they see an animal that the artist has somehow abused—it will be hard for them to recognize the nature of the artist's interest in and commitment to the work. Noting that his work often elicits "a negative (or at the very least a complex) response" from viewers, he comments: "I think that this is interesting because I think in many ways a lot of the work is beautiful and moving."[55]

British artist Chloë Brown's imposing work *A Fragile Happiness* (2002) adds further twists to the work of reading trophy-like imagery, not least in relation to questions of beauty (see figure 4.7). It consists of a mounted stag's head that appears to be shedding abundant streams of glass tears, while nine mounted birds perch nonchalantly on its antlers. It is (at least for this writer)

Jordan Baseman, *Bred* (1997), preserved rabbit's head. Courtesy of the artist.

Chloë Brown, *A Fragile Happiness* (2002), mounted stag's head, nine mounted birds. Courtesy of the artist.

quite difficult not to read this as an accusatory anti-hunting image, in which the incipient sentimentality of the weeping stag is perplexingly but successfully held in check by the singing birds.

Like Singer and Baseman, Brown is concerned to emphasize the care taken in sourcing her animal bodies. The taxidermist with whom she works uses donated roadkill for his specimens, as a result of which Brown had to modify her plans for *A Fragile Happiness*. She had initially hoped to use mounted British songbirds, but as it was not possible to obtain many of these, other specimens had to be substituted. She acknowledges that "the idea of a hunting trophy is definitely entwined in this work" and that it is an indirect comment on "the lack of dignity" afforded to such animals, but she insists that "this work is not a comment on bloodsports." What she was seeking to achieve seems to have involved a fine balance between pathos and comedy: "The birds are having a fine time, and the stag is not. The birds have mistaken the stag for a tree . . . and are oblivious to the suffering of the stag." She also relates the piece to "the use of imagery that one often finds in cartoons," such as the "horrible" visual joke of what appears to be a mounted trophy head turning out to be that of a living creature whose head "has been rammed through the wall behind the trophy." The profusion of teardrops is also intended to make "the 'cartoon' nature of this piece" evident to the viewer.[56]

She also makes a revealing comment about the beauty to be found in what some may regard as distressing imagery: "Part of the original idea came from a series of alchemist's etchings of animals with their throats cut, and the blood sprays out in profusion but it is drawn in a very beautiful way; it is aestheticized beyond what it means to cut an animal's throat, and I wanted to treat the tears in this way."[57]

Another artist whose animal imagery is shaped by a complex mix of influences and intentions is Lyne Lapointe, who lives and works in a fairly remote part of Quebec, not far from the border it shares with Vermont. A major exhibition of her work (entitled *La Tache aveugle*) at the Musée d'art contemporain de Montréal in 2002 included a number of pieces that engaged—in extremely elliptical ways—with her opposition to hunting. One of those pieces, *L'Éperon* (2001), is as much a trophy manqué as a painting (see figure 4.8).

Jutting out from its center is the real spur to which the title refers, its heel taking on something like the shape of a pair of antlers. Enclosed within it is a little piece of collage: a detail of a painting by Leonardo da Vinci. It shows

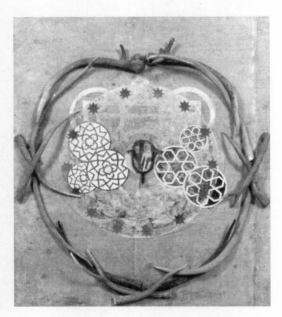

Lyne Lapointe, *L'Éperon* (2001), oil paint, collage, old spur, lead stars, metal amulet, antlers, on paper mounted on plywood, painted wooden frame. Courtesy of the artist.

a human hand holding an ermine, though the creature itself is all but invisible in this collaged detail. And surrounding the stellar geometry that occupies much of the painting are further animal fragments, this time in the form of the ring of real antlers that seem to allude indirectly to the idea of a hunting trophy.

The rural environment in which Lapointe works includes plenty of evidence of the decorative display of hunted animals' remains, in the form of rows of antlers secured to the wooden boards at the front of local hunters' houses. But *L'Éperon* seems also to have in its sights the more formal symmetry of the mounted hunting trophy, which is not only the frontal symmetry of the dead animal's head but also that peculiar symmetrical logic that wants to show the means of its destruction too. That kind of display can be seen at its most elaborate and explicit in the Musée de la chasse et de la nature in Paris, where conventional animal-head trophies are flanked by elephant tusks, guns, spears, and a variety of exotic blades. There, it seems, an attempt is made to aestheticize those clusters of inanimate and previously animate things through their symmetrical display, as though visual pleasure might distract the viewer from the deadly theme of the displays.

It would be quite wrong, however, to read Lapointe's echoes of such imagery as a direct critique of it, despite her opposition to hunting. Her works do not moralize in any way, and she says of them, "I want people to feel good when they see the work. I want to give a certain peace." This telling remark relates to her belief that even when her works show animals that may be the subject of a hunter's or a predator's attention, as in *Cerf albinos* (1999), those works can offer a form of "protection." It seems as though, in this regard, she sees them as operating rather like a traditional talisman, the purpose of which (as David Freedberg explains) was to "ward off hostility," not least through imagery that employed "the force of frontality, symmetry, repetition." Several of Lapointe's works, including *L'Éperon,* have this talismanic dimension, and if their protective role is in part a matter of offering what she calls "a place to hide," it is equally to be understood as "a place for the spectator to think."[58]

The examples of work by Baseman, Brown, and Lapointe have been presented here to emphasize that there is no simple or single way to read the empty, subverted, or turned trophies of contemporary art. Even Singer, whose work may seem far more single-minded in terms of its political purpose, admits that her taxidermic manipulations are open to a variety of readings. She suggests, for example, that "a viewer might completely miss the anti-hunting message" of a work such as *sore* (figure 4.5) but might legitimately read it as "a symbolic funeral effigy," because "*sore* references the medieval

funeral wax effigy, created to be mourned." More worrying are those instances where viewers sympathetic to the cause of animals completely fail to
register the effect of her deliberate botching of their bodies. She reports the
remarkable story of Bob Kerridge, executive director of the Society for the
Prevention of Cruelty to Animals, being asked by a journalist for a comment
on one of Singer's exhibitions in Auckland that featured examples of her
botched taxidermy pieces. He apparently commented: "It's all in the name
of art I suppose. I guess it's no different to having a stuffed deer in the
lounge."[59]

Addressing Killing

The dead animal of botched taxidermy is not the dead animal of the hunting
trophy, though each might be said to haunt the other. Hirst's aphorism "You
kill things to look at them" does at least have the value of recognizing that
what is at stake here is an intense and inventive looking, a rigorousness of
investigation, which has to be coldly unapologetic in its attitude to the
looked-at being. This, arguably, is what any serious art does. And in botched
taxidermic trophies, it seems, the killing is addressed by investigating the
looking. In this sense, far from being sensationalist, these works do indeed
constitute what Lapointe calls "a place for the spectator to think."

However, in the light of the varied intentions and interpretations that
cluster around the works discussed in the previous section, it is important
to return to the question of how effective the strategy of turning meanings,
and more specifically of turning the animal's gaze, might really be. In the
end, this is for readers and viewers to decide for themselves, but there is at
least one pertinent recent argument for the significance of seeing the human
world (including human killing of animals) "from the vantage of the animal."

That argument is presented in Jacques Derrida's ground-breaking essay
"The Animal That Therefore I Am" (the lengthy text of part of an even
longer lecture delivered in 1997), in which he comes close to proposing the
rewriting of his entire philosophy on the basis of attending seriously to his
relationship with his pet cat and in which the question of looking is central.
His understanding of the world and of his own secure place in it is unsettled
entirely when he stands "before a cat that looks at you without moving, just
to see." This particular form of unsettling impropriety [malséance] he calls
animalséance: "the cat's eyes looking at me as it were from head to toe, just
to see, not hesitating to concentrate its vision."[60] There is no need to elaborate
the idea that in this intense and serious looking the animal adopts something

rather like the role of the artist, for Derrida's direct concern is with how that looking turns and transforms the project of philosophy.

He alleges that the "invariable" concern of "Western philosophical discourse" has been with "what is proper to man, his superiority over and subjugation of the animal, his very becoming-subject," and in place of that discourse he calls for a recognition of human responsibilities to animals that, "were we to take it seriously, would have to change even the very basis . . . of the philosophical problematic of the animal." Imagining the world "from the vantage of the animal" and acknowledging "the seeing and not just seen eyes of the other" is exactly what philosophers have failed to do. "They have taken no account of the fact that what they call animal could *look at* them and *address* them," says Derrida, and "everything goes on as if they themselves had never been looked at . . . by an animal that addressed them."[61]

That address, as he presents it, explicitly includes the question of how to read the forms of contemporary animal abuse and slaughter. Noting the impact of "the joint developments of zoological, ethological, biological and genetic *forms of knowledge* and the always inseparable *techniques* of intervention" on the lives and deaths of animals, he alleges: "No one can deny seriously, or for very long, that men do all they can to dissimulate this cruelty or to hide it from themselves, in order to organize on a global scale the forgetting or misunderstanding of this violence that some would compare to the worst cases of genocide." For Derrida, therefore, it is clear that the killing of animals can indeed be productively addressed through the turning of looking and through philosophy's adoption of the vantage of the animal. The difficulty, discomfort, and awkwardness of adopting this unfamiliar perspective is unsurprising, calling as it does on the human to surrender "to the animal in itself, to the animal in me and the animal at unease with itself."[62]

The dead animal of botched taxidermy—"difficult to 'read' and far from 'beautiful,'" as Mieke Bal put it—is precisely Derrida's animal *at unease with itself*. Art gives physical form to that unease by botching the animal body. As Angela Singer observes, people "understand what an animal is meant to look like. If it has been altered they know it and they can question why." In many pieces she is directly concerned to create a difficult looking, an uneasy looking. Jeffrey Masson said to her, "I find your art hard to look at, which is the point, I imagine," and she herself states, "I want the viewer to feel discomfort when they see my work, because the work is born of my discomfort with the way that animals are treated as a resource available for exploitation by human beings." She offers a specific example: "When I made *sore* I tried to imagine the pain and terror of the animal. . . . I wasn't going to make its pointless death easy on the viewer." It is a matter of materials and technique as much as content: "I think some people fear the physicality of art that uses taxidermy. Taxidermy shrinks the animal and botching taxidermy gives the animal back its presence, making it too big to ignore."[63]

A description of one further piece will help to explain how Singer locks looking and killing together in her work. The installation *wild-deer-ness (Kill Joy)* (2002) positions an awkward-looking recycled trophy-kill taxidermy fawn in front of a "1970s decorative forest photo wall," at some distance from a recycled rifle scope mounted on a tripod, through which both can be seen (see figure 4.9).

Looking through the scope, the viewer "sees that the fawn has a glistening bloody bullet hole" (added by the artist) and that it "appears to be frozen attempting to stand from a lying position. When the viewer abandons the scope and walks closer to the fawn, viewing it from another angle, the chest of the fawn is revealed to be very obviously stitched up, thus ruining the life-like illusion of the taxidermy." The effect, she hopes, is to "concentrate" the image so that "the fawn becomes the small wretched bullet wound."[64]

In 2001, a year before this installation was made, Lyne Lapointe had offered what might be regarded as an alternative treatment of a very similar theme in a work called *No Man's Land* (see figure 4.10). At its center hangs an old enamel advertising sign, the words now difficult to decipher, but appearing to read "We use the De Laval Cream Separator." Found by Lapointe nailed to the outside of a milking barn on land used both for deer hunting and for

Angela Singer, *wild-deer-ness (Kill Joy)* (2002), 1970s decorative forest photo-wall, recycled trophy-kill taxidermy fawn, oil paint, recycled rifle scope and tripod. Courtesy of the artist.

agriculture at different times of year, the plaque is shot through with ragged bullet holes, having been used by local hunters for target practice. Here the animal's body may not be directly present, but the bullet holes are compellingly real. The artist has added little, positioning the plaque on the supporting field of a paper whose patterned texture might evoke that of an animal skin and on which a complex but only loosely target-like series of circles has been engraved.[65]

Lapointe's *No Man's Land* is an understated work, and some viewers may prefer it to the more elaborate drama of Singer's *wild-deer-ness (Kill Joy)* for exactly that reason. Both works address the killing of animals, both link the technologies of looking and of killing, and both present a stark image of the wound. Which of these two artworks is more effective in its address? The question is an unreasonable one, other than in pointing to the inescapability of aesthetic judgments and the expression of aesthetic preferences in almost any assessment of the ethical or political efficacy of art. That lesson, at least, may be worth remembering.

Lyne Lapointe, *No Man's Land* (2001), enameled plaque, pyrogravure on paper mounted on plywood, metal frame. Courtesy of the artist.

Notes

1. Roland Barthes, *Mythologies,* trans. Annette Lavers (London: Paladin, 1973), 101.

2. See, for example, Steve Baker, "Animal Rights and Wrongs," *Tate: The Art Magazine,* 26 (2001): 42–47; K. D. Thornton, "The Aesthetics of Cruelty vs. the Aesthetics of Empathy," in *The Aesthetics of Care?,* ed. Oron Catts (Nedlands: SymbioticA, University of Western Australia, 2002), 5–11; and Julia Lohmann, "The Death of Animals in Contemporary Art: Reasons, Processes, Reactions" (master's diss., Royal College of Art, London, 2003).

3. John Simons, *Animal Rights and the Politics of Literary Representation* (Basingstoke and New York: Palgrave, 2002), 207, 181–82. Although Simons's proposed reading of the photograph will be called into question here, Cindy Sherman has decided (for understandable reasons) that she prefers the image not to be reproduced in the context of this discussion of representations of animal death.

4. John Simons, review of *The Postmodern Animal,* by Steve Baker, *Anthrozoös* 15, no. 2 (2002): 183.

5. Steve Baker, *The Postmodern Animal* (London: Reaktion Books, 2000), 56.

6. Jacques Derrida, "'Eating Well,' or the Calculation of the Subject: An Interview with Jacques Derrida," in *Who Comes after the Subject?,* ed. Eduardo Cadava, Peter Connor, and Jean-Luc Nancy (New York and London: Routledge, 1991), 104, quoted in Baker, *Postmodern Animal,* 76.

7. E. H. Gombrich, "The Visual Image," in *The Image and the Eye: Further Studies in the Psychology of Pictorial Representation* (Oxford: Phaidon, 1982), 138; Sol Worth, "Seeing Metaphor as Caricature," *New Literary History* 6, no. 1 (1974): 204; Barthes, *Mythologies,* 101.

8. Mieke Bal, *Louise Bourgeois's "Spider": The Architecture of Art-Writing* (Chicago and London: University of Chicago Press, 2001), 3.

9. Mark Dion, "Some Notes towards a Manifesto for Artists Working with or about the Living World," in *The Greenhouse Effect* (exhibition catalog), ed. Ralph Rugoff and Lisa G. Corrin (London: Serpentine Gallery, 2000), 66.

10. Justice for Animals Arts Guild, e-mail correspondence with the author, June 2001, April 2003, and May 2003.

11. Sue Coe quotations drawn from two interviews: Susan Vaughn, "Staying True to a Unique Vision of Art," *Los Angeles Times,* 1 April 2001, reproduced at http://graphicwitness.org/coe/latimes.htm; and Elin Slavik, "Art<>Activism: An Interview with Sue Coe," *MediaReader Quarterly* 4 (2000), reproduced at http://www.mediareader.org/Issue4Stories/4_SueCoe.html.

12. Carol J. Adams, e-mail correspondence with the author, March 2000.

13. Mark Dion, "The Artist as Traveller in Foreign Lands," lecture at the School of Art History and Archaeology, University of Manchester, UK, November 6, 2000; Sue Coe, quoted in Slavik, "Art<>Activism."

14. Cindy Sherman, quoted in Amanda Cruz, Elizabeth A. T. Smith, and Amelia Jones, *Cindy Sherman: Retrospective* (London: Thames and Hudson, 1997), 8.

15. Simons, *Animal Rights,* 181–82.

16. Jonathan Burt, *Animals in Film* (London: Reaktion Books, 2002), 161–62, 25–26.

17. Brandon Taylor, "Beauty from Violence," *TwoNineTwo: Essays in Visual Culture* 3 (2002): 34–35.

18. Anthony Julius, *Transgressions: The Offences of Art* (London: Thames and Hudson, 2002), passim.

19. Ibid., 140, 142–43; Damien Hirst, *i want to spend the rest of my life everywhere, with everyone, one to one, always, forever, now* (London: Booth-Clibborn Editions, 1997), 279.

20. Julius, *Transgressions*, 143–44.

21. Ibid., 154.

22. John Isaacs, unpublished interview with the author, London, March 1999.

23. Sue Coe, conversation with the author, New York, May 2002.

24. Wendy Steiner, *The Scandal of Pleasure: Art in an Age of Fundamentalism* (Chicago and London: University of Chicago Press, 1995), 211.

25. This account of the event draws on two published reports: Fiachra Gibbons, "Lights, Camera, Let the Cutting Begin," *Guardian*, November 21, 2002, 1; and Steve Connor, "I Am at the Cutting Edge of Democracy, Proclaims Professor as he Defies Police over Public Autopsy," *Independent*, November 21, 2002, 1.

26. Anonymous editorial, "Cutting Edge Dilemma," *Guardian*, November 21, 2002, 23; Robert Baker, "A Deadly Serious Matter, Dressed Up as Entertainment," *Independent*, November 21, 2002, 21.

27. Jeremy Laurance, "Preventable Deaths Will Increase as Post-Mortem Exams Die, Say Doctors," *Independent*, November 21, 2002, 3; Baker, "Deadly Serious Matter," 21.

28. Richard Brooks, "Hirst to Pickle Three Crucified Cows," *Sunday Times* (London), April 13, 2003, 25.

29. David Usborne, "Fur and Loathing," *The Independent Review*, "Fur-y special issue" (the "y" being drawn as a bloody brush stroke throughout the issue), November 21, 2002, 10–11; and Hadley Freeman, "'There Is Nothing Creative about Skinning an Animal,'" *Guardian G2*, March 14, 2003, 8–9.

30. Jordan Baseman, e-mail correspondence with the author, April 2003; Angela Singer, e-mail correspondence with the author, April 2003.

31. Elaine Scarry, *The Body in Pain: The Making and Unmaking of the World* (New York and Oxford: Oxford University Press, 1985), 118, 117, 119.

32. Ibid., 121, 124, 125.

33. Julian Borger, "Here's the Evidence, Says US," *Guardian*, July 25, 2003, 1.

34. Scarry, *Body in Pain*, 126.

35. Julius, *Transgressions*, 146; Loura Wixley Brooks, "Damien Hirst and the Sensibility of Shock," *Art and Design* 10 (1995): 58.

36. Julius, *Transgressions*, 145, 154.

37. Kitty Hauser, "Coming Apart at the Seams: Taxidermy and Contemporary Photography," *Make* 82 (1998–99): 9.

38. William Gibson, *Pattern Recognition* (London: Viking, 2003), 137. The image of the towers as an opened body appears to have a certain contemporary currency: Susan Orlean's "Lifelike: What It Takes to Be a Great Taxidermist," *The New Yorker*, June 9, 2003, reports a "surpassingly weird" display at the 2003 World Taxidermy Championships in Springfield, Illinois, that showed "a coyote whose torso was split open to reveal a miniature scene of the destruction of the World Trade Center, complete with little firemen and rubble piles" (50).

39. Susan Shaw Sailer, "On the Redness of Salmon Bones, the Communicative Potential of Conger Eels, and Standing Tails of Air: Reading Postmodern Images," *Word and Image* 12, no. 3 (1996): 310.

40. Gilles Deleuze and Félix Guattari, *A Thousand Plateaus: Capitalism and Schizophrenia*, trans. Brian Massumi (London: Athlone, 1988), 160, and *Kafka: Toward a Minor Literature*, trans. Dana Polan (Minneapolis and London: University of Minnesota Press, 1986), 13, 35.

41. Hirst, *i want to spend the rest of my life everywhere* . . . , 285.

42. John C. Metcalf, *Taxidermy: A Complete Manual* (London: Duckworth, 1981), 66, 94.

43. Lynda Birke, "Who—or What—Are the Rats (and Mice) in the Laboratory?," *Society and Animals* 11, no. 3 (2003): 216.

44. Angela Singer, e-mail correspondence with the author, June 2001.

45. Ibid., March 2003.

46. Ibid., April 2003.

47. Metcalf, *Taxidermy*, 84.

48. Angela Singer, e-mail correspondence with the author, April 2003.

49. People for the Ethical Treatment of Animals, press release, "PETA to Give Away Fur Coats to the Homeless This Christmas," December 11, 2002.

50. Catherine Jones, "Furs Come Furs Served," *Liverpool Echo*, December 12, 2002, 3.

51. Julius, *Transgressions*, 108, 143.

52. Suzi Gablik, *Has Modernism Failed?* (London: Thames and Hudson, 1984), 74.

53. Donna J. Haraway, "A Companion Species Manifesto," lecture at Lancaster University, U.K., March 12, 2003.

54. Jordan Baseman, unpublished interview with the author, London, January 2000.

55. Jordan Baseman, e-mail correspondence with the author, April 2003.

56. Chloë Brown, e-mail correspondence with the author, May 2003.

57. Ibid.

58. Lyne Lapointe, unpublished interview with the author, Quebec, November 2001; David Freedberg, *The Power of Images: Studies in the History and Theory of Response* (Chicago and London: University of Chicago Press, 1989), 128, 132.

59. Angela Singer, e-mail correspondence with the author, April 2003.

60. Jacques Derrida, "The Animal That Therefore I Am (More to Follow)," trans. David Wills, *Critical Inquiry* 28 (2002): 372, 373.

61. Ibid., 413, 395, 390, 381, 382, 383.

62. Ibid., 394, 372.

63. Angela Singer, e-mail correspondence with the author, June 2001, March 2003, and April 2003.

64. Ibid., March 2003 and April 2003.

65. Martha Fleming, who knows Lapointe well, offers this thoughtful comment on the work's complementary agricultural dimension: "I think she's partly commenting on agricultural husbandry in dairy farming, where to get the 'CREAM' the calves must be 'SEPARATED' (killed) from the cows that bear them solely to be kept in milk. And cream separators work by centrifuge, hence the target-like ripple pattern on the surface of the work underneath the enameled plaque, a surface part pelt, cowskin, part meniscus of milk" (correspondence with the author, December 2003).

5 Two Ethics: Killing Animals in the Past and the Present

ERICA FUDGE

In *Man and the Natural World,* Keith Thomas states that "[i]n the case of animals what was normally displayed in the early modern period was the cruelty of indifference. For most persons beasts were outside the terms of moral reference. . . . It was a world in which much of what would later be regarded as 'cruelty' had not yet been defined as such." As evidence Thomas cites the popularity of baiting, hunting, cockfighting, hawking, bull-running, and the fairground contest of biting the heads off live chickens or sparrows. As well as these "sports," Thomas lists as his evidence schoolboy games that included flaying live frogs, stoning dogs, and throwing chickens into pike-infested ponds.[1] What emerges from just these few pages of a lengthy book is a vision of a world of savagery and, as he notes, grotesque indifference to animal suffering.

In this essay I want to argue, however, that to state as Thomas does that animals were "outside the terms of moral reference" is to fail to fully examine the nature of the ethical context of the early modern period and, as such, is to write off those events listed as evidence of a lack of a concept of cruelty to animals as mere barbarity rather than as important indicators of a complex attitude to animals. And, it is worth noting, a claim for the savagery of the period, which is implied in Thomas's statement, would also remove those elements of early modern culture that we do not regard as savage—Shakespeare's plays, the poetry of John Donne, and so on—from one aspect of their historical context. In this essay I will argue that in early modern England, the ethical context of human relationships with animals—and in particular, the killing of animals—was much more complex than Thomas allows for. I will also argue that recognizing this complexity might allow us to re-evaluate not only the early modern period but also modern human-animal relations. I begin with what is the central mode of ethics in the period and will then shift my focus, as numerous early modern thinkers did, to trace another ethic that undercuts Thomas's assertion and offers another way of thinking about the past.

Self-Serving Kindnesses

Philip P. Hallie proposes a useful title for what is the most orthodox ethical framework in the early modern period: "Inward Government" theory. This theory—emerging from the classical as well as the Christian tradition—proposes that "a good person is one whose passions are under control of his reason. To be good one's soul must be a harmonious, smoothly running state with reason at its head. To be good is to be self-controlled, or rather reason-controlled."[2] Such a theory was based upon a belief in a struggle between the body and the soul, the flesh and the spirit, in every human, and it was the passions—the appetites of the body rather than the mind—that must be controlled. These passions, in the words of Nicholas Coeffeteau, "reside onely in the sensitive appetite, and . . . they are not fashioned but in the ir-rationall part of the soule."[3] To live through direction only of one's passions (which include such things as love, hatred, desire, pleasure, and fear) without using one's mind was, in this theory, to descend to the level of the beast, and this descent was literal, not merely metaphorical. The key division in Inward Government theory was between human and animal and was based upon an analogous binary: the possession or lack of reason. Animals, so the tradition argues, lack reason and therefore lack self-awareness and self-control. Humans possess reason and should therefore exercise it in self-awareness and self-control. It is the role—perhaps a better word would be duty—of humans to ensure that they are self-controlled; that they govern their urges and live reasonably.

Within this theoretical framework, animals are the absolute other; despite the prospect of the human becoming a beast, animals are perceived to have no community with humans. They are the things *against* which humans position themselves. But the theory uses this opposition of human and animal to reiterate the centrality of not merely humanity but the individual human, the self. The focus is not upon the community as a whole—the government of others—as much as it is about the government of one's own being (although the former can emerge out of the latter—a tyrant rules through passion rather than reason).[4] In discussions of cruelty, for example, writers do not deal with the moral patient, the individual suffering, but instead focus on the moral agent, the individual being cruel, and as such self-control, not suffering, is key. This is something that can be traced in a text that had a massive influence on Renaissance thinking: Seneca's *De Clementia*.[5]

Seneca's work was translated into English by Thomas Lodge in 1614 as *A Discourse of Clemencie*. In it Seneca writes: "Crueltie is humane evill, it is unworthy so milde a minde: this is a beast-like rage to rejoice in bloud and wounds, and laying by the habite of a man, to translate himselfe to a wilde beast."[6] No mention is made here of the individual suffering the infliction of cruelty: the effect of cruelty is discussed only in relation to its impact upon the moral agent, the person being cruel. The cruel man becomes, for Seneca, a "wilde beast." This is not mere exaggeration or imagery, but the transformation is logical: because he has ceased to use his reason, has become unreasonable; the distinction between human and animal that underpins Seneca's (and so many others') work has broken down; and the cruel self therefore is—logically—translated into the beast.

Such an "egocentric theory" (Hallie's phrase) is central to numerous writings in early modern England, and it finds a clear illustration in texts that look at the human relationship with animals. Many of these take as their source not only classical ideas but also the work of thirteenth-century theologian Thomas Aquinas, in which classical and Christian thought were brought together. Aquinas took from Plato and Aristotle a belief that within God's creation there is a chain of being that organizes that world. Arthur O. Lovejoy, quoting from Aristotle, has defined such a "conception of the universe" as one in which there was

> an immense, or . . . an infinite, number of links ranging in hierarchical order from the meagerest kind of existents, which barely escape non-existence, through "every possible" grade up to the *ens perfectissimum*—or, in a somewhat more orthodox version, to the highest possible kind of creature, between which and the Absolute Being the disparity was assumed to be infinite—every one of them differing from that immediately above and that immediately below it by the "least possible" degree of difference.[7]

Human superiority to animal is, as in Inward Government theory, based on possession of reason, while animal superiority to plant is based on the capacities for movement and perception (these are the degrees of difference). Both of these forms of superiority are presented as natural and are evidenced in use: Aquinas states, "It is, therefore, legitimate for animals to kill plants and for men to kill animals for their respective benefit." In fact, that legitimacy is regarded as a natural duty: as Dorothy Yamamoto succinctly presents it, for humans in Aquinas's theory, "there is no sin in killing animals. In fact, to refuse to eat meat is to spurn the careful provisions which God has made to sustain human life on earth."[8] But this is not the end of the uses of animals given to humans on the basis of their superiority, and in a passage only a couple of pages after the above quotation from Aquinas, it seems that so superior is the human, the distinction between animal and plant appears to disappear. Aquinas writes: "He who kills another's ox does indeed commit a sin, only it is not the killing of the ox but the inflicting of proprietary loss on another that is the sin. Such an action is, therefore, included not under the sin of homicide but under that of theft or robbery."[9] Killing an ox, it would seem, is little different from, say, stealing a cart.

However, even as he appears to present animals as mere objects, there is, in Aquinas's theory, the possibility of kindness, but this kindness, once again, does not represent a vision in which animals are humans' moral equals; far from it. Animals, Aquinas writes, can be "loved from charity as good things we wish others to have, in that by charity we cherish this for God's honour and man's service."[10] That is, animals should be cared for, not for their own sakes, but for the sake of their owners or of God. This perception of animals is taken up in England in the early modern period, and a summary is offered that is clear, to the point, and wholly in keeping with Inward Government theory: in his 1612 sermon *Mercy to a Beast,* John Rawlinson wrote, "Save a beast's life and save a mans."[11]

Taking, like Rawlinson, their lead from Aquinas and from Proverbs 12:10— "A righteous man regardeth the life of his beast"—numerous other early modern theologians were led into discussions of the moral responsibility of humans toward animals, but their discussions remain strangely, although logically, egocentric, self-interested. Writing in 1589, Thomas Wilcox stated: "[H]ee is mercifull, if to beastes, much more to men."[12] Likewise, in 1592 Peter Muffett wrote, "[I]f he be so pitifull to his beast, much more is he mercifull to his servants, his children, and his wife."[13] Here, we have a glimpse of the natural world in microcosm, of a domestic chain of being: animals are at the bottom, with the master/father/husband at the top. However, even in this inferior position, animals are still perceived to be within the moral compass of humanity, but for a particular reason: becoming inured to viciousness to animals, so the Thomist argument goes, makes one more likely to be vicious to humans, something that would endanger not only other humans (a concern, but not the most important one here) but also one's own immortal soul (the greatest concern of all).

Keith Thomas has labeled this early modern perception of animals as beings within the moral compass of humanity as a "new attitude" and argues that it is paradoxical that such a vision should come from "the old anthropocentric tradition."[14] What he fails to take full notice of is that the "new" ideas not only merely repeat what can be found in the much older Thomist model but that they also remain absolute in their anthropocentrism. Kindness to animals is asserted, not because animals deserve to be treated with kindness, but because it is self-serving: as Joseph Hall wrote, "The mercifull man rewardeth his owne soule; *for* Hee that followeth righteousnesse and mercy, shall find righteousnesse, and life, and glory; *and therefore,* is blessed *for ever.*"[15]

But, there is something that can be labeled as "new" in early modern English ethics, something of which Thomas doesn't fully take notice. In fact, he seems, initially, to dismiss out of hand the importance of the work of those thinkers—Montaigne and his followers—who can be traced as a source of this new ethic in England in the early seventeenth century: "[M]ost contemporary readers," Thomas writes, "would have thought them extravagant nonsense."[16] This dismissal of the influence of ideas voiced by Montaigne comes in part, I think, because Thomas regards what he terms the "new sensibility"—what might actually be called the "generous anthropocentrism" of Thomism—as a positive enough response. But the other proposal about animals that gets such short shrift from Thomas comes from another way of looking at the world. This is not a focus upon inward government; rather the gaze is outside of the self and onto the other, and that other, it turns out, can be an animal.

The Community of the Self

Montaigne's essay "Of cruelty" was first published in 1580 and expanded as Montaigne returned to his essays between 1580 and 1588. It is, so Hallie argues, "one of the most powerful essays on ethics ever written. . . . In a few pages it manages to explore and explode one of the main traditions in the history of man's thought about good and evil, and then—again with remarkable brevity—it makes a statement about ethics that illuminates and gives vitality to the usually heartless abstractions of Western ethics."[17] What Montaigne does that is so remarkable at that date is turn away from the self that is central to Inward Government theory and look instead at the other, at the individual on whom cruelty is inflicted. But as if this turn in itself was not noteworthy enough, Montaigne goes further and makes the crucial distinction in his worldview not reason but sentience, not the ability to rationalize the world but the capacity to feel in it. He argues, "Savages do not shock me as much by roasting and eating the bodies of the dead as do those who torment them and persecute them living."[18] The reason for this statement is clear: at least the bodies that are cannibalized are already dead, while those that are tortured still live and are therefore able to feel. He cannot even look, he writes, "on the executions of the law, however reasonable they may be . . . with a steady gaze." Punishment should be, instead, upon the bodies of dead criminals, not live ones, "against the shell, not the living core."[19]

This emphasis on sentience rather than reason, on the capacity to feel rather than the capacity to rationalize, inevitably leads Montaigne to a discussion of animals. "I have not even been able without distress to see," he writes, "pursued and killed an innocent animal which is defenseless and which does us no harm." His distress is not sentimental, however—that is, it is not emotional or anthropomorphic—it is based on this new logic. He writes of animals: "There is some relationship between them and us, and some mutual obligation."[20] The fact of the relationship leads, for him, logically to a sense of obligation; animals, unlike the dead bodies of humans, are sentient and can, if only by basic means, communicate their suffering. There is, on this basis, recognition, and from that recognition should come society, fellow-feeling. Montaigne writes that when, in the hunt, "the stag, feeling himself out of breath and strength, having no other remedy left, throws itself back and surrenders to ourselves who are pursuing him, asking for our mercy by his tears . . . that has always seemed to me a very unpleasant spectacle."[21] The spectacle is unpleasant because the stag can communicate its suffering, or rather because Montaigne is willing to believe that what is being communicated in the tears in the eyes of the stag can—and must—be interpreted as suffering. Where in Inward Government theory the focus is on the beast within—the unreasonable part of that reasonable creature, the human—for Montaigne, the focus is upon the creature outside of us.[22]

While in Montaigne's work there is a turning away from assertions of human superiority and the significance of the rule of reason that is rare in this period, his inclusion of animals within the human moral framework can be found in other writers. Strangely, in relation to his earlier dismissal of the influence of Montaigne on English ethical thinking, Thomas seems to change his mind when he notes not only that Montaigne's *Essais* were translated into English twice during the seventeenth century but also that "[m]any shared the view expressed by Montaigne" in "Of cruelty."[23] Thomas's ambivalence toward the power and influence of Montaigne's attitude to animals is not unusual. Numerous critics of Montaigne have also refused to take his views in and of themselves wholly seriously. In his study of the ethical and political themes in Montaigne's *Essais,* for example, David Quint writes, "The essayist will advocate kindness toward animals less because of sentimental notions of creaturely kinship, than because 'humanity' separates us from the cruelty of an animal world of predators and victims—which the hunt too closely resembled. Our capacity for humanity counters our bestial instinct to inhumanity."[24] Quint here seems to be reading Montaigne as an Inward Government theorist and is ignoring the fact that in the longest of his *Essais*, "Apology for Raymond Sebond," Montaigne writes, "We recognize easily enough, in most of their works, how much superiority the animals have over us, and how feeble is our skill to imitate them."[25] Such a statement as this (and there are numerous other similar ones) goes against the interpretation of animals as images of predation and violence that Quint proposes. And, because he ignores this aspect of Montaigne's work, Quint has nothing further to say about Montaigne's attitude toward animals.

Another refusal to take Montaigne's vision of animals wholly seriously can also be traced in *The Happy Beast in French Thought of the Seventeenth Century*, George Boas's study of Montaigne and his followers. Boas regards Montaigne's "theriophily" (love of animals) as an exercise within the popular "*genre* of the *Paradoxes*," in which writing was "for literary effect and not for demonstrating truth."[26] Animals are, it would seem, merely part of a literary game that Montaigne is playing; they are never real animals. It is as if, so often, critics are unwilling to contemplate the possibility that a key thinker of the early modern period might have something radical (still radical) to say about nonhuman beings. It is as if it is not quite possible to reconcile the centrality of Montaigne with the perceived marginality of thinking about animals. This is not a view that was shared in Montaigne's own time. Sir William Cornwallis, for example, wrote in 1610 of Montaigne's "womanish" discussion of the "death of birdes and beasts": "[A]las this gentlenesse of Nature is a plaine weakenesse."[27] There is nothing to suggest in this dismissal that Cornwallis didn't take Montaigne at his word, that he didn't read Montaigne's views about animals as serious. It's just that he didn't agree with them.

However, I also want to argue that Montaigne's views about animals are worth taking seriously and that to dismiss them is to undermine the coherence of his wider ethical statements. In addition, I want, as a historian, to take Montaigne's views seriously because there is evidence that his ideas were taken up by a number of writers in England, and while it is difficult to attribute them at origin directly to Montaigne, these writers do reiterate arguments that are present in the *Essais*. What perhaps links Montaigne to these English writers is not nationality or religion—the works that follow are by English Protestants while Montaigne was a French Catholic—but the sense in which it is the everyday rather than the abstract that is the focus. Where Seneca detailed cruelty as an abstract concept, Montaigne wrote not only about the concept but also about actual events, often events that he was directly involved with. Likewise, the English writers I will look at wrote manuals to direct everyday living and gave sermons to address ordinary concerns. They came from a background in theology, certainly, but for them the Bible was the source of ethics, and ethics, for Joseph Hall, one of the most renowned sermonizers of the age, was "*a Doctrine of* wisedom and knowledge to *live wel . . . the end wherof is to see and attaine that chiefe* goodness of the children of men."[28] We are dealing with what might be termed good lives, not just with the Inward Government theory's focus on good selves. Although the two—good lives and good selves—are inseparable, in Montaigne's new ethics a good life must take note of the world in which it is lived; it must include in its contemplation not only its own actions but also the impact of those actions on other beings in that world. This is very different from attempting to attain a good self. But, as well as emphasizing the importance of Montaigne's attitude to animals, it is also possible to see how another context made the notion of the community of all creatures more acceptable than might be expected in early modern England.

The Other Ethics

During the sixteenth and early seventeenth centuries, natural philosophy, the study of the natural world, was a very different practice from modern zoological or ethological investigations. On one level, the natural world was studied, not because it was of interest in itself, but because it offered a further understanding of the Creator. In his *Historie of Foure-Footed Beastes,* for example, Edward Topsell, a cleric, proposed that animals were created in order "that a man might gaine out of them much devine knowledge, such as is imprinted in them by nature, as a tipe or spark of that great wisedome whereby things were created."[29] What follows in this lengthy text is an attempt to outline the workings of God through an analysis of animals, and the implication of that intention was, as Peter Harrison has written, that "the literary context of the living creature was more important than its physical environment. Animals had a 'story,' they were allocated meanings, they were emblems of important moral and theological truths." As well as this, another early modern conception added to the meaning of the natural world. This conception emphasized animals' connection with humans: as Harrison notes, the human was perceived as "an epitome of all the animals. Birds and beasts could thus symbolise distinct passions, virtues and vices."[30] The cunning of a fox, the loyalty of a dog, the timidity of a hare, all of these apparently predetermined animal behaviors were used to explain more generally the concepts of cunning, loyalty, and timidity in humans.

In these terms, animals were represented as meaningful and recognizable to humans. To offer just one example, Topsell begins his chapter "Of the Elephant" with the following statement: "There is no creature among al the Beasts of the world which hath so great and ample demonstration of the power and wisedome of almighty God as the Elephant: both for proportion of body and disposition of spirit." The spirit of this animal includes, in Topsell's analysis, its generosity: "They are so loving to their fellowes, that they will not eat their meat alone, but having found a prey, they go and invite the residue to their feastes and cheere, more like to reasonable civill men, then unreasonable brute beasts."[31] Here, a mere animal is presented as being capable of the "civill" behavior that humans so frequently fail to display. As such, the elephant offers to Topsell's readers a vision of how a good human might behave. God has sent this sign, and the natural philosopher's argument is that humans should learn to interpret it correctly and from that interpretation become better—more godly—people.

The outcome of this understanding of the study of animals is, then, that animals are often anthropomorphized. The male bear, to offer another example, has the decency to leave the female bear alone when she is pregnant, and the clear meaning of this zoological "fact" is that male humans should act in the same way toward pregnant women.[32] What this anthropomorphism does is reduce the distance between humans and animals. Animals remain lesser beings—their virtuous behavior is not willed; it comes from natural instinct rather than a process of moral decision-making, also known as reason—but the naturalness of an animal's virtue reinforces the need for humans themselves to be virtuous. "For yf," as the translation of one French text of 1585 presented this argument, "the beastes do better their office accordyng to their nature, then men doe theirs, they deserve more to be called reasonable, then men."[33]

This sense in natural philosophy of the closeness of humans and animals feeds into other discourses and offers, I suggest, a context into which Montaigne's assertion of the human community with animals may have comfortably fit. When tracing Montaignean ideas in England, then, we are tracing not only the emergence of a new ethic but also recognition that this new ethic was not absolutely at odds with preexisting ideas in a different discourse. What both have in common is the assertion that it is through animals that humans can live good, ethical lives.

Robert Cleaver's *A Plaine and Familiar Exposition of the Eleventh and Twelfth Chapters of the Proverbes of Salomon* (1608) begins to show how a shift in focus from the good self to the good life might manifest itself in ethical discussion. Looking at Proverbs 12:10 once again, Cleaver writes: "Mercy is to be shewed not onely to men, but to the unreasonable creatures also. As all creatures doe taste of, and live by the aboundant liberality and bountifulness of Gods hand, so would he have them to feele by sense, though they cannot discerne it by reason, that there is also care for them and compassion in his children."[34] Here animals' lack of reason is regarded as a lack (in this Cleaver is very different from Montaigne), but that lack is not all that is regarded. Instead, and more like Montaigne, Cleaver asserts animals' ability to feel as the more important ethical point. It is for this reason that humans are to show mercy to them. By acknowledging the sentient nature of animals—their God-given capacity to feel in the world—Cleaver shifts his ethics to allow for this fact. Reason is not all that is worth recognizing.

A different aspect of Montaigne's thought can be traced in Joseph Hall's 1625 discussion of Balaam and his ass (Numbers 22:21–33). Hall begins with the miracle of the speaking ass "whose common sense is advanced above the reason of his rider" and argues that this is an example of the power of the Almighty: "There is no mouth, into which God cannot put words: and how oft doth hee choose the weake, and unwise, to confound the learned, and mighty." This theological discussion, however, leads to something very different. The theory, in fact, leads, as it often does in Montaigne's work, to something much more practical. Hall writes: "I heare the Angell of God taking notice of the cruelty of *Balaam* to his beast: His first words to the unmercifull prophet, are in expostulating of this wrong. We little thinke it; but God shall call us to an account for the unkind and cruell usages of his poore mute creatures: He hath made us Lords, not tyrants; owners, not tormenters."[35]

Nothing, it seems, could be more different from the Thomist perspective. Here, cruelty to animals is something that is not a path to sin (Aquinas's view) but is sinful in and of itself. Animals, not the owners of the animals, in this interpretation can be worthy recipients of kind acts by moral agents. In this Hall has moved the boundaries of community and has included animals within his moral framework. He continues, however: "[H]ee that hath given us leave to kill them, for our use, hath not given us leave to abuse them, at our pleasure; they are so our drudges, that they are our fellowes by creation."[36] This seems to return to Aquinas's sense that animals are on earth to serve humans, but here Hall is making an important distinction. While it is acceptable to kill animals for use, that is, that their role as our "drudges" will include them being our meat and clothing as well as our servants, animals are not to be the victims of our pleasure, that is, they are not to be killed for no practical reason. Animals, in Hall's representation, are "our fellows by creation": they share our world. Even though they have a lower place than humans, they still have a place. This is significantly different from the egocentric view that presented animals as mere objects, whose deaths were to be regarded as robbery rather than homicide, and the abuse of whom was regarded as detrimental to human salvation, not to the experience of the animal.

However, it is worth remembering that Hall was also cited earlier in this essay as evidence of the continuation of the Thomist tradition in England: "The mercifull man rewardeth his owne soule," he stated. What is clear from this is that these two visions of ethics—that of the good self and that of the good life—not only existed at the same time but also actually *coexisted* in the early modern period: Hall could be simultaneously a Thomist and something of a Montaignean. But it is not merely on an individual basis that this apparently contradictory ethical framework can be seen. It is also to be traced in institutions.

Baiting and Justice

In "Of cruelty" Montaigne writes, "We owe justice to men, and mercy and kindness to other creatures that may be capable of receiving it."[37] Here Montaigne makes a distinction between justice and mercy, and the implication is, I think, that justice is something that only humans can experience as both recipients and benefactors. On the other hand, animals, while within the compass of human care, are not capable of either receiving or distributing justice, one of the four cardinal virtues. Montaigne's assertion that justice cannot be directed toward animals is also evident in a very different context: in the English legal system. While in continental Europe trials of animals did take place, English law was different.[38] Instead of a trial of the animal, in England the animal that had killed or caused injury was declared deodand (from the Latin *deo dandum*—given to God), and the owner either paid a fine to retrieve the animal or the animal was destroyed and so the owner lost the economic value of that animal. This distinction between continental European and English law stems from the fact that in English law, an animal was perceived to be incapable of intent and therefore of committing a crime: only a reasonable creature could intend something. A death resulting from the actions of an animal was termed a "Casuall death," a death without meaning because it was without purpose.[39] But on top of this denial to animals of a sense of intention, if the animal was declared deodand, that placed it within a category that included not human criminals but objects. In a case of drowning from Essex in 1576, for example, a set of blown-up bladders (early modern water wings) that failed to keep a child afloat were declared deodand. The objects had not fulfilled their function and were taken from their owner. The punishment was not, of course, directed at the objects but at the owner of the objects.[40]

This legal practice can be witnessed on two occasions in the Bear Garden, home to the baiting of bears on London's Bankside. The killing of bears in the Bear Garden was unusual in this period for one very practical reason: bears were specially imported—brought over from continental Europe (there were no indigenous bears in England, Scotland, or Wales)[41]—and were too expensive to kill on a regular basis.[42] It is for this reason that, during a baiting contest, human bear-wards would step in to defend the bear from the attacking dogs. One bear would be baited numerous times over a number of years. But on two occasions the value of the animal was set aside and the bear was killed. The reason for these killings shows how the apparently contradictory ethical frameworks available in early modern England existed not only in the minds of individuals but also on an institutional level.

In 1609 James VI and I went to the Tower "to see a triall of the Lyons single valour, against a great fierce Beare, which had kild a child, that was negligently left in the Beare-house." The entertainment was actually a kind of chivalric ritual that might allow the spectators to see right overcome might, the law (in the shape of the lion, of course) overwhelm the savage bear. John Stow and Edmond Howes recorded the event:

> This fierce Beare was brought into the open yard, behind the Lyons Den, which was the place for fight: then was the great Lyon put forth, who gazed a while, but never offred to assault or approch the Beare: then were two mastife Dogs put in, who past by the Beare, and boldly seazed upon the Lyon: then was a stone Horse put into the same yard, who suddenly sented & saw both the Beare and Lyon, and very carelessly grazed in the middle of the yard between them both: and then were six dogs put in, the most whereof at the first seazed upon the Lyon, but they sodaily left him, and seazed upon the Horse, and hadde worryed him to death, but that three stout Beare-wards, even as the K[ing] wished, came boldly in, and rescued the horse, by taking off the Dogges one by one, whilest the Lyon and Beare stared uppon them, and so went forth with their Dogs: then was that Lyon suffered to go into his den againe, which he endevoured to have done long before: And then were divers other Lyons put into that place, one after another, but they shewed no more sport nor valour then the first, and every of them so soone as they espied the trap doores open, ran hastily into their dens. Then lastly, there were put forth together the two

young lustie Lyons, which were bred in that yard, and were now grown great: these at first beganne to march proudly towardes the Beare, which the Beare perceiving, came hastily out of a corner to meete them, and sodainely offred to fight with the Lyon, but both the Lyon and Lionesse skipt up and downe, and fearefully fled from the Beare, and so these like the former Lyons, not willing to endure any fight, sought the next way into their denne.

The animals' failure to live up to royal expectation—the cowardice of the lions before the bear—meant a failure of this "triall" before the king. Instead, James VI and I proposed something else, something more popular: "And the fift of July, according to the kings commandement, this Beare was bayted to death upon a stage: and unto the mother of the murthered child was giuen xx.p. out of part of that money which the people gave to see the Beare kild."[43] This seems quite simply to be the law of deodand in action: the Master of the Bears lost the value of his bear in its death, and compensation was paid to the mother for the loss of her child out of the day's profit, "xx.p." here apparently meaning twenty pence, a pitifully small sum.

Almost fifty years later, virtually exactly the same "trial" by baiting took place. *Perfect Proceedings of State Affaires* from September 1655 records that a child "between four and five years of age" was accidentally locked in with the bears and had his face bitten off. The child died. The outcome for the bear is described as follows:

> [T]he *Bear* for killing the Child fell to the Lord of the Soil, and was by the Bearward redeemed for fifty shillings; and the Bearwards told the Mother of the Child that they could not help it, (though some think it to bee a design of that wicked house to get money) and they told the Mother that the bear should bee bated to death, and she should have half the mony, & accordingly there were bills stuck up and down about the City of it, and a considerable summe of mony gathered to see the Bear bated to death; some say above [6] pound, and now all is done, they offer the woman three pound not to prosecute them.[44]

Once again the killer bear was declared deodand—in the terms of the report, it "fell to the Lord of the Soil, and was by the Bearward redeemed for fifty shillings." In the eyes of the law, this was the punishment, and it was a punishment that fell not on the bear but on its owner, who lost a valuable animal and who made only about £3 in compensation from the baiting (one should also note that the compensation for the death of a child had gone up considerably by 1655).

But, to say that these killings in the Bear Garden were evidence of the law of deodand in action is only partially true. What is also possible is that the killing of the killer animal in the Bear Garden was a punishment, that what was witnessed was a kind of execution—more like the putting to death of a human criminal at Tyburn than what happened at the knacker's yard. For this interpretation to be available, the animal must have been understood to have deserved punishment, and as such must have been perceived to be a member (albeit a somewhat marginal one) of the community and so answerable to that community's rules. In fact, the interpretation of the baiting to death as a punishment rested upon the possibility that the animal knew, or ought to have known, the rules that the deaths of these children were anything but "Casuall."

These two events in the Bear Garden can be read, then, as evidence that there were two different ethical frameworks available to early modern English men and women. On the one hand, there is the Thomist, anthropocentric vision in which animals are not in themselves worthy of kind acts and in which they have the status of objects—like a cart or some water wings. This vision is clearly present in the law of deodand and would make sense as a way of understanding the prevalence of cruel sports in the period. But in the killing of the killer bears there can be read another view of animals. In this view, they are perceived as capable of feeling pain, fear, and so on (remember the lions running away in Stow and Howes's description) and can be understood as fellow beings. On this basis, animals are baited and are given intent; they are other, and they are same.

The different perceptions of killing that emerge in early modern ideas, then, are based upon different conceptions of animals: between that faith in the idea of the animal as an unreasonable object that can be stolen but not murdered, baited but not punished, and the idea of the animal as fellow being that can feel cruelty and should experience compassion, that can be killed for use but not for pleasure. Recognizing the existence of such diverse ways of thinking about animals in this period is important, challenging the notion of the apparently unproblematic violence of the early modern Bear Garden and questioning Keith Thomas's somewhat one-sided modern understanding of that period. But these differences do not end there. Where we have found animals objectified and anthropomorphized, we can trace in this distinction another division, one that is still being felt and lived with today.

Thinking Theoretically

The division that I have characterized within ethical discussion is that between concentration upon the good self and the dedication to leading a good life, and such a distinction opens up very different responses to animals and to the world more generally. If the focus of the Inward Government theory is toward directing the actions of the self, then by logical extension all discussions of the outer world must remain purely theoretical. These are not discussions of real moments—real ethical decisions—but possible ones that might be faced by any individual and are laid out in discussion in order for individual readers to prepare themselves for similar experiences. In his work *A Treatise of Anger* (1609), for example, John Downame writes:

> Though therefore anger be a perturbation of the mind it doth not follow that it is evill, for not the perturbation it selfe but the cause thereof maketh it good if it be good, and evill if it be evill. Furthermore whereas they object that anger blindeth and confoundeth reason, I answere first, that if anger bee temperate and moderate, it doth serviceably waite upon reason, and not imperiously over rule it: and rather maketh a man more constant and resolute in walking the path of truth.[45]

All this is purely theoretical—it is establishing the place of anger within the Inward Government theory. And when something close to a real situation emerges, Downame remains within this framework: "Many," he writes in the chapter entitled *"the properties of unjust anger,"* "are not onely incensed against the persons of their enemies who are men like unto themselves, but also with brute beasts, which are not capable thereof." The possibility of anger toward animals Downame regards as a futile loss of control on the part of the angry self—it is likened to "children, who having gotten a fall beate the earth."[46] Anger is not to be directed toward the unreasonable, and animals, like earth, lack reason and, by implication, all else that might link them with humans. Animals are not worthy of inclusion as patients, especially where the focus is the agent.

Montaigne's ethics are very different. In his essay on the same subject as Downame's later treatise, for example, Montaigne begins with theory—Plutarch and Aristotle—and moves swiftly to practice: the brutality directed toward children that he has witnessed "as I passed along our streets."[47] This is no mere theoretical discussion (although it has elements of that); it is an argument about the use and abuse of a real and powerful passion and the effects of that passion on the lives of moral patients. As such, Montaigne's self—and the *Essais* are an exploration of himself—is a real self, not an abstract one; he is living in the world rather than only in the realm of theory and faces the problems that the world throws up as real, not theoretical ones. This is how he can see that cruelty is being directed toward animals and that cruelty needs to be assessed within the logic of the day-to-day existences we share with animals. But we can once again go further than this.

There is also a difference, I would argue, between Downame's animal and Montaigne's animal, a difference that is characteristic of the wider difference between ethical focus on the good self and on the good life. Downame's animal is a theoretical one—there is no particular animal, no specific situation. Montaigne, on the other hand, thinks about the stag that "surrenders to ourselves who are pursuing him, asking for our mercy by his tears," about "the scream of a hare in the teeth of my dogs."[48] Here there is a sense that the animals he represents are real ones, that the situations have actually been experienced. Most famously, Montaigne refers to his cat in "Apology for Raymond Sebond." He asks, "When I play with my cat, who knows if I am not a pastime to her more than she is to me?"[49] This is a philosophical question that emerges from what seems to be a real experience. Montaigne has looked at his cat and is asking about that cat, not a theoretical one.

There is a difference, then, between Downame and Montaigne (and from them, a difference between the study of the good self and the study of the good life) that is a difference between the concept of "the animal" and of "that animal": that is, between a theoretical situation in which "man and beast" confront each other and a real one in which Montaigne and a stag, or a cat, come face to face. When Montaigne thinks about stag hunting, it is not as a theoretician but as a practitioner, and as a practitioner—paradoxically—he knows that a stag feels its death; he has seen its tears.

In a recent essay, Jacques Derrida has highlighted the significance and implications of the difference between what I am terming "the animal" and "that animal," between the abstract and the concrete perceptions and representations of nonhuman beings that are available to us in different kinds of ethical thought. For Derrida once again it is animals' capacity to suffer that is key, and, again, reason—here characterized by Derrida as the *logos*—is undermined as the determining attribute. Derrida represents this shift as moving from Descartes's "indubitable certainty"—*cogito, ergo sum,* I think, therefore I am—to Jeremy Bentham's statement, "The question is not, can they reason? Nor, can they talk? But can they suffer?"[50] Derrida writes, "No one can deny the suffering, fear or panic, the terror or fright that humans witness in certain animals."[51] The shift is from a metaphysical concept of animals—as machines in Descartes's thought—to an empirical account.

While I agree wholeheartedly with Derrida's distinction, I would want to argue that that distinction was already in place by the time Descartes wrote his *Meditations* (it may also have urged Descartes to propose the "beast-machine" hypothesis).[52] But, whatever my disagreement with Derrida over the source of this philosophical shift, he does contextualize it in a way that reinforces the significance of the modes by which philosophy has characterized human relationships with animals and from that the ease with which animals can be killed. Derrida proposes that "this word *animal* that men have given themselves at the origin of humanity" allows for a relationship with the world that would be impossible if the foundation was not "the animal" (the general singular) but "that animal" (the particular singular). He argues that human "interpretive decisions (in all their metaphysical, ethical, juridical, and political consequences) . . . depend on what is presupposed by the general singular of this word *Animal*."[53] It is the way we have theorized real animals out of our conceptual frameworks—how we deal with animals as a general grouping rather than as individuals—that has allowed for interpretation in the first place. Without this concept—the animal—understanding as it exists now would cease.

If we take the possession of reason as the central organizing principle of Western philosophy (and it is hard not to see this as so), then it is possible to see that Derrida is correct. Humankind has traced the foundation of all knowing to the presence of that invisible essence known in Aristotelian philosophy as the "inorganic soul."[54] What this has entailed is a certain positioning of animals not as animals (as in *real* animals) but as ideas first and real second. It is this disjunction in the way in which humans think with and about animals that allows, I think, for the simultaneous existence of bear baiting and the emergent ethics of fellow-feeling with animals in the early modern period and as such might help to explain the killing of the killer animals in the Bear Garden. While the law does not allow for such an event to be understood as punishment, it is possible that the spectators, caught as they were between two very distinct ethical positions, were able simultaneously to enjoy the spectacle of animal death and to comprehend it as some kind of justice. They could, in fact, see the animals both as mere objects and as members of the community.

But to focus attention on historical interpretation alone is, perhaps, to imply that things are simply better now, that history has been a slow process of improvement, that we now—in ethical terms—strive for good lives rather than for good selves and that the position of animals has been changed forever. Such, of course, is not the case: Derrida's essay is not historical, it is polemical. The disjunction between the desire for the good self and the good life continues, and it is this disjunction that allows for the co-existence of pet-ownership and meat eating, of anthropomorphism and experimentation.[55]

We maintain in some areas of our lives that we—the good selves—remain central and all other beings remain marginal. In other parts of our lives, however, something very different occurs. We turn from ourselves to look at the world around us; we take on the possibility of suffering in beings other than ourselves and as such find some killing unnecessary, distasteful. We turn, in fact, from "the animal" to "that animal." As such it is worth returning to think again about the quotation at the beginning of this essay. Perhaps Keith Thomas's assertion that there was no concept of cruelty to animals in early modern England not only blanks-out the contradictions of that period but also helps us to blank-out the fact that we still live with these contradictions. There is, after all, nothing more reassuring than thinking that we are better humans than those men and women of the past. Nothing is more comforting than a history that allows us to maintain the status quo.

Notes

1. Keith Thomas, *Man and the Natural World: Changing Attitudes in England 1500–1800* (1983; repr., London: Penguin, 1984), 144–48, quotation 148.

2. Philip P. Hallie, "The Ethics of Montaigne's 'De la cruauté,'" in *O Un Amy! Essays on Montaigne in Honor of Donald M. Frame,* ed. Raymond C. La Charité (Lexington, Ky.: French Forum, 1977), 158.

3. Nicholas Coeffeteau, *A Table of Humane Passions* (London, 1621), 2. In this and other early modern texts, I have silently modernized *j, u,* and *v.*

4. See, for example, Owen Feltham, *Resolves. Divine, Morall, Politicall* (London, 1628), 90–91.

5. For a discussion of the influence of Seneca's work on medieval and Renaissance theories of cruelty, see Daniel Baraz, "Seneca, Ethics, and the Body: The Treatment of Cruelty in Medieval Thought," *The Journal of the History of Ideas* 59, no. 2 (1998): 195–215.

6. Seneca, *A Discourse of Clemencie,* in *The Workes of Lucius Annæus Seneca, Both Morall and Naturall,* trans. Thomas Lodge (London, 1614), 601.

7. Arthur O. Lovejoy, *The Great Chain of Being: A Study of the History of an Idea* (1936; repr., Cambridge: Harvard University Press, 1976), 59.

8. Dorothy Yamamoto, "Aquinas and Animals: Patrolling the Boundary?" in *Animals on the Agenda,* ed. Andrew Linzey and Dorothy Yamamoto (Urbana: University of Illinois Press, 1998), 80.

9. Thomas Aquinas, *Summa Theologiae,* trans. R. J. Batten (London: Blackfriars, 1975), 19–21. On Aquinas, see Judith Barad, "Aquinas' Inconsistency on the Nature and the Treatment of Animals," *Between the Species* 88, no. 4 (1988): 102–11; and Peter Drum, "Aquinas and the Moral Status of Animals," *American Catholic Philosophical Quarterly* 66, no. 4 (1992): 483–88.

10. Aquinas, *Summa Theologiae,* 91.

11. John Rawlinson, *Mercy to a Beast* (Oxford, 1612), 33.

12. T. W. [Thomas Wilcox], *A Short, Yet sound Commentarie* (London, 1589), 38r.

13. P. M. [Peter Muffett], *A Commentarie Upon the Booke of Proverbes of Salamon* (London, 1592), 103.

14. Thomas, *Man and the Natural World,* 156. It is worth noting that in recognizing these "new" ideas, Thomas is somewhat contradicting the statement with which I began this essay.

15. Joseph Hall, *Salomons Divine Arts* (London, 1609), 64. In this period there were few vegetarians, and the two non–meat eaters who recorded their ideas before 1660—Thomas Bushell and Roger Crab—can both be firmly placed within the Inward Government ethic. In avoiding animal flesh, both men were searching for purity. They did not regard it as wrong to eat animals because of the suffering of the animals. See Erica Fudge, "Saying Nothing Concerning the Same: Dominion, Purity and Meat in Early Modern England," in *Renaissance Beasts: Of Animals, Humans and Other Wonderful Creatures,* ed. Fudge (Urbana: University of Illinois Press, 2004), 70–86.

16. Thomas, *Man and the Natural World,* 129.

17. Hallie, "Ethics," 156.

18. Michel de Montaigne, "Of cruelty," in *The Complete Works,* trans. Donald M. Frame (1943; repr. London: Everyman, 2003), 380–81.

19. Montaigne, "Of cruelty," 381, 382.

20. Ibid., 383, 385.

21. Ibid., 383. The tears of the stag is an image repeated before and after Montaigne. See, for example, Ovid, *The XV. Bookes of P. Ouidius Naso, entytuled Metamorphosis, translated oute of Latin into English meeter, by Arthur Golding Gentleman* (London: William Seres, 1567), book 3, 63, for the tears of the transformed Acteon; Stephen Bateman, *Batman vppon Bartholome, his Booke De Proprietatibus Rerum* (London, 1582), 358r; and Robert Chamberlain, *Nocturnall Lucubrations: Or Meditations Divine and Morall* (London, 1638), 30.

22. It seems a paradox to note that, even as he condemned the cruelty of hunting, Montaigne continued to hunt. He himself was aware of this paradox when he wrote, "I cannot bear to hear the scream of a hare in the teeth of my dogs, although the chase is a violent pleasure" ("Of cruelty," 379). As Hallie notes, "Compassion is strong in him, and it guides his conduct, though the violence of the chase is pleasurable to him. The point is that this pleasure is not something he tries to conquer by reason, by philosophic precepts; this pleasure is something his own deepest feelings must combat." Hallie, "Ethics," 167.

23. Thomas, *Man and the Natural World,* 159.

24. David Quint, *Montaigne and the Quality of Mercy: Ethical and Political Themes in the Essais* (Princeton, N.J.: Princeton University Press, 1998), 55.

25. Montaigne, "Apology for Raymond Sebond," in *Complete Works,* 404.

26. George Boas, *The Happy Beast in French Thought of the Seventeenth Century* (1933; repr., New York: Octagon, 1966), 9, 13. Similarly, Zachary S. Schiffman, for example, has argued that Montaigne's emphasis on the fragility of human power and reason is a product of the humanist education system in which emphasis was placed on the scholar's ability to argue "*in utramque partem,*" on both sides. Zachary S. Schiffman, "Montaigne and the Rise of Skepticism in Early Modern Europe: A Reappraisal," *Journal of the History of Ideas* 45, no. 4 (1984): 500, 502.

27. Sir William Cornwallis, "Of Affection," in *Essays* (London, 1610), N7v–N8r. The

idea that Montaigne's beliefs are "womanish" fits within the structure of Inward Government theory, as in that theory women were perceived to have a weaker command of reason and therefore to be more susceptible to the descent into passion.

28. Hall, *Salomons Divine Arts,* 1–2.

29. Edward Topsell, *The Historie of Foure-Footed Beastes* (London, 1607), A4r.

30. Peter Harrison, *The Bible, Protestantism, and the Rise of Natural Science* (Cambridge: Cambridge University Press, 1998), 2, 185.

31. Topsell, *Historie,* 190, 196.

32. Ibid., 37.

33. Pierre Viret, *The Schoole of Beastes, Intituled, the good Housholder, or the Oeconomickes,* trans. I. B. (London, 1585), 4r–v.

34. Robert Cleaver, *A Plaine and Familiar Exposition of the Eleventh and Twelfth Chapters of the Proverbes of Salomon* (London, 1608), 140–41.

35. Joseph Hall, *Contemplation, Lib. VII, "Of Balaam",* in *The Works of Joseph Hall Doctor in Divinitie, and Deane of Worcester* (London, 1625), 934–35.

36. Hall, *"Of Balaam,"* 935.

37. Montaigne, "Of cruelty," 385.

38. For a detailed record of many trials from the medieval to the modern period, see E. P. Evans, *The Criminal Prosecution and Capital Punishment of Animals: The Lost History of Europe's Animal Trials* (1906; repr., London: Faber and Faber, 1988).

39. Michael Dalton, *The Countrey Justice* (London, 1618), 218.

40. The emphasis placed by the deodand legislation on the behavior of animals did overturn this object status, however, as it required owners to know their animals in a way that was rather different from the sense of the character of animals found in the animal trials of continental Europe. This argument is expanded in Erica Fudge, *Perceiving Animals: Humans and Beasts in Early Modern English Culture* (Basingstoke: Macmillan, 2000), 123–24, 139–42.

41. Little is known about the exact details of the origin of the brown bears, but it is recorded that in 1609, two "white bears" were captured in Greenland and brought over to England where they were presented to James VI and I. The king, in turn, gave them to Philip Henslowe, the Master of the Bears. It may have been one of these "white bears" that was baited in the Thames before the Spanish ambassador in 1623. See Barbara Ravelhofer, "'Beasts of Recreation': Henslowe's White Bears," *English Literary History* 32 (2002): 287, 291.

42. At a time when the average annual wage of a laborer in the south of England was somewhere between £9 and £15, a replacement bear is estimated as costing £8. Wage averages in Keith Wrightson, *English Society 1580–1680* (London: Unwin Hyman, 1982), 34; the cost of a bear cited in S. P. Cerasano, "The Master of the Bears in Art and Enterprise," *Medieval and Renaissance Drama in England* 5 (1991): 198.

43. John Stow and Edmond Howes, *The Annales, Or Generall Chronicle of England* (London, 1615), 895–96.

44. *Perfect Proceedings of State Affaires. In England, Scotland and Ireland, with the Transactions of other Nations. From Thursday 20 Septem, to Thursday the 27 of September. 1655.* (no. 313), 4971–72. The original has "60 pound," but I have silently amended it here to 6,

as this means that the mother received her promised half of the takings; £60 also seems an excessive amount of money to be made from one baiting.

45. John Downame, *A Treatise of Anger* (London, 1609), 7.

46. Ibid., 37.

47. Montaigne, "Of anger," in *Complete Works,* 655.

48. Montaigne, "Of cruelty," 383 and 379.

49. Montaigne, "Apology," 401.

50. Jeremy Bentham, *Introduction to the Principles of Morals and Legislation* (1789), cited in Richard Sorabji, *Animal Minds and Human Morals: The Origins of the Western Debate* (London: Duckworth, 1993), 210. Sorabji, like Derrida, sees the shift of philosophical focus from reason to feeling as beginning with Bentham.

51. Jacques Derrida, "The Animal That Therefore I Am (More to Follow)," trans. David Wills, *Critical Inquiry* 28 (2002): 396.

52. It is particularly odd that Derrida does not cite Montaigne as an important source for the shift from reason to sentience in contemplating the status of animals as he refers to Montaigne's cat early in his essay. Derrida, "The Animal," 375.

53. Ibid., 409.

54. For extremely useful overviews of this idea, see Katherine Park, "The Organic Soul," and Eckhardt Kessler, "The Intellective Soul," in *The Cambridge History of Renaissance Philosophy,* ed. Charles B. Schmitt and Quentin Skinner (Cambridge: Cambridge University Press, 1988), 464–84, 485–534.

55. I develop this idea in *Animal* (London: Reaktion, 2002).

6 Conflicts around Slaughter in Modernity

JONATHAN BURT

> In these chutes the stream of animals was continuous; it was quite
> uncanny to watch them, pressing on to their fate, all unsuspicious—a
> very river of death.
> —Upton Sinclair, *The Jungle* (1906)

> "Killing," in relation to an animal, means causing the death of the
> animal by any process other than slaughter; "slaughter," in relation to
> an animal, means the death of the animal by bleeding.
> —UK Government Regulations (1995)

> Jews need hardly be lectured on the prevention of cruelty to animals.
> They introduced the whole concept long before any other civilisation
> or any other faith cared about animal welfare. To inflict any suffering
> on animals is a religious offence.
> —Lord Jakobovits, House of Lords, *Hansard* (1990)

In this chapter I address the question of what the slaughter of animals for
meat in modernity can mean to humans. There are two main strands to this
inquiry. The first focuses on the mechanized process of slaughter, and the
second analyzes the attitudes and responses to that process by different social
groups such as religious, professional, or political ones. However, the technology of slaughter and meat processing is not a separate domain, a distant
and other mechanical process, that is evaluated or fought over in varying
ways from the outside. Rather, technology is fully interlocked with, and is to
some extent constitutive of, the cultural conflict that exists around slaughter.
I begin with some descriptions of the industrial side of meat production,
particularly in the United States, because it offers a good example of the
industry at its most intensive and highlights the manner in which it is inte-
grated with so many other technologies that touch on almost every area of
human life. I then focus on aspects of slaughterhouse history in Britain as it
concerns those efforts to clarify what is meant by "humane" slaughter. A

specific analysis of the debate around *shechita*, the Jewish method of slaughter, in the late nineteenth and twentieth centuries is used to highlight the contradictions, fault lines, and diversity within the slaughter industry as it seeks to make slaughter as orderly, hygienic, and uncruel as possible.[1]

* * *

There is a much-quoted remark of Upton Sinclair's concerning his 1906 novel, *The Jungle*, about the horrific working conditions in the Chicago Union Stockyards: "I aimed at the public's heart, and by accident I hit it in the stomach."[2] The reference is to the fact that despite his exposure of the appalling working conditions in the meatpacking industry, the outraged response to his descriptions contributed, in part, not to the alleviation of the plight of migrant workers but to the 1906 Pure Food and Drug Act, which banned from interstate commerce any adulterated or mislabeled food and drugs.[3] In other words, improving the quality of meat was more important than improving the quality of the overall structure of the industry. This was ironic given that Sinclair was very much concerned with the impact of this kind of labor on the human body and psyche. As Sinclair toured the yards for his research, carrying a metal pail and pretending to be one of the laborers, he wrote, "I went about, white-faced and thin, partly from undernourishment, partly from horror. It seemed to me I was confronting a veritable fortress of oppression."[4] He writes in *The Jungle*:

> When Jurgis had first inspected the packing plants with Szedvilas, he had marvelled while he listened to the tale of all the things which were made out of the carcasses of animals, and of all the lesser industries that were maintained there; now he found each one of these lesser industries as a separate inferno. . . . The workers in each of them had their own peculiar diseases.[5]

As with many accounts of large-scale slaughter, the totalizing nature of the picture reveals that the ramifications of the business of killing animals affects almost every dimension of life.

Just as all parts of the animal are used for everything from, for example, meat to fertilizer, from soap to shoe blacking, from household items like combs and hairbrushes to glue ("They use everything about the hog except the squeal" is a running joke in *The Jungle*), so too are all the networks of modernity—transport, labor, technologies—implicated in the manufacture. What probably would have made Sinclair so white-faced is no one particular element of this process but the cumulative horror of the whole picture, of which the actual killing is only a small part. In an almost paradoxical manner, the scale of the picture and the fact that so many humans as well as animals are subject to brutalization erase each individual moment of death as it occurs hundreds of times an hour. One cannot see the animals for the industry. As Noëlie Vialles notes in her anthropological study of slaughter-house workers in France, "In a place where animals are slaughtered each person is able to say what he does: one anaesthetises, the other bleeds. Two men are necessary for neither of them to be the real killer. The double disjunction of repeating the fatal moment, only evades it the more effectively."[6] This idea that it is important not to be the killer does not always apply universally or historically, and is not an issue in Sinclair either, though it does indicate the fact that at the heart of industrial slaughter, various cultural—and also in some instances, ethical—factors can be found at work that indicate difficulties around the idea of slaughtering. Most important, it indicates that slaughter is always more than simply killing.

In the United States, a primitive assembly line had been introduced as early as the 1830s in Cincinnati's hog slaughterhouses. Although by the 1880s, the slaughtering and butchering was still done by one man in some houses, changes had already occurred and the speedup of the process was in place by the middle of the decade. One indication of the increasing speed of slaughter can be seen in the fact that in 1884, 5 splitters handled 800 head of cattle in a ten-hour day, whereas a decade later 4 splitters would handle 1,200 a day.[7] By the turn of the century, the single butcher had been replaced by a killing gang of 157 men divided into 78 different "trades."[8] This system was part of a much greater interconnecting network of the kind so well described by William Cronon in his account of the Union Stockyards in Chicago that opened in 1865. Everything affected and was in turn affected by the needs of the meat industry: the extension of railway networks to carry cattle; the development of refrigerated cars; ecological changes in the landscape; new connections between grain farmers, stock raisers, and butchers; the need to manage pollution through the tons of waste produced; and the increasingly sophisticated packaging and marketing techniques for particular beef cuts.

A combination of industrialization and the circumstances of history had a powerful influence. The Civil War confirmed Chicago's dominance in American pork packing, for instance. Some 1.5 million men enlisted in the Union army and consumed over half a billion pounds of packed meat. By the early 1870s, Chicago was processing over 1 million hogs a year.[9] Time was also a key consideration in the quest for enormous profits, both in terms of the processing of cattle and the speeding up of the growth of the animal body. The old seasonal alternation between fat summers and lean winters gave way to a system of continuous growth in which food supply was stored "so that there need be no interruption to the steady accumulation of future cash in well-muscled flesh."[10]

Many of the features of this industry that were shaped by the early meat factories such as in Chicago are still in evidence today: the cheap migrant labor forces, the high rate of injury and death, the cavalier attitude to safety and diseased meat, the monopoly power of the big meat companies. None of these features is alien to Upton Sinclair's fictional description of the industry published over a century ago. Nowadays workers may labor on kill lines that process up to 300 cattle in an hour, while the rate of cattle killed in the United States every 24 hours is approximately 100,000.[11] The changing patterns over time of the transportation of beef from live cattle to carcasses to boxed beef and packaged cuts reflect not only the increasing distance between live animal and finished product but also the way in which the industry has increasingly sought to optimize every aspect of its process. In this particular transition from live to dead, less and less space is wasted in transport and less and less unusable material is transported in the first place.[12]

The mode by which this increasing efficiency is linked to the changing technology of distribution, as shown by the importance of the development of refrigeration for railways and shipping in the nineteenth century, has a parallel in the twentieth century too. Eric Schlosser, for example, has shown how car culture in the 1940s, especially in Southern California, was crucial in the development of fast food, particularly in its distribution through roadside restaurants.[13] In a more intriguing link between technology and the economic geography of meat, Schlosser describes how the burger chain McDonald's has long analyzed roads and regional development from the air to assess potential restaurant locations. The company later developed computer software to combine information from satellite photography with other forms of geographical and economic information, effectively automating its site selection process.[14]

There are other comparable examples of this in food history in which the interconnection of improved transportation networks, refrigeration technology, and the colossal exploitation of animal life to meet demand come together in similar ways. An interesting comparison with the example of meat is that of the fish industry in Britain. As John Walton notes in his study of the history of the fried fish trade, the dish fish and chips was "central to the growth and transformation of the British fishing industry from the later nineteenth century onwards and its impact on agriculture should not be underestimated. It generated its own specialist engineering and hardware industries and it stimulated demands for oils and fats, paper, fuel, salt, vinegar, mineral waters and a range of other products."[15] Especially important to the increasing volume of catches was the impact brought on by the introduction of the steam trawler in the 1880s, which massively extended the range for the exploitation of fishing grounds.[16] In fact, the processing of fish parallels that of packaged meat with the increasing popularity of frozen fish fillets in America in the 1920s and especially the development of fish sticks (or fishfingers, as they are known in Britain) whereby blocks of frozen fillets are sawed into slabs and then into sticks.[17]

Once one begins to take a large-scale perspective of the networks of which slaughter is a part, then the cultural attitudes to meat, by which I mean how we assume meat is perceived and what it means symbolically, need to be understood as more than simply an abstract version of the human relation to the animal kingdom. Certainly, it is the case that meat-eating expresses control over animals and that the distance between the animal and the finished meat product exemplifies an alienation that characterizes a more general structure of exploitation and dominion. As Nick Fiddes notes, "Our use of meat as a food reflects our categorization of and our relations towards animal competitors, companions and resources. . . . Consuming the muscle flesh of other highly evolved animals is a potent symbol of our supreme power."[18] However, these cultural attitudes are also a particular product, not of the universals of human-animal relations, but of a particular configuration of technology, the animal, and discourses of efficiency, breeding, health, and ethics. It is easy to forget, due to certain notions of naturalness around the idea of the animal, that human-animal relations are mediated by technology and that these conjunctions are far from new.

The conjunction of the values of the humane together with notions of efficiency can be found at the very beginning of thinking about slaughter along something like factory lines. Interestingly, such thinking also incorporated ideas that such methods would improve social order, reminding us that the technology of slaughter is always imbued with a general idea of control that applies to both animals and humans. In Richard B. Grantham's 1848 *Treatise on public slaughter-houses,* he directly links notions of meat to the economy of efficiency, cleanliness, and a basic plan for a prototype "disassembly" line. An animal yields "to man in a concentrated form what it has amassed at so great expense of time and labour, [and] gives him leisure for those pursuits which raise him so immeasurably above the animals on which he feeds."[19] Given, in principle, the efficiency of this system of hierarchical conversions, achieved through time and labor, the issue of waste is crucial. The sheep that are thrown down the steps of the cellars under Newgate

Market, where they are unable to rise due to broken bones and injuries from the fall, are subject to a wasteful and unsanitary slaughter. In an efficient cycle of processing, one finds both profits and benefits to health:

> The blood and other animal matter rejected would, if produced in a proper locality, contribute materially to the income of the butcher, while it furnished increased fertility to the land, and consequently would contribute to cheapen the food, the basis of national prosperity. This economy might be effected in a well organised establishment without nuisance and yet without adding to the contaminations of our already deadly sewers.[20]

What Grantham proposes is the building of public slaughterhouses and, in anticipation of the later disassembly lines, a "travelling frame" on which carcasses can be raised and dressed and then moved on so another can take its place. Being raised would also expose the carcass to a free current of air. Underneath the rooms, according to his plans, vaults containing ice would provide cold air that would come up through gratings in the floor.[21] An important implication of the optimization of the animal product is that it reflects a proper degree of civilization. If animals are neglected, and by implication mistreated, disease and its attendant evils of poverty and crime ensue.

As the example of Grantham shows, it is impossible to disentangle these interconnected ideas of efficiency, the decent treatment of animals, and profitability that proliferate around the practice of slaughter and still hold true today. The ever-reinforcing cycle of technological development and shifts in food fashions can also be seen in the rise of ready meals, a market that has grown enormously since the 1970s and also feeds the demands of new devices like the microwave oven.[22] This can also be seen in factory farming. One of the most important shifts in meat production from the 1950s onward has been the industrialization of poultry, which has the further advantage of minimizing land use.

> Apart from computerised feeding and formation of feed composition, themselves associated with nutritional research, the intensive feeding of animals requires cost-effective "housing," specialised and timely veterinary services, and drugs to treat and prevent diseases and to enhance digestive performance. Particularly "advantaged" by these developments have been pig and poultry, especially chicken, due to the "high conversion efficiency of these species." . . . The number of days taken to fatten a bird to 4lb has declined from sixty to thirty-nine days between 1966 and 1991 and the amount of feed has fallen from 9lb to 7.75lb.[23]

Of course, what this language of efficiency and optimization conceals is the ironic fact that meat manufacture is the most inefficient system for the production of protein in terms of the amount of energy needed to produce a given quantity of protein.

In the light of this complex and totalizing system, it seems to me that ethical debates and humane considerations concerning animals that are being prepared for slaughter have to be regarded in relation to the system as a whole. However, it has usually been the case that the attempt to promote humanitarian values in slaughter have focused on the killing alone. Paradoxically, although the defining of humane slaughter may promote methods that diminish the trauma and pain that animals experience in the slaughter process, at the same time these "humanitarian" methods are complicit in the process itself and in fact contribute to its efficiency and its overall acceptability. The phrase "humane slaughter," when considered in the light of the scale of killing for meat and the deanimalizing (and dehumanizing) technologies that meat production entails, is a contradictory one. As I shall demonstrate in the discussion below on the debate over the acceptability or not of religious methods of slaughter, the distinction between what is civilized and what is barbaric—mainly on the grounds of whether a creature is stunned before slaughter or not—takes place within a system that is deeply inhumane by virtue of its scale. Furthermore, the accusation that other methods of slaughter that do not conform to the clinical conditions of modern slaughter are barbaric and the assertion that the reduction of pain and stress in "humane slaughter" represents, by implication, a higher civility remind us that the meat industry of modernity has its own highly partial form of cultural differentiation where boundaries are drawn based on slaughter methods. In a sense, the overall picture of the cultural conflict around slaughter reveals that the manner in which we adhere to this or that mode of animal slaughter is one of the constituting elements of our particular social identity.

* * *

In Britain in 1904, the Admiralty appointed a committee to consider the question of humane slaughtering.[24] Although the main object of the inquiry was a humanitarian one, the notion of the humane was tempered by the point that "it would be futile to recommend any methods of slaughter, however humane, which would be impracticable on the score of complication, time, or expense, or which would in any way depreciate the utility or market value of the carcasses for human food."[25] One of the main recommendations of the committee was that all animals without exception should be stunned before slaughter. This would also mean the establishment of a uniform system of slaughter with a proper standard of supervision and licensing of workers. Reforms were in the interests "not only of humanity, but of sanitation, order, and ultimately economy."[26] This also benefited meat quality given that the reduction of sources of fear or pain for the animal prior to slaughter would benefit its "palatable and marketable qualities."[27] As one respondent, a butcher, put it, "There is no man going more tender-hearted than a butcher to an animal. He does not want to punish the animal, and he saves it from all the pain he possibly can. . . . Certainly he wants [the slaughtering] done as quickly as possible; the quicker the animal is killed the better the flesh is."[28]

Another important feature of the committee was its investigation of Jewish slaughter, which it deemed was not of "equal humanity" with those methods in which a pole-axe was used. Most commonly in this latter instance, the animal would be struck on the head and then pithed, whereby a rod inserted through the hole made by the pole-axe broke the connections between the spinal cord and the brain. In its critique of Jewish slaughter, the committee was particularly disturbed by what was known as casting. This is a process by which the animal is roped and secured down onto the floor with its head pulled back and its neck exposed for the cut.

A succession of witnesses with various connections to slaughter and the meat trade, such as butchers, health inspectors, and veterinarians, were called and were asked questions about things like the most efficient ways to dispatch an animal, whether animals showed pain or fear, what happened when animals witnessed slaughter, their reactions to smell and sound, how one might license slaughterers, and whether Jewish slaughter was humane or cruel. Interestingly, there were wide variations in answers to questions about how animals reacted to the slaughter around them, leaving the committee's findings inconclusive as to whether animals were afraid of things like the sight or smell of blood. It was, however, remarked on by a number of respondents that they considered Jewish slaughter to be cruel. James King, the Veterinary Inspector to the Corporation of the City of London, claimed that he had timed cattle undergoing Jewish slaughter and that they had taken three or four minutes before they lost sensibility.[29] John Colam, the secretary of the Royal Society for the Prevention of Cruelty to Animals (RSPCA), also objected to this method, particularly the casting, but pointed out that great care was taken with the actual cutting of the throat. Interestingly, Colam used the term "killer" for Jewish slaughterers rather than the term "butcher," which he used when discussing other aspects of slaughtering. Indeed, the clash between the committee and Sir Samuel Montagu, the president of the Board for Shechita, reflects the deep divisions of a debate that recur throughout the twentieth century whereby what are considered by the Jews to be divinely ordained codes of slaughter cannot be compromised by the humane "secular" version of slaughter, which involves pre-slaughter stunning. As the committee noted, "We are only examining these methods on their merits, entirely apart from any question of religious observances."[30] Whether animal welfare issues can be separated from specific cultural practices becomes a key question in subsequent arguments.

It is evident from many of the remarks in the report that the idea of the humane is an integral part of slaughter and not simply an additional consideration to satisfy things like public guilt or a more general code of humanitarian sentiment. In G. R. Leighton and L. M. Douglas's five-volume handbook, *The Meat Industry and Meat Inspection,* published in 1910, the idea of optimization is directly linked to the well-being of the cattle: "Wherever animals are to be used for human food, it is a preliminary necessity that they should be in every case in a sound and healthy condition; not only is this a necessity from an economic point of view, but it is also desirable from the point of view of public health."[31] The authors also recommend that stunning of the higher animals "ought to be compulsory in all *civilised* communities" (emphasis added).[32] It is vital "to kill the animal as quickly as possible in such a way as to avoid any unnecessary pain to the beast, not to mention any actual cruelty . . . [and] to kill the animal in such a way as will serve that the carcass, when dressed for food, will have what is known as good keeping quality."[33] In what the authors see as a textbook for the meat industry to encourage the production of healthy meat and establish standards for things like the best conditions for maximizing protein output for the least feed input, *civilized* standards of treatment are proposed as essential components of this process.

H. B. Cronshaw and D. J. Anthony's textbook for meat traders, *The Meat Industry,* published in 1927, again reiterates this. In the act of slaughter, the butcher has to consider both the avoidance of pain for the animal and the quality of meat. Again the practical and humane are combined: "There is public health as well as the sentimental point of view to be borne in mind."[34] Cronshaw and Anthony do, however, take a more positive view of Jewish slaughter, pointing out that it has good keeping qualities. As they stress, the key point is that carcasses have to be well bled, preferably where the heart and respiratory functions are in action for as long as possible, to ensure that residual blood does not spoil the meat. When considering different methods of pre-slaughter stunning, something that comes to be essential to the ethos of humane slaughter, it is considered necessary to avoid the possibility of damage through the wrong sort of bleeding. Thus, hammers, pole-axes, and various types of bolt mask or spring bolt apparatus (where a mask is fitted onto the animal's head and a fitted bolt is then driven with a hammer into the brain) are preferable to shooting instruments. One cannot, for instance, control the track of a free bullet nor its possible effects on internal bleeding.

At the time of the publication of Cronshaw and Anthony's textbook, preliminary experiments were being carried out on a new form of stunning using electricity.[35] The advantages of this seemed numerous. Ideally it was cheap, efficient to use, and without the problems of accuracy sometimes associated with striking the head by pole-axe. In fact, it represents another aspect of the trajectory of labor in slaughterhouses, especially seen in the big slaughterhouses in the United States, whereby workers are effectively deskilled. The historical trend toward smaller and smaller tasks on the disassembly lines means each worker needs less ability for a smaller set of actions. One of the advertised advantages of electrical stunning equipment was that it required little skill because the voltages would be pre-set and all that needed to be done was to place the electrodes against the correct part of the cranium. The promise of this technology was that it was hygienic, time efficient, and, above all, "civilized."

In the first experiments reported in England in 1929, the prototype apparatus was evidently crude and inefficient. Bacon pigs were rendered unconscious, but the process was not so effective with sows. The convulsion produced by the shock evidently affected the bleeding qualities of the carcass: "In its present state of development, this method of stunning by electricity is unsuitable for application to bacon pigs, owing to the damage to the carcass, inferior appearance, and reduced keeping qualities of the meat due to its increased blood content."[36] Early work focused on pigs, and there was no demonstration of stunning cattle in Britain until 1931. By the early 1930s, a great deal of experimental work had been done, and electrical stunning was used in a variety of countries such as Germany (where the machinery had been pioneered by Max Müller and Anton Weinberger), Austria, Czechoslovakia, Holland, Denmark, Sweden, China, Japan, and the United States.[37] Improvements were made to avoid the extensive convulsions in reaction to the shock. Also, as a number of observers pointed out, slaughterhouses were quieter places when electrical stunning was being used. Commenting on one of the improved devices, known in England as the S.R.V. Electrolethaler 2, D. J. Anthony produced what to me epitomizes the mantra of humane slaughter: "The claims made on behalf of this latest device are that it is humane, instantaneous in action, economical in use, causing no 'splashing' in the meat [that is, residues of blood], is safe, and ensures complete bleeding."[38]

All the advantages of electrical stunning, such as its image of clinical cleanliness and the manner in which stunning can in theory be objectively standardized by the calibration of electrical doses, made it a perfect blend of the humane and the technological. As a method of technology, it was seen as being above partisan attitudes to slaughter, answering only to the abstractly conceived higher cause of humanity: "The setting up of electric stunning devices for the slaughtering of animals will further the cause of humanity. The question of the stunning of animals for slaughter, to the humane slaugh-terman, is a matter which is not a party, political, or religious one, but one that must be answered from the point of view of humanity and justice to animals."[39] In other words, it offered the classic image of an objective and neutral technology that rose above cultural differences in slaughter, which, in any case, were seen as backward-looking in the progressive ideology of humane slaughter.

Comparative studies on exsanguination and meat quality were not neces-sarily conclusive as to which of the then current methods was best. Thomas Parker described a 1925 experiment in which the carcasses of four heifers were examined after being killed in different ways: stunned with a felling hammer, shot with a humane killer, stunned with a captive bolt, and *shechita*. In all cases, the quality of meat was good.[40] With little to choose between different methods of slaughter, it was argued that the issue of the best method should be settled on humane grounds. Müller made claims on the meat quality of pork produced through electrical stunning and suggested that he could see no objection to this method being used by Jews, as the head and brain of the animal appeared uninjured prior to slaughter. The irony of his recommenda-tion to the Jews that they should consider this technology because it produced good pork might have bemused them were it not for the unavoidable asso-ciations with anti-Semitism that, particularly by the early 1930s, the animal welfare movement in Germany was inextricably linked with.

In 1934, two Dutch scientists, J. Roos and S. Koopmans, questioned the idea that stunning actually produced unconsciousness and suggested that the paralysis brought on by the stunning was due to an overexcitation of the central nervous system.[41] In other words, it was possible that the animal could still feel things; it was just physically immobilized. Interestingly, they were challenged on both scientific and political grounds. For Weinberger, the ob-ject of stunning was not to produce a narcosis but a strong stunning to last a few minutes that would "render bleeding possible in the unconscious state."[42] Müller took his opposition a little further by suggesting that these objections were flawed because the science was compromised by Jewish mo-tives, such as those of Professor Roos and his "co-religionists." In a later article, Roos remarked that "in Holland a Jewish professor is as credible as any other."[43]

The image of the slaughterhouse as a quiet place in which pigs do not squeal before they are stuck convinced some that electrical stunning was the best form of pacification: "I have watched dozens of pigs being anaesthetised by the electro-lethaler in a most easy and perfect way. After each one was narcotised it was hoisted, stuck and bled without struggle or squeal; the slaughterhouse was thus made a place of peaceful quiet. There is no struggle whilst the animal is bled, the heart and respiration are in action the whole time and the blood flows freely."[44]

The goal of pain reduction, or its complete disappearance, also entails slaughter at its most orderly and mechanistic. There are no sounds of pigs squealing in agony, nothing to indicate to a wider world, neighbors, or passersby the extent of the life-taking going on within the slaughterhouse. Slaughter is both unseen and unheard. What is done in the name of removing the animal from sources of pain and distress also means that a perfect ideal of slaughter is reached in modernity: slaughter without quite the horror the word "slaughter" should connote. As Neville Gregory notes in his recent book on scientific aspects of slaughter, carbon dioxide is also an efficient method of stunning pigs as well as other creatures such as poultry. He, in fact, suggests that poultry plants might move from electrical stunning to gassing, the great advantage being that birds can be stunned in their transport crates en masse, which avoids the pre-slaughter stress of removing them from their crates and hanging them on the killing lines.[45]

Although it is possible at one level to distinguish the well-intentioned animal welfare arguments from anti-Semitic currents in the attacks on *shechita,* from a historical point of view the enacting of anti-*shechita* legislation in Europe has always been political. One certainly cannot read the writings of Müller, for instance, outside this context. J. A. Dembo, a physician in St. Petersburg, noted in 1894 how the tenor of attacks against *shechita* had changed over the last few decades. Looking at the earlier publications of animal protection societies during the period 1850–60, he noted how *shechita* had been objected to as being a torturous method. In more recent years, he thought that the character of the attack had changed particularly in Germany and had taken on a much more anti-Semitic character.[46] In the 1890s in the Reichstag, anti-Semitic politicians repeatedly proposed that preslaughter stunning should become compulsory as it had in Saxony in 1892.[47] Interestingly, in Dembo's own comparative study of slaughter methods, which comes out in favor of *shechita,* he noted that there was no possible "ethical" position on slaughter: "The killing of a living creature is *per se* to some extent an immorality, to be excused only in view of the requirements of our stomach, and in an immoral action the ideal is not to be sought."[48]

In Germany, the struggle between the Jewish community and those who wished to ban *shechita* became an increasingly extensive one from the 1890s until Hitler's ban on the practice in 1933. Fighting their defense on both scientific and religious grounds, various Jewish organizations published large amounts of evidence allegedly showing that animals suffered no more under their method than under any other.[49] To give an idea of the range of arguments, in 1931 the reorganized Reichszentrale für Schächtangelegenheiten (Central Committee for Shechita Affairs) created three advisory boards. One was made up of physiologists and vets who dealt with the humaneness of torture and examined stunning methods; the second was comprised of engineers and slaughterhouse technicians for the investigation of improved casting and restraining devices; and the third dealt with legislation. The aim was to answer all possible objections to *shechita* and revealed at the same time how many aspects of society animal slaughter touched upon. Incidentally, the 1933 ban was not reversed in the Federal Republic of Germany until 1960.[50]

The position in Britain, which made it clear that *shechita* was permissible, was coincidentally enshrined in law in the same year as Hitler's ban in Germany. The 1933 Act to Provide for the Humane and Scientific Slaughter of Animals (note the juxtaposition of "scientific" and "humane") contains the following opening provision: "No animal to which this section applies shall be slaughtered in a slaughter-house or knacker's yard except in accordance with the following provisions, that is to say, every such animal shall be instantaneously slaughtered, or shall by stunning be instantaneously rendered insensible to pain until death supervenes." Permitted exceptions to this were the slaughter of pigs, boars, hogs, and sows in a knacker's yard or slaughterhouse where there was no possible supply of electricity and "by the Jewish method for the food of the Jews and by a Jew duly licensed for the purpose by the Rabbinical Commission constituted in accordance with the provisions of the first schedule to this Act; or by the Mohammedan method for the food of Mohammedans and by a Mohammedan." The schedule mentioned refers to a commission set up by the act to be run by Jewish representatives for the licensing of *shochetim*, the Jewish slaughterers. Bills to repeal this section of the act exempting *shechita*, and also *dabh* (the Muslim method), were put before Parliament repeatedly in 1955, 1956, 1962, 1968, 1981, and 1984. None of these bills succeeded.[51]

The historical background to the debates over *shechita* means that issues of animal welfare and issues of ethnicity cannot be disentangled, even if one wished they were. Mary Dudley Ward's pamphlet on kosher published in 1944 and revised in 1951 was viciously anti-Semitic in its tone, despite her

protestations to the contrary.[52] Indeed, the problem for animal welfare cam-
paigners, in the light of this legacy, is that even when distancing themselves
from issues of race, in this case anti-Semitism, the communities under attack
do not find it easy to distinguish one position from another. Due to the history of anti-*shechita* campaigns in Europe, some British welfare campaign-
ers bent over backwards to dissociate themselves from these past associations.
In 1962, the House of Lords debated a bill against religious slaughter proposed
by Lord Somers. He was at the time the president of the Council of Justice
to Animals and Humane Slaughter Association. Somers was at great pains,
when opening the debate, to separate his bill from any charge of anti-Semitism.[53] This was, for him, purely an issue of animal welfare, and the argument
ranged widely over the issue of whether the rights of animals should be
given priority over the values of particular religious communities. In his
summing up of the debate, Viscount Hailsham offered a number of objections as to why the bill should not go forward, the most significant of which
was that the House, whatever its good intentions, would be seen to be anti-
Semitic. In the end, Somers withdrew the bill to avoid precisely that situation.

It is important to stress that there are, and have long been, differences of
opinion concerning *shechita* within the Jewish community, as Todd Endelman shows in his analysis of the response by the Jewish establishment to
Nathan Salaman's attack on *shechita* in 1953 in a lecture given to the Jewish
Historical Society of England. Salaman raised the uncomfortable question
that Jews may not be so observant of *kashrut* (the Jewish dietary code) because it was no longer universally accepted that *shechita* was humane.[54] However, the battle lines between the different camps pro- and anti-Salaman were
not necessarily defined by animal issues per se. Both Orthodox and Reform
Jews, many of the latter not strictly observant of dietary laws, united because
this was seen as a matter above all of defending religious liberty. Their sensitivity to anti-Semitism in relation to the issue was not misplaced.[55] In the
Second World War, the dispersal of people out of London, including Jews,
brought *shechita* into prominence in areas of Britain previously unfamiliar
with the practice, particularly the areas just outside London. Arguments
appeared in local newspapers. As one letter writer put it, "Jews have sanctuary and protection in this country and they should therefore be compelled
to toe the line, and to adopt British methods of slaughter."[56]

It has been claimed that the campaigns against religious slaughter in Britain have been particularly marked in periods of high racial tension: the 1900s,
1930s-40s, and the 1970s-80s. Contacts between the RSPCA and the Board
of Deputies of British Jews in the late 1930s indicated the awareness of anti-

Semitism in considerations of *shechita*. Indeed, the RSPCA suggested, and
it was an argument that would be used more than once, that there would be
more racial tolerance toward the Jews if they gave up the practice of *shechita*.[57] To show that the parameters of the debate have rarely changed much in
the ensuing years, an RSPCA officer made exactly the same argument to
Muslims concerning *dabh* in 1977.[58] Brian Klug, in an article on anti-Semitism
in animal rights literature, notes the manner in which, despite the disavowal of animal welfarists to the contrary, the animal welfare position can so
easily fall into racism. Citing a Compassion in World Farming leaflet on
slaughter, he points out the organization's desire to distance itself from racism: "There is nothing inherently political about having a view, one way or
the other, on the technical questions of which methods of slaughtering animals cause least distress and suffering." However, the leaflet also presents a
picture of *halal* slaughterhouses expanding in number to the point where
the "secular/Christian sector" will be unable to have meat from humanely
stunned animals.[59] The fear that these "ethnic groups," as Compassion in
World Farming terms them, will take over is a familiar trope in all racist
literature. In 1984, the British far right party, the National Front, marched
against religious slaughter in Brighton.[60] During the same year, the eventually successful efforts by Muslims to have *halal* meat served in schools in
Bradford led to the chair of the Bradford Education Committee, who was
incidentally a Conservative, receiving abuse and death threats for his support
of the scheme.[61]

The rhetoric of animal welfare in relation to slaughter declares itself to be
universal, transcending multicultural issues, and one finds an uncanny echo
of Max Müller's sentiments in articulations of this principle. For example,
as Lord Houghton said in Somers's debate in 1962, "We shall have to decide
as a matter of constitutional principle, whether our laws relating to cruelty
to animals shall apply universally throughout the land to all people who deal
with animals, no matter what their religion, creed, nationality, or activities.
The standards applied by law to safeguard animals from unnecessary cruelty should not be open to variation to suit religious practices or beliefs."[62]
The problem, of course, is that animal welfare values are themselves culturally embedded rather than transcendent, and it is impossible to disconnect
them from the structures of human-animal relations in which they are located, and this includes the industry of slaughter. In fact, by focusing on the
act of slaughter and the question of pre-slaughter stunning rather than on
the overall system of meat production, the animal welfare argument must
acknowledge its own partiality.[63]

The campaign against religious slaughter intensified in the 1970s when animal welfare groups discovered that Muslim entrepreneurs had developed a substantial export market for *halal* meat.[64] In 1985, the Farm Animal Welfare Council produced a *Report on the Welfare of Livestock When Slaughtered by Religious Methods.* Interestingly, no Jews, Muslims, or Sikhs were represented on the investigating committee. The report described the different methods of slaughter and the regulations pertaining to them in the United Kingdom at the time. A number of telling faults were noted in *shechita.* For instance, members of the council found a variation in skill when making the throat incision: "We are concerned that some animals may be subjected to shackling, hoisting, thoracic incision and internal examination while they retain some degree of sensitivity."[65] The issue of whether the animal might remain conscious for a period of time after throat-cutting was central to the argument for pre-slaughter stunning, even for animals decapitated in the Sikh method of slaughter known as *jhatka.* However, council members were not without sensitivity to the problems that the report was raising and diplomatically recognized that they were crossing a "minefield" with their recommendation for pre-slaughter stunning. The report fully acknowledged the traditions of care for animals in both Jewish and Muslim religious doctrine.

In the same year, in reaction to the report, the Campaign for the Protection of Shechita was launched. It is worth noting that in the subsequent lobbying of government, many of the arguments familiar from earlier decades were rehearsed again: whether electrical stunning might be acceptable to Jews, how long it took for an animal killed by *shechita* to lose consciousness, reports on inadequate and inefficient stunning slaughterhouses, and generally whether other methods of slaughter were as pain-free as was claimed. However, more important, the eating of kosher meat was seen as a defining characteristic of Jewish identity, so this was a direct threat to Jewish custom: "Whatever intentions Ministers may express the effect of the proposed measures will be the deprivation of tens of thousands of Jews of the right to eat meat."[66] In fact, it has been an important strand of the Jewish argument that this is never simply a question of religious symbolism—"a mere historical symbol of purely historical value"—but that the eating of kosher meat makes the "physical act of eating into an expression of divine service."[67] Another complaint of the campaign was that the humane attitudes to animals as enshrined in Jewish doctrine were not recognized by a law that made *shechita* merely a tolerated exception to general rules of slaughter rather than humane in its own right.[68] This contrasted with the situation in the United States where it was defined by statute in 1958 as a humane method. In an effort to avoid the implications of a terminology that implied that Jewish slaughter was somehow backward, the issue of words became crucial: "There is nothing ritualistic or cultural about the Jewish method of slaughter. The banner 'ritual slaughter' is a description offensive to those familiar with *shechita*."[69]

The idea of what is considered "humane" has a different connotation in both Muslim and Judaic thinking. Although there are important differences between the two religions with regard to animals and rules for slaughter, both believe that animals have to be well treated in life and that the act of killing is a recognition of lives that are divinely given. Also, both religions see slaughter as a form of purification. *Dabh* in Arabic connotes purification or rendering something good or wholesome, while the knife used by the *shochet* in *shechita* is termed a *chataf,* so named because it is the instrument that changes the state of that which is forbidden into that which becomes permitted. "The taking of an animal's life therefore involves a great responsibility, must fulfill a real human need—i.e. food—and must be performed in the prescribed manner, with the person performing the act concentrating on the fact that, at the time of *shechita,* he is actually bringing the life of one of God's creations to an end."[70] In *dabh,* the slaughterer has to pronounce the name of Allah at the moment of killing. In Islam, animals that die of natural causes are considered unfit to eat because their death was not brought about for the purpose of food. There has to be an opportunity to declare an intention, or *niyyah,* of taking the animal's life for food. Also, animals and birds cannot be hunted except for the purpose of providing food, and one is not allowed to use animals for trophies or target practice.[71] In an attack on the idea that Muslim slaughter is seen as "ancient" and "barbaric," Ghulam Khan writes:

> Animals that are stunned and strangled and animals that died through beating or through falling headlong from a height or being drowned (the meat of all of which is prohibited) represent animals that are shot in the head, gassed and electrocuted in the post-mechanical era. The processes and end result are essentially the same. There is no difference between mechanical and non-mechanical stunners from the point of view of cruelty and hygiene.[72]

I noted earlier how the German Jews attempted to fight the attacks on *shechita* on different fronts. In Britain, there have been similar efforts to base the justification of a humane act on scientific measurement. In this case, the question asked is, At what point does the animal lose consciousness and the ability to feel pain in the killing process? Furthermore, how might one measure the secession of pain? In *shechita,* it is held that slaughter and stunning are combined in a single act, partly derived from the claim that the animal's consciousness is lost almost instantly on having its throat cut. In an account of the debate between the government and Jewish lobbyists between 1985 and 1990 over *shechita,* Geoffrey Alderman notes how many of the arguments turned on scientific issues around the measurement of the periods of time between throat-cutting, the swiftness of the loss of blood supply to the brain of the animal, and loss of consciousness rather than on the matter of religious faith and the freedom to practice it.[73] One significance of the scientific justification for notions of the humane is that it shifts the notion of acceptability a degree away from the act of killing itself. The criterion for the most "humane" method thus incorporates a clinical element that determines, and objectivizes, the idea of the animal's pain and awareness through EEG patterns and other forms of electro-cortical reading. In moving between scientific, secular humanitarian, and moral/religious arguments to ensure a sense of minimum suffering, the emphasis in these arguments becomes centered on time: the potentially measurable rapidity of the loss of consciousness and the efficient rapidity of the dispatch of the animal. In that sense, the notion of the humane maps neatly onto the logic of efficiency, and, in its use of scientific data to justify its own humaneness, religious slaughter becomes likewise complicit with such a logic.

One of the main changes that was introduced in the reform of slaughter practices in 1995 in the light of a number of reports by the Farm Animal Welfare Council was the upright restraining pen.[74] The introduction of these pens had been resisted by defenders of *shechita* in Britain, although they had long been acceptable for producing kosher meat in the United States since 1958.[75] This meant that the *shochet* would have to make an upward cut to the throat, with the animal upright, which would also require more strength, rather than having to cut when the animal was below him, as had happened when animals were cast or turned upside down in an inverting pen. The pens also required a suitable head restraint to pull up the head and expose the neck and had to take the weight of the animal as it was slaughtered. Temple Grandin, commenting on inverting pens with reference to the United States, noted how slow the Weinberg casting pen—one of the main makers of inverting pens—was with a top speed of 30–40 cattle per hour. A more humane upright apparatus was developed in 1963, whose patent was bought by the American Society for the Protection of Cruelty to Animals in 1964. It was considered not only more humane but could also handle 50–75 cattle per hour. The next development for kosher meat was a high-speed V conveyor restrainer with a capacity for 200 cattle per hour. In this machine, cattle ride along between two conveyors that form a V, the animal's body supported by angled conveyors on its flanks with its feet protruding through an opening between the bottom of the conveyors. When it reaches the head of the V, its head is raised by a hydraulic device and *shechita* is performed.[76] Although the upright pens may not involve the same intensity of throughput in Britain as found in some American slaughterhouses, there is still the irony that the more humane restraints are developed within a system that becomes more efficient by their introduction.

In June 2003, the Farm Animal Welfare Council produced a new report on the slaughter of red meat animals. One of its conclusions was that preslaughter stunning should finally be made compulsory for all forms of slaughter, and the report was convinced that, particularly for cattle, there was too great a length of time in *shechita* between the cut and insensibility.[77] Again, this was to be primarily understood as a welfare argument first and foremost: "We make no moral judgement."[78] There was also a repeat of the idea that the debate around the ethics of killing and slaughter was not of concern in this context but that the sole intention of the committee was to find a way to minimize the distress to the animal. In fact, in a remark that almost borders on black comedy, the council found that killing might not be the worst experience for an animal in a slaughterhouse but "may only be the final stressor in a sequence of equally or *more* stressful events" (emphasis added).[79] At the very end of the report, a number of quantifiable indicators are described that might give some measure of the standard of animal welfare. These include ratings for animals that slip or fall, rates of goading and hitting, levels of vocalization by the animals, and effective types of behavior "from the animals' point of view." Effective behaviors indicate that "animals are moving well through the system."[80]

I have chosen to highlight the rifts between different types of slaughter that exist within the overarching structure of meat production because it demonstrates the variety of meanings of meat and slaughter for different groups within the same society. In other words, the killing of animals for meat is not simply a monolithic edifice. In modernity, where the slaughter industry is so mechanized and intensive, it is important not to lose sight of the fact that competing moral, religious, and scientific positions do justify and, above all, shape practices of slaughter. However, the weakness of all these positions lies in their focus, their unit of analysis if you like, on the act of killing rather than on the whole system of *mass* slaughter and what it entails. The progressive outlook of technologized slaughter is thus undermined when we refuse to restrict the concept of humane slaughter to the single act of slaughter per se but see it as central to a language of efficiency and control that underpins a system engaged in the killing of millions of

animals every year. In addition, the fact that both secular and religious out-
looks seek to justify slaughter on the same terrain, by referring equally to
scientific authorities in attempting to define what is cruel and what is not
cruel, brings them uncomfortably close together. It suggests, as far as the
proponents of the religious argument are concerned, a flexibility and a willingness not to restrict the argument to one of faith. By the same turn, there
is no reason, therefore, why the issue of the mass slaughter of animals on an
almost uncountable scale might not likewise be debated from within religious
traditions themselves. By inevitably avoiding the overall question of killing
and restricting the argument to the kill itself, neither side can claim a moral high ground, and the debate over cruelty will, for all its efforts, always be
a competing one rooted in a series of pragmatic trade-offs between different
social interest groups. Despite the claim to neutrality by some animal welfarists, there is no self-evident, transcendent moral position around the mass
slaughter of animals, divine or secular.

Notes

1. It is important to bear in mind that this study does not seek to generalize too much
from the examples that are specifically offered here to other countries. There are important differences of detail in, for example, the slaughter industry, the structure of the
butchering professions, notions of animal welfare and animal rights, and the cultural
responses to *shechita* in Germany, France, Scandinavia, North America, Britain, and so
on. I am grateful to Dorothee Brantz for pointing this out to me.

2. Upton Sinclair, *The Autobiography of Upton Sinclair* (London: W. H. Allen, 1963),
135.

3. Jimmy M. Skaggs, *Prime Cut: Livestock Raising and Meatpacking in the United States
1607–1983* (College Station: Texas A&M University Press, 1986), 118–24. On the continued
plight of migrant workers in the slaughter industry, see the contemporary account by
Charlie LeDuff, "At a Slaughterhouse, Some Things Never Die," in *Zoontologies: The
Question of the Animal,* ed. Cary Wolfe (Minneapolis: University of Minnesota Press,
2003), 183–97.

4. Sinclair, *Autobiography,* 117.

5. Upton Sinclair, *The Jungle* (Harmondsworth: Penguin, 1982), 118–19.

6. Noëlie Vialles, *Animal to Edible* (Cambridge: Cambridge University Press, 1994),
46.

7. James Barrett, *Work and Community in the Jungle: Chicago's Packinghouse Workers
1894–1922* (Urbana: University of Illinois Press, 1987), 27. See also Jeremy Rifkin, *Beyond
Beef: The Rise and Fall of the Cattle Culture* (London: Thorsons, 1992), part 3.

8. Barrett, *Work and Community,* 23–28.

9. William Cronon, *Nature's Metropolis: Chicago and the Great West* (London: Norton,
1991), 230.

10. Cronon, *Nature's Metropolis,* 224.

11. Rifkin, *Beyond Beef,* 127, 154. Of course rates of killing of other animals can be even higher. Gail Eisnitz points out that poultry plants can process as many as 340,000 birds an hour, while one plant in Iowa has a capacity for 75,000 hogs per week (or one every four seconds). See Eisnitz, *Slaughterhouse: The Shocking Tale of Greed, Neglect, and Inhumane Treatment inside the U.S. Meat Industry* (New York: Prometheus Books, 1997), 167, 63.

12. "To produce Branding Iron boxed beef, one cattle is transformed into seven heavy cardboard boxes 22.5 inches long by 17.5 inches wide by 10.5 inches deep." Ken Erickson, "Beef in a Box: Killing Cattle on the High Plains," in *Animals in Human Histories,* ed. Mary Henninger-Voss (Rochester: University of Rochester Press, 2002), 90.

13. Eric Schlosser, *Fast Food Nation* (London: Penguin, 2002), 15ff.

14. "'Geographical information systems' . . . are now routinely used as site selection tools by fast food chains." Schlosser, *Fast Food Nation,* 66. For comparable material on Britain and the connections between railways, refrigeration, meat markets, and things like the impact of the changing fashions in meat tastes, see Richard Perren, *The Meat Trade in Britain 1890–1914* (London: Routledge and Kegan Paul, 1978).

15. John Walton, *Fish and Chips and the British Working Class 1870–1940* (Leicester, UK: Leicester University Press, 1992), 6. Fish and chips began in London and the Pennine manufacturing towns in the 1870s.

16. Ibid., 42–43.

17. Mark Kurlansky, *Cod: A Biography of the Fish That Changed the World* (London: Vintage, 1999), 134–40.

18. Nick Fiddes, *Meat: A Natural Symbol* (London: Routledge, 1991), 2.

19. Richard B. Grantham, *A treatise on public slaughter-houses, considered in connection with the sanitary question. Describing the practice of slaughtering in France and England, with an historical and statistical account of the abattoirs of Paris, and accompanied by plans, with the view to the introduction of similar establishments into England* (London: J. and H. Cox, 1848), 5.

20. Ibid., 79.

21. Ibid., 110–12.

22. Ben Fine, Michael Heasman, and Judith Wright, *Consumption in the Age of Affluence: The World of Food* (London: Routledge, 1996), 206.

23. Ibid., 207–8.

24. On debates around humane slaughter in Britain prior to the 1904 report, see Ian MacLachlan, "*Coup de Grâce:* Humane Slaughter in Nineteenth Century Britain," unpublished manuscript cited with the kind permission of the author.

25. *Report of the Committee appointed by the Admiralty to consider the Humane Slaughtering of Animals, Cmd. 2150* (London: HMSO, 1904), 5.

26. Ibid., 6.

27. Ibid., 7.

28. Ibid., 23.

29. Ibid., 20.

30. Ibid., 51.

31. G. R. Leighton and L. M. Douglas, *The Meat Industry and Meat Inspection* (London: Educational Book Co., 1910), vol. 2, 675. They wrote, "The time has surely gone by when any ethical value should be attached to a method of slaughtering, except on grounds of

humanitarianism." Vol. 3, 765. See other grounds for objection to Jewish slaughter in vol. 2, 401.

32. Ibid., vol. 3, 743.

33. Ibid., 737.

34. H. B. Cronshaw and D. J. Anthony, *The Meat Industry: A Text Book for Meat Traders and Others Engaged in Various Branches of the Meat Industry* (London: Baillière, Tindall, and Cox, 1927), 121.

35. For a broader cultural historical perspective on electrical stunning, see Jonathan Burt, "The Illumination of the Animal Kingdom: The Role of Light and Electricity in Animal Representation," *Society and Animals* 9 (2001): 203–28.

36. C. H. Ducksbury and D. J. Anthony, "Stunning of the Pig by Electricity before Slaughter," *Veterinary Record* 9 (1929): 433–34.

37. Leonard Hill notes that Benjamin Ward Richardson experimented on electricity as a method of slaughter in 1896. See his "Electric Methods of Producing Humane Slaughter," *Veterinary Journal* 91 (1935): 51. Müller and Weinberger continued Leduc's experiments on the application of electricity to the animal body in 1927; in 1930 Letterschmidt and Weinberger constructed a mains operated apparatus; during the years between 1933 and 1940 Roos and Koopmans at Utrecht University experimented with electricity on dogs, cats, rabbits, young goats, and calves. J. Hickman, "The Electrical Stunning of Animals Prior to Slaughter," *Veterinary Record* 66 (1954): 498. Solomon Lieben, who had been working on electrical stunning in Prague from at least 1928, experimented on electrical stunning to see if it could be incorporated into *shechita*. See Michael Munk and Eli Munk, eds., *Shechita Part II of "Edut Ne'emana": Religious and Historical Research on the Jewish Method of Slaughter* (New York: Gur Aryeh, 1976), 21.

38. D. J. Anthony, "Electricity for the Slaughter of Animals," *Veterinary Record* 12 (1932): 380. The definition of "splashing" is "the term commonly applied to a more or less disfigurement of dressed carcasses which takes the form of haemorrhagic areas." Thomas Parker, "Humane Slaughtering and Some Experiments by Various Methods of Stunning, with Special Reference to the Condition Known as Splashing," *Veterinary Journal* 85 (1929): 197. On the causes of splashing, see W. Tweed, G. A. Clark, and J. W. Edington, "Splashing of Meat in the Slaughter of Animals," *Veterinary Record* 11 (1931): 23–27.

39. Max Müller, "The Electric Stunning of Animals for Slaughter from the Humane Standpoint," *Veterinary Journal* 85 (1929): 166.

40. Parker, "Humane Slaughtering," 199–200.

41. J. Roos and S. Koopmans, "Studies on the So-Called Electrical Stunning of Animals," *Veterinary Journal* 90 (1934): 244.

42. Anton Weinberger, "Electrical Stunning of Animals," *Veterinary Journal* 90 (1934): 339.

43. J. Roos, "The So-Called Electrical Stunning of Animals," *Veterinary Journal* 91 (1935): 64.

44. Hill, "Electric Methods," 53.

45. Neville Gregory, *Animal Welfare and Meat Science* (Wallingford, UK: CABI, 1998), 239. Gregory notes that there are a number of other uses for electricity when applied to the animal. Sometimes a second current is applied after the stunning either before or during bleeding out. This is done as part of an electromobilization procedure to stop

convulsions and avoid injury to workers. It can also be applied after sticking to accelerate postmortem muscle metabolism and allow rapid chilling without producing tough meat (88–89).

46. J. A. Dembo, *The Jewish Method of Slaughter: Compared with Other Methods from the Humanitarian, Hygienic, and Economic Points of View* (London: Kegan, Paul, Trench, Trübner, 1896), 103–4.

47. Dorothee Brantz, "Stunning Bodies: Animal Slaughter, Judaism, and the Meaning of Humanity in Imperial Germany," *Central European History* 35 (2002): 187–89.

48. Dembo, *Jewish Method*, 53.

49. For a description of this, see Munk and Munk, *Shechita*, 17ff. See also Boria Sax, *Animals in the Third Reich: Pets, Scapegoats, and the Holocaust* (New York: Continuum Books, 2000), esp. 142–44.

50. Sebastian Poulter, *Ethnicity, Law and Human Rights: The English Experience* (Oxford: Clarendon Press, 1998), 142.

51. Roger Charlton and Ronald Kaye, "Defending the Religious Slaughter of Animals: A Study in Ethnic Issue Management," *Politics* 5 (1985): 27.

52. Mary Dudley Ward, *Jewish "Kosher": Should It Be Permitted to Survive in a New Britain?* (Ilfracombe, UK: Arthur H. Stockwell, 1944). In the 1951 edition, she writes, "I do not want my animal welfare campaign to be confused with racial prejudices. The time comes, however, when honest opinions must be expressed, regardless of what offence may be taken; and I condemn kosher slaughter wholeheartedly as a most appalling barbarity . . . not because it is Jewish but because the normal horrors of the slaughterhouse are in this way multiplied with savagery" (v).

53. *Hansard* (Lords), December 3, 1962, 5th ser., vol. 245, 8. Robert Crouch, when moving a similar amendment to the 1933 Slaughterhouse Act in the House of Commons in 1956, said, "I should like to make it clear that I'm not anti-semitic and that I have a number of friends of the Jewish faith." *Hansard* (Commons), December 12, 1956, 5th ser., vol. 562, 439.

54. Todd Endelman, "'Practices of a Low Anthropologie Level': A *Shechita* Controversy of the 1950s," in *Food in the Migrant Experience*, ed. Anne Kershen (Aldershot, UK: Ashgate Publishing, 2002), 80.

55. Ibid., 82.

56. *Oxfordshire Times*, November 19, 1943, quoted in Tony Kushner, *The Persistence of Prejudice: Antisemitism in British Society during the Second World War* (Manchester: Manchester University Press, 1989), 95.

57. Tony Kushner, "Stunning Intolerance: A Century of Opposition to Religious Slaughter," *Jewish Quarterly* 133 (1989): 17. He also notes an anti-Semitic riot in Liverpool in 1947 after abattoir workers refused to handle kosher meat.

58. D. Wilkins, "Ritual Slaughter, RSPCA's Point of View," *Muslim Herald*, June 1977, 30.

59. Brian Klug, "Overkill: The Polemic against Religious Slaughter," *Jewish Quarterly* 134 (1989): 41–42.

60. Keren David and Simon Rocker, "Shechita Row: Experts Reply," *Jewish Chronicle*, August 2, 1985, 5.

61. Wendy Berliner, "Bigotry Boils Up over Asian Meat," *The Guardian*, March 26, 1984, 4.

62. Lord Houghton of Sowerby, *Hansard* (Lords), July 13, 1990, 5th ser., vol. 21, 611.

63. The potential for double standards by focusing on kosher and ignoring other aspects of intensive animal husbandry is discussed in Sebastian Poulter, *English Law and Ethic Minority Customs* (London: Butterworths, 1986), 279. On European Union and other international rulings on religious freedom, see also Poulter, *Ethnicity, Law,* 142.

64. Poulter, *Ethnicity, Law,* 134.

65. Farm Animal Welfare Council Report, *Report on the Welfare of Livestock When Slaughtered by Religious Methods* (London: HMSO, 1985), 19.

66. Letter from Neville Kesselman to Margaret Thatcher, June 13, 1989, in Neville Kesselman, *A Guide to the Law on Shechita in Great Britain* (London: Neville Kesselman, 1995), app. 5.

67. These remarks are made in a statement against the 1984 Farm Animal Welfare Report, *Report on the Welfare of Livestock (Red Meat Animals) at the Time of Slaughter,* quoted in Poulter, *Ethnicity, Law,* 140. See also the comments on the spiritual justifications for kosher in Munk and Munk, *Shechita,* 35–37. "Different methods of killing can bring about different material conditions in the body and consequently lead to different effects when the flesh is consumed. This difference need not be of a hygienic nature; it can have an effect in a purely spiritual way" (35).

68. For a summary of Jewish attitudes to animals and some specific doctrinal arguments against the proposals to alter *shechita*, see "Comments Submitted by the Campaign for the Protection of Shechita 14 June 1990" in Kesselman, *Guide,* app. 2; and also Anon., *Shechita: A Humane Method* (London: The Board of Deputies of British Jews, 1990).

69. Kesselman, "Comments," 3.

70. Anon., *Shechita,* 3.

71. Ghulam Khan, *Al-Dabh: Slaying Animals for Food the Islamic Way* (London: Islamic Medical Association, 1982), 16.

72. Ibid., 37.

73. Geoffrey Alderman, "The Defence of *Shechita*: Anglo-Jewry and the "Humane Conditions" Regulations of 1990," *New Community* 21 (1995): 81.

74. I refer here to "The Welfare of Animals (Slaughter or Killing) Regulations 1995," *Statutory Instruments 1995: Part I Section 3* (London: HMSO, 1996), 2610–44. The two other influential Farm Animal Welfare Council reports were the *Report on the Welfare of Poultry at the Time of Slaughter* (1982) and the *Report on the Welfare of Livestock (Red Meat Animals) at the Time of Slaughter* (1984). On European directives on *shechita* at the same time and approaches to animal protection generally, see Berel Berkovits, "Challenges to *Shechita* in Europe," *Judaism* 39 (1990): 470–87. Interestingly, Berkovits sees *dabh* as "in reality, so different—and so inferior—that we cannot join forces with them in our battle for *shechita*. Indeed, we often find ourselves tarred with the same brush by non-discriminating opponents of all forms of religious slaughter" (472). It is not clear if she means that Muslims should be subject to secular rules and Jews exempt.

75. Though as Temple Grandin pointed out writing in 1990, not all cattle in kosher plants were killed in a restraining pen in the United States. "In many shackle and hoist

cattle plants, a clamp is placed in the nostrils and the neck is stretched by a powerful air cylinder, which may apply as much as 400lbs of pull. Suspending a 1300lb steer by one back leg is also very stressful." "Humanitarian Aspects of *Shechita* in the United States," *Judaism* 39 (1990): 438. On a case study of kosher slaughter in the United States, see Stephen Bloom, *Postville: A Clash of Cultures in Heartland America* (New York: Harvest, 2001).

76. Grandin, "Humanitarian Aspects," 439–41.

77. Farm Animal Welfare Council, *Report on the Welfare of Farmed Animals at Slaughter or Killing Part 1: Red Meat Animals* (London: FAWC, 2003), 32–36.

78. Ibid., vii.

79. Ibid., 2.

80. Ibid., 70.

7   BSE, Hysteria, and the Representation of Animal Death: Deborah Levy's *Diary of a Steak*

ROBERT MCKAY

Prolegomenon: A Story of BSE

On March 20, 1996, the UK Secretary of State for Health, Stephen Dorrell, announced to Parliament that he had been advised of the likelihood of a link between bovine spongiform encephalopathy (BSE) and new variant Creutzfeldt-Jakob disease (vCJD). This contradicted his government's denials of such a link over the preceding decade. Now he was admitting that a disease that had caused people, many of them young, to become anxious, depressed, and then withdrawn and to lose their memory, sense of balance, all of their physical functions, and finally their life was indeed the human form of BSE. This was the disease that had caused cows to become irritable, foam at the mouth, lose their balance, stagger, and collapse. The pictures shown over and over again on television of deranged cows stumbling and thudding into the ground in a muddy farmyard could no longer be viewed by meat-eating Britons secure in the knowledge that the species barrier protected them from a similar fate. Instead, in the aftermath of Dorrell's announcement, the pathos (and for some, the humor) of those images took on a more frightening aspect, and that earlier impervious security gave way to the fear of contagion. For the implication of the BSE-vCJD link was that the eating of meat cut from cattle any time in the preceding ten years, an act apparently so innocuous before the announcement was made, could have belated life-shattering effects. The "Roast Beef of Old England" once had life-affirming power, both literally and as a national symbol. It was suddenly resignified as a bringer of illness and death: a disturbing and abject reversal.

March 20, 1996, was the day that "mad cow disease" stopped being predominantly a problem of animal health and became the "mad cow crisis," perhaps the most important political and social event of 1990s Britain. Beyond the terrible immediate fact of the deaths of humans from cases of vCJD (150) and of cows diagnosed with BSE (180,780), its ramifications were and are widespread. Epidemiologists still cannot calculate accurately the number of people who continue to incubate vCJD. The response to export controls imposed by the European Commission on the British meat industry repeatedly exposed the Conservative Party's schism over the issue of UK-European relations. This was a rift that (along with the handling of the BSE epidemic itself) must be seen as a huge factor in the Labour Party's general election win in 1997. BSE's cost to the UK treasury reached £3.9 billion by the end of the 2001–02 financial year, a cost largely brought about by the removal from the food chain of all cows over thirty months old. To date, the UK cull of animals in the wake of BSE has required the slaughter and disposal of 7,990,012 animals.[1]

Such a figure as this last may still have the power to shock. Yet as one draws a breath at the sheer scale of death involved here, it is easy to overlook the complicated interplay of empathy and disavowal involved in such a response. For expressions of dismay at BSE's mass slaughter, or indeed at the modern-day hecatombs that blighted the British countryside during 2002's foot-and-mouth outbreak, may give evidence of a real sense of loss at the demise of these beasts. Yet at the same time, the mourning of these animals acts as a screen for a more profound loss to the psyche of the meat-eating public: that of a quasi-pastoral ideal in which meat is produced without the visible reality of death by farmers whose intimate relationship with their living herd counteracts the meat consumer's alienation from the animal that is slaughtered.[2] Indeed, despite appearances, it is not strictly the *death* of the animal in the aftermath of BSE or foot-and-mouth that is mourned but also its *waste* as a commodity. There is a salient difference between the demise of the animals condemned during these epidemics and the 46,000 cows that are killed each week in Britain's meat industry.[3] Although the latter disappear into an efficient market where gastronomic and economic consumption are combined, the deaths of the former remain visible, languishing with no use value and hence no economic destination. The condemned animals' burning, whether in pyres or incinerators, bears witness to the hard facts of an industry where death is essential to production and consumption. The decision was made to eradicate foot-and-mouth because it reduces milk yields and animal growth (that is, profit); the decision to cull cattle over thirty months

was made primarily to retain public confidence in British beef after BSE
rather than to meet the explicit requirements of human or animal health.

BSE Narratives

I have begun this essay with a foray into some of the meanings of BSE because
in surveying the cultural aftermath of the crisis, it is fascinating to note this
surprising fact: BSE spawned a great number and variety of narratives but
very little literary response. Newspapers and television documentary, news,
and discussion programs attempted to manage the ongoing story for the
public.[4] As Richard Kerridge notes in his analysis of these, two particular
narratives emerged: one of a return to normality as BSE itself was gradually
eradicated; the other of a crisis ever harder to control as blood transfusions
and growth hormones were implicated and information about possible longer incubation periods forced reconsiderations of the eventual number of
vCJD cases.[5]

Accompanying these, however, were two highly politicized narratives. First,
the nationalist Euro-phobia, which turned the international politics of BSE
into a "beef war," tapped into Britain's repertoire of cultural imagery from
beefeaters to John Bull in order to promote a flagging industry by making
the eating of beef a matter of national pride.[6] The second accompanying
narrative, the description of the reaction to BSE as "hysteria," tried to reas-
sure the public by characterizing its response (a turn away from beef consumption) as irrational panic. Elaine Showalter has followed this trend by
suggesting (without evidence or argument) that "the furor over Mad Cow
Disease in 1996 owed some of its intensity to British fear and denial of anything mad."[7] She mentions neither the complex manipulation of such a
denial by politicians, marketers, and press to promote the interests of the
meat industry, which was surprisingly effective, nor the genuine life-preserv-
ing self-interest, which might have been behind the original turn away from
beef.

Accompanying the journalistic response were books whose titles exem-
plify the way that BSE reportage was a modern form of the quest story, a
drama of search and revelation.[8] Storytelling was also central to the report
of the official public inquiry into the events leading up to the government
announcement. It relied on a narrative-led style and metaphorical conceits,
telling the story of the approaching announcement with subheadings such
as "The Storm Clouds Gather," "Rumbles of Thunder," and (inevitably)
"The Storm Breaks."[9] The fact that an essentially bureaucratic report with a

main readership of health professionals and parliamentarians should have such an unlikely reliance on narrative plotting only goes to insist that any understanding of the politics of BSE-vCJD should not be separated from the analysis of its formal representation.

Taking all of this into account, I want to suggest here one consequence of the prevalence of these particular narrative types in our understanding of BSE. The animals at the source of the epidemic are in effect effaced from the general cultural response to it. This is not to say that popular and official BSE narratives do not talk about cows. Rather, they follow the pattern that I documented in my opening paragraphs of appearing to be about cows yet all the while being about commodities. The BSE Inquiry Report is a good example. Second in its list of thirteen key conclusions is the following: "A vital industry has been dealt a body blow, inflicting misery on tens of thousands for whom livestock farming is a way of life. They have seen over 170,000 of their animals dying or having to be destroyed, and the precautionary slaughter and destruction within the United Kingdom of very many more."[10]

Here, the deaths of the cows are unsurprisingly secondary in importance to the survival of an industry facing a collapse that is the chief cause of the farmers' "misery." Such misery is in turn the main concern of the report's authors. The telling word "precautionary" is the signal for the emotional dynamic by which a professed sadness in response to animal death acts as a conduit for a more profound, economic loss. One can see that the misery annotated in this passage would be out of place if conditions allowed the replacement of that adjective with "productive" or something similar.

However, the interesting point here is not that there is an ideology inherent to the meat industry, reiterated in the report, which masks the fact that meat is predicated on death. Indeed, one recent development in the narratives of meat-eating in the wake of foot-and-mouth disease has seen a major shift in this ideology away from masking the conditions of meat production and toward a persistent focus on the ideal of organic consumption: knowing where one's meat comes from and purchasing accordingly. Rather, the interesting point is that pathos for the demise of what is essentially an economic endeavor can only find its expression precisely and ironically via an impossible identificatory mourning of the very animal deaths that are the raison d'être of the industry. Moreover, such an overlaying of animal by industry closes off the possibility of mourning the animal itself.

Of course, it is not surprising that narratives produced for consumption by a public that is largely meat-eating and so is fully invested in a productive meat industry should have this sort of focus. Obviously, too, the narrative drive of scientific research into the nosology and epidemiology of both BSE and vCJD is to document a specifically human teleology. And the shift of the gaze from animal to human is understandable when the passage from animal to human misery is the essence of the disaster of vCJD. Yet even in the *London Review of Books*, one of Britain's premier cultural reviews, BSE becomes a drama about the recruitment policy of the civil service. Hugh Pennington's main conclusion in reviewing the *BSE Inquiry Report* was that the most important lesson of BSE is that we need more scientists in the executive branch of government.[11]

As I mentioned earlier, there has been only a small number of literary responses to BSE-vCJD.[12] On the one hand, this is perhaps an understandable result of the oft-noted dilemma for the postmodern fabulist that the contemporary world offers such fantastic narratives that fiction can barely keep up. On the other hand, however, the lack of a literary response remains surprising given the fact that if BSE were a novel, it would be a distinctly postmodern one. As Joan Leach notes, "The BSE event offers no narrative closure, no ending by which the truth is recovered, boundaries stabilised, or uncertainties made certain."[13] Obviously, there is the human tragedy involved for sufferers of vCJD and the possibly national scale on which it was predicted to appear. There is also the arresting repertoire of the bovine imagery of BSE, replete with staggering cows and infernal incinerators. Then there is the challenge to narrative technique itself of representing the traumatic belatedness of a disease with such a complex chronology, a point remarked by Barbara Adam. As Kerridge applies Adam's argument, "The timescapes of the dominant forms of contemporary narrative, from thrillers to documentaries and news reports, cannot accommodate the timescape of BSE/CJD, with its unknown rates of infectivity and unknown incubation period."[14] The prevalence of other kinds of traumatic narrative in recent years, covering such diverse social phenomena as slavery and race, the Jewish Holocaust, and HIV-AIDS, only serves to bring into relief their dearth in the case of BSE-vCJD. There is, however, one literary story of BSE that responds to each of these exigencies of its representation, as well as counteracting the particular effacement of the animal during the portrayal of animal death that I have documented in other modes of BSE narrative. It is this work, Deborah Levy's *Diary of a Steak,* that will be the focus of the rest of this chapter.

* * *

I will begin with a description. Published in 1997, *Diary of a Steak* is a fascinating addition to the emergent cultural narrative of BSE first because of the potential of its avant-garde form to expose and undermine the ideology of representational strategies. Standard literary generic categories, such as the novel, cannot accommodate this extremely unusual piece of writing. Formally, it is made up of fractured stretches of prose, but it also resembles at times the text of a performance artwork, containing both transcribed conversations and declamatory statements that explicitly address a public audience. The meaning of the prose itself is extremely enigmatic, with plenty of unexplained extratextual allusion. And throughout, language itself is broken down, losing coherence at all semantic levels: words often have letters missing; there is erratic grammar and frequent non sequiturs; and the text itself is heteroglot, incorporating both a host of European languages and also, strangely, English words transliterated into ancient Greek.

Responding to this heteroglossia, one good way of describing the text is in terms outlined by Russian cultural theorist Mikhail Bakhtin.[15] In addition to the journal form, it accommodates a range of other genres and modes of writing that are put into dialogic interaction, from medical and cultural history to psychoanalytic case study, news reportage, and surrealist free-association poetry, from parliamentary speeches to popular celebrity magazines like *Hello!*, private letters, and even bureaucratic documents like faxes. This all contributes to a remarkably pluralist, even anarchic, textual arena in which the reader has to make a meaning of the text as much from the clash of these discourses as from the insight of any one of them. The resulting text is certainly a grotesque one, its language decomposed and difficult to make any sense of. It is filled with allusion to food, illness, the exigencies of time, and death (not surprising in a text about BSE) as well as to sexuality and other bodily processes. The final entry of the diary, which comments on the cause of BSE's spread at once with punning humor and melancholy, suggests that BSE-vCJD is in a way the most Bakhtinian of social phenomena. In its sad indictment of a fact structural to the dairy industry—the forcible removal of calves from their mothers—it also introduces to the narrative of BSE a gender-based inflection that will be of central importance to my reading of the text: "My momm y went to the incinerator. She was not allowed to suckle me. I'm a herbivore but I was made into a carnival."[16]

This entry is (ridiculous as it may seem) attributable to the eponymous steak, but the panoply of discursive modes that I have described in fact relates two interwoven stories. It is a record of the last six days in the (shelf-) life of a steak culled from the body of a cow that has been slaughtered while incubating BSE, and it incorporates both individual memories of the cow's actual life and what we might call "cultural memories" of her bovine grandparents. But it is also a diachronic memoir of the treatment of women during the various stages of psychotherapeutic medicine, stages that correspond to chapters in Elaine Showalter's book on that subject, *The Female*

Malady. This, along with *Diary of a Steak*'s allusion to Gogol's *Diary of a Madman,* is its most obvious intertext. The summary moment of this history, for Levy as well as for Showalter, is the explosion of hysteria across fin-de-siècle Europe, which saw the high-water mark of incidence of female psychiatric illness as well as the foundation of psychoanalytic therapy as we know it today. In addition to all of this, *Diary of a Steak* stages a veritable polyphony of voices, including unnamed politicians at the time of the BSE crisis as well as famous physicians and hysterical patients such as Jean-Martin Charcot, Josef Breuer, Sigmund Freud, Augustine, Anna O., and Dora among its characters.

In surveying the book, I especially want to flag the problem of how to categorize it since, as I will argue later, one of its chief concerns is to undermine the notions of conventional aesthetic authorship and interpretation. It is therefore very difficult to talk about the book as a novel or other such literary genre. This is something that one might feel compelled to do when confronted with a text that, despite its titular claim to be a non-artistic form of self-disclosure, is clearly confected by an author called Deborah Levy, a writer of several highly regarded works of avant-garde fiction.[17] These are concerns to which I will return later, for I want to suggest that *Diary of a Steak* tackles the difficult task of telling the *animals'* story of BSE, confronting (and thus exposing) the way in which the singular reality of millions of animals' deaths has been obscured by the dominant human-centered narrative. This requires a very complex renunciation of the ability to define the animal that conventional narratives of BSE happily assume.

Questions about BSE and how animal death is represented prove especially important for understanding how animals are represented in general in contemporary fiction. However, the point is not, as can be argued, that any representation of animals is anthropomorphic, a part of human culture that must therefore destroy what is essentially "animal" about them. *Diary of a Steak* makes clear the false logic in this understanding of animal representation. For BSE-vCJD marks the moment when the structurally related oppositions of human to animal, of language to body, and of culture to nature—oppositions that subtend any literary representation of the animal—simply will not hold. This is all encapsulated in one brief extract. The text gives words to a BSE-cow that bring into the open the fact of human responsibility for infecting cows with BSE and the devastation of the slaughter that we have visited on them. "I lost my mind before they culled it. Loss is not the equation. I gained mindlessness, memories of knives and psychic anguish in the English countryside. The mind gentlemen is closely related to the flesh . . . the mind is a body . . . the mind falling falling falling."[18]

In the case of vCJD, humans became infected with a disease that began as

BSE in the bodies of Britain's cows but that only disseminated throughout the herd because of a process integral to the postwar industrialization of farming: the replacement of grass with meat and bone meal made of rendered cattle carcasses (a high-protein cattle feed that increases milk yields). One could say that the infection of animals with BSE is in a sense the completion of their being turned into texts, their very bodies being inscribed with a disease that is the most explicit manifestation of agriculture's denaturalization of the animal. Seen in this light, BSE repositions the animal body from the so-called silent realm of nature into a circuit of cultural meaning. That human bodies should then be infected with the disease after another essentially enculturating device, the conversion of the animal body into meat during culinary preparation, makes it even more difficult for such binaries as human/animal or culture/nature to hold.

So, it is in the context of these implications of BSE and meat that *Diary of a Steak* emerges, for in such a confusion of human, animal body, and text, any complaint that giving words to an animal is anthropomorphic seems entirely beside the point. In this context of a permeable boundary between body and text, I now turn to the key guiding concept in *Diary of a Steak:* hysteria. For such a boundary transgression is perhaps a key facet of this illness in which mental traumas manifest themselves on the physical body in the form of culturally recognizable symptoms. The hysterical body, like the BSE-infected steak, is at once body and text.

Mad Cows? Parallels of Women and Animals in *Diary of a Steak*

I want to preface my explanation of the link between hysteria and BSE with a quotation that will perhaps give a sense of the interlinking of the two in the text. Here the cow-steak is addressing a gathering of "learned gentlemen" at Charcot's famous *leçons de mardi,* his lectures on hysteria at the Salpêtrière hospital in Paris in the late nineteenth century. In *Diary of a Steak,* however, this scene is merged with a post-BSE European Commission meeting room, and the aforementioned "learned gentlemen" now comprise "vets, journalists, leading personae of Europa, scholars, journalists, poets, more vets." We hear about the cow's own conception, and she also touches on a possible cause of BSE, the feeding to cattle of sheep infected with scrapie (a disease related to BSE), as well as humorously alluding to the BSE symptom of intense itching. In addition, her narration merges with that of someone who appears to be one of Charcot's patients. The cow's actions with the ammonia, charcoal, and top hat are actually paraphrased from a contemporary book about the *leçons,* although these were exhibited by different women.

> Gentlemen: Pank you for calling me to the lecture theatre today and in such a pretty nightie too. Do you think my nose is too big? I tell you what. We do have something in common after all. You eat sheep and I eat sheep. I'll scratch your back if you scratch mine. If you want milk just tee heee. Mother was an eating machine. Father never got to breathe on her neck. He copulated with a large leather mock-up of mother and his semen was transferred via a glass tube into her womb. I think I was a Friesian Hereford cross, with plentiful width. Mother showed me how to do it. Hysteria. I learnt all I know from her milk. She taught me everything. Perfected my falls. Rolled my eyes.
>
> [. . .] They gave me a bottle of ammonia to smell, I said it was rose water. They gave me charcoal to eat, I told them it was chocolate. They gave me a top hat and I told them it was a baby and suckled it in front of the distinguished gentlemen farmers and independent experts on brain disease.[19]

Here, I would argue, the text indicates *parallels* between hysteric and BSE-cow, a term that indicates similarity between the two while insisting on a necessary difference between them. Thus, while it remains possible to recognize that there is an obvious political necessity not to *equate* women and animals (an age-old patriarchal gesture), this notion of a parallel between hysteric and BSE-cow allows me to use insights gained from the feminist study of hysteria to understand the figuration of animals.

Now, within feminist criticism, there has been much debate in the past twenty years over the political potential of hysteria as a conceptual category. However, one factor does remain constant across the competing approaches: the critical leverage gained by the fact that in hysteria, body and culture meet. "Hysteria is a mimetic disorder," Showalter writes; "it mimics culturally permissible expressions of distress."[20] As a psychosomatic illness, hysteria formulates its symptoms by tapping into the image repertoire of the culture of its sufferer. The hysterically suffering body is therefore both body and text, like the BSE-infected cow.

Through the parallel of hysteria and animal, *Diary* offers a radicalization of the conventional philosophical idea that language is what is added to a shared bodily nature to separate humans from other animals: humans are animals with language. Such a thesis is problematized because the animal (or hysteric's body) itself is seen as a text provoking or requiring interpretation rather than as blank matter. Under those circumstances, as we shall see, making any sense at all of the animal or of hysteria means, to be sure, looking closely at the politics of their interpretation. That said, I can now analyze in more detail the ways in which hysteria and BSE find their way into this text.

I have already touched on the way that the word "hysterical" became a key epithet in the political management of the public refusal of beef in the wake of Dorrell's announcement. *Diary* uses this fact as a launching pad for its much more thoroughgoing mutual implication of the two realms (hysterical illness and BSE and vCJD). This might at first seem only a theoretically in-genious parallel, but the symptomatology of hysteria (at least as it is re-corded most famously by Freud and Breuer) and of vCJD are remarkably similar, including as they do uncontrollable emotional states, aphasia, mem-ory loss, and a variety of bodily dysfunctions.[21] In fact, my own (and Levy's) looking to hysteria for meaning about animal ethics only repeats in reverse the work of Victorian anti-vivisection activists who condemned the "no less disgusting experiments practised on the lunatics and hysterical patients in the Salpêtrière."[22]

Looking specifically to BSE, *falling* is the symptom that is virtually syn-onymous with the disease, just as the conventional feminine swoon is one of the most pervasive cultural signifiers of nineteenth-century hysteria.[23] The repetition of "falling" in the following quotation from *Diary* recalls the repetition in the phrase "tormenting, tormenting, tormenting" spoken by Anna O., one of the first hysterics studied by Breuer. Breuer remarks this as the key indicator of her aphasic speech disorganization: "The camera has been crucial to the study of my hysteria, just as the microscope was crucial to histology. I have become partial to the status the lens has given me and my falls . . . falling falling falling keeling and shuffling on sawdust."[24]

This quotation is particularly packed with meaning. In addition to its introduction (via the invocation of Anna O.'s aphasia) of the theme of the hysteric's *failed speech,* it also introduces the fact that *visibility* is central to the understanding of hysteria: hysteria in this text is explicitly a performance before an interpreting viewer. Elizabeth Bronfen has summarized the com-plex play of hysterical performance and medical interpretation at Charcot's Salpêtrière. "Doctors, insatiably seeking images of hysteria (be these live performances or photographic representations) and hysteric patients, com-plying with this spectacle, outmatching each other with the theatricality of their poses, came together to stage a scene where hysterical suffering could be invented and fabricated as an art form, both as a spectacle and as an im-age."[25]

A last important message to be read in the above quotation from *Diary* is that its series of implications about hysteria, failed speech, and the visibility of the hysterical performance are made by way of quotation from Showalter.

As such, it is one clear example of the text's construction from a tissue of such quotations. For in *The Female Malady,* we learn that "one of [Charcot's] admirers remarked that 'the camera was as crucial to the study of hysteria as the microscope was to histology.'"[26] In fact there are more than thirty such quotations from Showalter placed throughout the book, indicating that this particularly direct form of intertextuality is a formal method vital to the text's meaning. For just as the text's notion of hysterical performance presumes, following Bronfen, a certain dialogue or at least mutual complicity in the patient-doctor relationship, the incorporation of Showalter's words ensures that Levy's avant-garde presentation of that performance comes into dialogue with Showalter's historicism. It may seem a long way from this to the images of dying cattle with which I began this essay. However, the links will become clear in my final section, in which I will explain how the two major themes I have mentioned (failure of speech and the performative nature of hysteria) hold the key to *Diary of a Steak*'s rendering visible of the animals in the BSE crisis.

Textualizing the Animal: The Failure of Speech

The first entry in *Diary of a Steak* begins with the apparently affirming words that "it's good to talk," although the affirmation is not a little undermined by the fact that the phrase is overcoded with ideology in the form of a national advertising campaign by British Telecom. As the week's worth of entries progresses, however, this axiom passes through various stages of corrupted mutation. It appears as "goo o alk," "o alk," "it's od to ta," and "goo tal," until on Friday the entry reads:

> good to talk
> gd talk
> o a tlk.[27]

By this time, the original notion of "good talk"—which, bearing in mind the rationalist prejudice of Western thought, is as much an anthropocentric credo as it is a barely masked piece of canny marketing—has been radically undermined. Considering the notion of "talk" more specifically than just as a synonym for language, this very *textual* destruction of talk (how would one pronounce "goo o alk"?) indicates a certain denigration of the value of the spoken word itself in favor of writing. *Diary* recapitulates the familiar critique of the sovereign subject, a subject that is always, of course, human and whose self-certainty is underwritten by speech's prevalence over writing in Western thought.

Diary's turn from speech to textuality is also a consequence of its representation of hysteria, which has a very ambivalent relationship to speech. Its symptoms are essentially the result of patients' silencing, of their inability to find a valid cultural expression of their trauma. *Diary of a Steak* finds an ingenious way to imbue this fact with meaning about the political manipulation of BSE by staging a meeting between the steak and Josef Breuer:

> Das ist frauelin . . . ?—This is Miss . . . ?
> **—Buttercup**
> Ein beefsteak?
> **Yes.**
> Aha.
> **I was born in East Grinstead[. . . .]**
> Haben Sie etwas zu vorzollen?—have you anything to declare?
> **May I have the bill?**
> Es war mir ein Vergnugen—It was nice meeting you
> **May I have the bill please**
> Alles ist inbegriffen—all is included.
> **Pank you very much**
> Gutentag Buttercup—Good afternoon Buttercup. From now on I will call
>   you Buttercup O.
>
> He called me Buttercup O[28]

Here, the scene of psychoanalysis is melded with the scene of the ignorant Brit abroad in continental Europe. The heteroglot result makes a telling comment not only on the deafness of the analyst to the hysterical voice; with Breuer's German tongue so uncomprehending or ignorant of the steak, it also manages a wicked joke at the expense of a certain kind of English xenophobia, one that resurfaced so tellingly during the BSE debacle. For although all of Europe banned British beef, it was the *German* refusal of it that so incensed the tabloid press.

Breuer's naming of the steak "Buttercup O" obviously reaffirms the parallel with Anna O.

> I, Buttercup O
> Craisy Daisy
> invented the talking cure that is psychoanalysis . . .
> mute. I was mute[29]

Muteness characterizes the hysteric as well as the animal. As Mary Jacobus notes: "It is an irony of the history of psychoanalysis that the patient credited with the invention of 'the talking cure' . . . should have had as her major hysterical symptom the inability to talk. Afflicted by a 'deep-going func-

tional disorganisation of her speech,' Anna O . . . successively 'lost her command of grammar and syntax.'"[30] Avant-garde writers from the surrealists
to Cixous, Irigaray, and Kristeva have played with language in an attempt to
capture at the level of the text this challenge to subjectivity and signification
posed by Anna O.'s aphasia. Levy's development of this tradition is to take
its challenge for the fictional representation of postmodern human subjectivity into the realm of representing the animal.

The diarist's self-introduction on the opening page aligns Buttercup with
a roll call of now famous hysterics: "At times I will lose control of grammar
and syntax. Call me Emmy, Dora, Bertha, Anna O, Augustine, Buttercup."[31]
This passage has several implications and contradictions for the understanding of a work that tries to represent cows. Primarily, it inscribes on the very
first page of the work the slippage from spoken to textual word. To introduce
herself by way of the idiomatic phrase "call me" implies two-way communication with the reader. And yet written on the first page of a work of fiction,
that phrase cannot but seem explicitly intertextual, evoking Herman Mel-
ville's—and his character Ahab's—attempt to capture in literature a very
different (cetacean) kind of cow. Indeed, we can see that the diarist is a specifically *textual* sort of animal when we recognize her further self-expression,
in this most personal of written forms, by way of a slight modification of
Breuer's words about Anna O., which are quoted by Jacobus above.

Furthermore, that the diarist should imply an estranged reader who would
need to "call her" anything immediately makes a problem of the notion of
self-reflexivity inherent to the diary's conventional mode of construction,
which presumes that it will be read only by its writer. In construction, the
diary might at first appear to differ from the narrative nature of autobiography, structured only by the real condition of its writer's temporal existence,
rather than by more aesthetic concerns. The diary is implicitly perspicacious
because it has no apparent addressee (other than, as with the "Dear Diary"
approach, the diary itself). Yet, as a written document, the diary must have
an implied reader, even if only an unacknowledged part of the writer's own
subjectivity. In a sense, the diary is an ever-failing attempt to shore up the
identity of the writing subject. The writer attempts to control his or her
personal history through the very act of revisiting it in writing. Yet once the
diary passes from process to product and is read, it can reveal only the self's
ongoing construction in time. In *Diary of a Steak,* moreover, the writing
subject not only is split across a variety of selves (from Emmy to Buttercup)
but also explicitly emerges as the result of a dialogic performance with the
text's implied reader. And this dialogism is spread into a larger cultural realm
by the fact that the performance interpolates intertextual utterances.

Such a dispersal of the first person in writing is of course a familiar lesson of post-structuralist readings of enunciation. Far from being a signifier of self-presence, as a general singular form in grammar the "I" can always be possessed by others. Recently, however, Derrida has noted the link between this sense of the "I" and the word "animal":

> It happens that there exist, between the word *I* and the word *animal*, all sorts of significant connections. They are at the same time functional and referential, grammatical and semantic. Two general singulars to begin with: the *I* and the *animal* designate an indeterminate generality in the singular and by means of the definite article. The I is anybody at all; I am nobody at all and anybody at all must be able to say I.[32]

And in a surprisingly lyrical passage, Derrida goes on to suggest what might be at stake for the representation of animals in Levy's deconstruction of the bovine diarist's position of enunciation: it grants this represented animal a certain kind of *freedom*. He suggests that by using the general singular and effacing animal difference, philosophers' talk of humanity's difference from "the animal" enacts a kind of imprisonment. Derrida metaphorically connects that philosophical gesture to literal animal abuse.

All of this is a far cry from the simple validation of self-expression, "it's good to talk." Indeed, as we shall see shortly, the other constituent factors of the *Diary*'s deconstruction of speech—performativity and dialogic construction—are essential components of Levy's representation of the hysteric-animal parallel. For I want to argue that the text's method of representing both hysteric and animal as particular kinds of performer whose act seduces the desire of the viewer to interpret it evidences a commitment to the radical singularity of both. In the case of hysteria, the viewer of this performance is of course the examining doctor; in the case of the animal, it is the human who would wish to know the animal other.

The interest of the scene of hysteria for the critic attuned to animal politics as well as feminist politics is that it describes a drama of power and resistance that is *unconscious*. This unconsciousness separates the hysteric's protest from conventional liberal political action, which presumes a rational human subject. The parallel of hysteric and BSE-cow thus offers a space for *animal* protest, something that otherwise seems ridiculous in conventional terms. The task of the next section will be to explain just how a highly confected artistic text manages to promote a protesting agency that is predicated on the effacement of authorial power. To do so, however, first requires understanding that despite its insistence that the hysteric enacts a bodily performance, the agency behind that performance has become central to the feminist politics of hysteria.

The Performance of Hysteria

> Aberdeen Angus?
> I don't know who I am.
>
> I don't know who I am.
> What am I?   *barking*
> I am what?
> Who
>
> I can feel some erotic hysteria coming on
>
> barking
>
> It's coming
>
> my theatre of rib and shadows
>
> here it comes
> nearly there
> my hysteria[33]

The words of the diarist here chime with Luce Irigaray's suggestion that the female hysteric performs the masquerade of femininity, a mimicry that is a result of the "phallocentrism" of representation, which leaves no space for an authentic voice of the feminine. Irigaray devises from this reading of hysteria the notion that mimicry might be made into a feminist critical strategy, in which a space is created for "a possible operation of the feminine in language" by parodically miming the masculinist discourse of philosophy. Importantly, what distinguishes Irigaray's work from a naive celebration of the tragic heroism of the hysteric is her explicit redefinition of the hysterical symptom, from a counter-patriarchal language of the body into a textual strategy. For it is not a matter of celebrating the disease of hysteria and its supposed unconscious rebellion; rather, by textually performing hysteria, one can "assume the feminine role deliberately," Irigaray writes.[34]

Irigaray's insistence on a deliberate, strategic performance of hysteria implies that should be at essence an artifice, its performer an aesthetic creator, describing hysteria in terms of avant-garde poetics. She inveigles the feminine writer to "turn everything upside down, inside out, back to front" and to "overthrow syntax by suspending its eternally teleological order."[35] Such textual strategies, not unlike those of *Diary*, reveal the deliberate parodic intent behind Irigaray's grand theoretical strategy of miming rationalist masculine discourse, which thereby encounters its constitutive exclusions.

In fact, Judith Butler takes up where Irigaray falls short here, noting that Irigaray incorrectly insists that women form the only constituency oppressed by philosophy and forgets that many have suffered the same fate. "After all," Butler writes, "Plato's scenography of intelligibility depends on the exclusion of women, slaves, children and animals."[36] Butler adapts this critique of Irigaray into her own queer theory, but the implication that pro-animal meaning might be voiced by a strategic miming of discourse is brought to bear in *Diary of a Steak*.

The diarist pastiches the meetings of various British politicians, health professionals, and veterinarians with their European counterparts that took place in the wake of the March 20, 1996, announcement. These discussions eventually resulted in the Over Thirty Month Scheme, the slaughter of millions of healthy cattle over that age as a public relations exercise. A particularly sharp example of the diarist's mimicry involves a parody of John Major's and his government's policy of noncooperation in Europe, put into effect on May 21, 1996, which involved Major's exercising the United Kingdom's power of veto on much European Union legislation. This apparently petulant behavior succeeded in rewriting the BSE crisis, for Britain's more xenophobic contingent at least, as an anti-European "beef war." As the quotation opens, the diary incorporates the genre of news reportage, although that discourse itself is dialogically contaminated by the diarist's animal-obsessed imagination:

> The minister from Whitebait has promised Europa he will do everything in
>   his power to avoid lunacy in the English herd—
>
> He made a speech
>
> Tell the Greeks.
> Tell Luxembourg
> Tell the Portuguese they're
> Tell the French
> Tell the Italians their gnocci has a mental disorder
> And the Danish they've lost the plot
> The Neverlands
> The Germans and their bratwurst holograms
> Tell the Spanish about their poppies salamis
> Tell Belgium they're silly.
> Tell Denmark
> Finland

Sweden
Republic of Ireland
Tell Poland they're homosexual
Don't cry, please don't cry[37]

   As the shocking final line makes clear, there is obviously disquiet, caused
by BSE and the encroachment of animal disease into humanity, in the heart
of the faceless ministerial official. The speech's repetitive form also shows
that his disquiet is answered by an appeal to xenophobic, and latterly homo-
phobic, discourse. The repelling force of the repeated imperative, "tell," attempts to compel by the power of word alone the repulsion of a European
otherness that encroaches on the British subject. The collapse in normal
national stereotypes seems only to underline the obsessive and frantic nature
of this xenophobia. But the real need at the heart of government to silence
any disruption of society's carnivore hegemony by the BSE-cow—and here
I return to the transversal of the species barrier with which I began this
chapter—comes across most clearly as the quotation continues. The official
discourse can now only attempt to silence the BSE-cow's rupture of anthropocentrism via an act of pure will that evidences a pathetic desire to "legis-
late" the disruptive cows into the proper patriotic/xenophobic state, as if
that could make BSE and its worries for humanity go away. Printed in a large
bold red font reminiscent of "red top" tabloid newspapers, the text presents
this legislation in a way that parodies the Fleet Street mentality of the government's response to BSE:

   The official (eyes still closed)
   Telepathic legislation to the herd

   You are
   normal

   You are
   the
   National
   Anthem.[38]

   It appears, then, that *Diary of a Steak* is formally constructed of an Irigarayan textual hysteria, a parodic inhabitation of anthropocentric political
discourse, which aims to give voice to the animal by making clear that it is
that political discourse's excluded other. However, we must bear in mind
Irigaray's insistence on the *strategic agency* of the parodist in such matters.
The problem with this is that the very interest of hysteria in terms of pro-
animal politics was that it offered a form of protest that was of the body,

nonlinguistic, and without agency. These were hysteria's parallels with the animal. However, by inscribing an artistic human subject as the agent at the root of hysteria's feminist-political power, the Irigarayan reading rules out that parallel.

This problem is perhaps best explicated by following up the implication of the text's Bakhtinian ending, in which the diarist insists: "I'm a herbivore but I was made into a carnival." As it stands alone on the final page, it is hard to overestimate the power of this summary moment of a text that represents so much that is grotesque: from anorexia and self-harm to the rotting steak that lingers on a butcher's shop shelf. The connection between the Bakhtinian carnivalesque and hysteria has been a fruitful one in terms of understanding the political potential of non-official or agentless discourses. And focusing on the carnival as a site of meaning in this text seems apt indeed. For if the feast of carnival originally was the taking up of meat after lent (*carnelevare*), then the culture to which *Diary of a Steak* responds, with its daily consumption of six thousand cows, is certainly carnivalesque. Further, as the quotation and much of my discussion suggest, the animals who stumbled to the ground in the iconic images of BSE were themselves transformed into carnivalesque performers by television, just as, of course, animals are still so transformed in today's vestigial carnival performances of the circus. The problem with the BSE-cow's image-performance, though, is that because it makes explicit a trans-species disease, her freak show cannot so easily be objectified by the viewer.

With the transgression of the human-animal binary that goes on when human carnival-goers perform various kinds of animality, as well as carnival's more general re-coding of high-low power relationships, it would seem a fruitful sphere of discussion for pro-animal politics. And, as with hysteria, the fact that carnival seems to offer a mode of creative and political action that foregoes conventional artistic-individual agency also begins to explain Levy's recourse to the carnivalesque search for a textual voice for the animal. Another intriguing link between animal and carnival in terms of animal representations lies in Peter Stallybrass and Allon White's argument that the literary carnivalesque form is a space of nostalgia that remembers the scene of popular carnival forms at the same time that it signifies their disappearance.[39] It is worth speculating that this influential thesis is a descendant of John Berger's claim about the zoo in his groundbreaking 1980 essay on visual representation, "Why Look at Animals?" In modernity, metropolitan humans have completely abjured their premodern link with animals, and representational forms such as the zoo nostalgically mourn its passing.[40]

This allows us to keep animals in mind while looking at a key implication of Stallybrass and White's work on the nostalgia of the carnivalesque, which is to undermine the latter's celebration in contemporary society as a space for political transgression of bourgeois-patriarchal hegemony. Hence, of course, the methodological link with hysteria, which has suffered the same fate.

The very nature of the Irigarayan hysterical performance in *Diary of a Steak* as I have described it highlights the dilemma of what happens to carnival's potential when it is incorporated into an avant-garde literary text. For if we are to accept that Levy's parody of the anthropocentric discourse of government BSE policy opens a space (to paraphrase Irigaray) for "the possible operation of the animal in language," then a key problem remains. Stallybrass and White criticize the inherent political romanticism of avant-garde writers' nostalgic appeals to the carnivalesque as transgression. For them, it is a fact that "bourgeois writing smashes the rigidities of its own identity by projecting itself into the forbidden territories of precisely those excluded in its own political formation." This, however, only proves that the bourgeoisie "is perpetually rediscovering the carnivalesque as a radical source of transcendence."[41] We can turn this suggestion toward *Diary of a Steak.* Were it to be the case that the pro-animal meaning of Levy's avant-garde representation of the animal is visible *only* with the presumption of Levy's authorial intent, then it seems impossible for the text to avoid the taint of Stallybrass and White's critique. *Diary of a Steak* appears as just one more way for the hegemonic group (in this case, a specifically human as well as bourgeois one) to spend itself in nostalgic mourning for its always-already abandoned other: animals. In this sense, it is just like Berger's zoo. Neither the cow nor its death is really present in the text, we might say; rather, their carnivalesque representation acts as a screen for a romantic transcendence of the author's modern humanity. Here, we are reminded of the invisibility of the actual animals in popular cultural bemoanings of BSE and foot-and-mouth disease.

The text manages to undermine this problematic reading, however, and *does* put a pro-animal inflection on Berger's belief that the space of representation puts an unbridgeable distance between human and animal. For this to be explained, we need to revisit the text's own avant-garde practice in the context of its dramatization of hysteria. The text explicitly includes the actual historical personages of hysteria: Charcot, Breuer, Anna O., and others. But it also includes in this scene extracts from *The Female Malady,* Elaine Showalter's feminist critique of the psychotherapeutic institution, which argues that doctors have enforced their interpretive will on their patients. These extracts are italicized in the quotation below. Showalter explains the performative nature of hysteria, inspired by the photographs that the text describes being taken by Charcot's assistant Albert Londe, in perhaps *Diary of a Steak*'s most telling scene. With characteristic wit, Charcot's analysis of his patients at the *leçons* is presented as a "grilling," whose metaphorical status shifts to a literal one in the context of the hysteric-animal parallel. This parallel is expanded to correlate Charcot's audience with European BSE officials. It also includes a connection between the Parisian doctor and the xenophobic British politician discussed earlier, made clear when Charcot's own discourse is similarly dialogically polluted by animality:

> I am Jean-Martin Charcoal.
> I will etch and icon you in *full hysterical seizure. I will draw you in coloured chalks* on the blackbird. I will create with you your hysterical vocabulary . . . but first we doctor I want your baby will rehearse some of the *exaggerated gestures of French classical theatre* doctor I want your baby we will watch *stills* doctor I want your baby *from silent movies,* we will observe together *the paintings of Millais* doctor I want your baby *in particular his Ophelia.* You will learn timing and perform on cue for my photographer, Albert [. . .]
>
> I will Charcot grill you
>
> Buttercup
> Crazy Daisy
> Aberdeen Angus
> Augustine
> Emmy
> Dora
> Anna O
> Bertha
> Blanche
>
> serve you to a venerable audience of actors, vets, journalists, leading personae of Europa, scholars, journalists, poets, more vets.[42]

Bronfen's incisive analysis helps to explicate the drama of the original *leçons* that are re-described here. She explains that they offer a "scene of mutual representative complicity, with the physician requiring the poses of the patient to confirm the scientific text and the patient, accepting this desire, performing the symptoms the physicians sought to discover."[43] The hysteric's unconscious desire for affirmation by the doctor (represented in the quotation by the small-font allusion to Anna O.'s hysterical pregnancy) is manifested by her performance of the symptoms that the doctor wants to see. These symptoms, as many have noted, mimic cultural representations of femininity such as Millais's *Ophelia*. The patient's symptomatic performance is thus inextricably bound up with the doctor's desire to interpret it, and vice versa, adding a further layer of meaning to the critique that complains of the doctor's exertion of interpretive power over the patient. For "the cost of visualising and objectifying is not simply that it silences the hysteric performer but also that it cruelly delineates the limits of the empiricist medical enterprise."[44] Empiricism fails because the entity that Charcot wishes nosologically to describe, hysteria, is produced by his very attempt to analyze it.

The parallel of animal and hysteric—of Buttercup and Bertha Pappenheim and of Aberdeen Angus and Augustine—makes clear that *Diary of a Steak*'s representation of animals needs to be understood in terms of Bronfen's analysis. The text's parody of Charcot goes one step further than an Irigarayan strategic imitation designed to expose the silencing of the hysteric or animal. For in the context of the unconscious circuit of interpretation between doctor and patient that Bronfen describes, the "meaning" of hysteria emerges as a dialogic compendium from their encounter. It therefore seems ridiculous to suggest that anyone acts strategically or with agency in such a mutually implicated scenario. This is especially relevant in terms of the text's representation of animals given the description of Charcot as a sort of butcher. If Charcot "grills" the narrator of *Diary* in the process of his analysis, then it is in preparation for a consumption that is obviously a work of power pertinent to hysteric and animal. Levy's pun makes clear that when it comes to human-animal relations, and especially the case of BSE, the stakes in the politics of interpretation are enormous. As my introduction explains, not only is any sense of cows' right to an autonomous life rendered invisible by dominant narratives of the disease (a kind of killing in itself), but their very death is too.

Diary of a Steak's avant-garde form finds its raison d'être in the textual realization of these oppressive possibilities of interpretation in the context of animals. For the text in fact makes a major problem of its own meaning and interpretation by representing the animal and dramatizing the scene of hysteria with the sort of extremely difficult language and form that I have been describing throughout this chapter. The result of this avant-garde form is that the reader who would wish to read about cows (or, for that matter, BSE or meat) from the *Diary of a Steak* is drawn into precisely the same interpretive position as Charcot. By representing both animal life and death in the form of the cow-steak's hysterical performance, so difficult for the reader to make sense of, the text seduces the reader's desire to know the animal. As readers, we assume the place of the doctor whose interpretive power is so radically undermined by hysteria. A fundamental aporia is therefore produced at the site of representation: in this work, animals are essentially unreadable. The reader wants to make meaning of the textual representation of the animal but cannot without exhibiting his or her own desire to know, a desire that constructs the object of interpretation. Just as in the above quotation Charcot's desire to make meaning of the hysteric patient consumes and silences her, so will the reader's desire consume the represented animal.

It is precisely this supremely convoluted hermeneutic environment that makes a tortuous process of writing about this text and its avant-garde animal representation. For one cannot discuss *Diary of a Steak* as if Levy, its author, shows her readers that the reality of the meat industry or the BSE crisis is the commodification of animals' lives and deaths. This is because one key implication of the text's hysterical performance of the animal is that *any meaning* can arise only from the interaction of hysterical text and interpreting reader. Yet there is a second implication, one that has serious knock-on effects for those who would wish to unmask the ideology of conventional representations of BSE, or of animal death more generally. By interpreting this text (as I have obviously been doing), one must always consume and silence the animal that it is the text's apparent point to present. Only in the process of admitting that, as a textual representation of the animal, the artwork must, so to speak, be about a steak (an animal objectified and made ready for consumption) can the reader sense that it will be always-already about the animals whose death such a consumption requires. Now, this may be compromised as an assertion about the ability of representation to betray the facts of animal killing. It is certainly devoid of any grand ethical potential. But as we look back over all the other stories about BSE, it describes the only text that manages to create a place, albeit an uncertain one, in the consistently anthropocentric cultural narrative of BSE for living (or indeed dying) animals.

One final thing must be said about this compromised representation of animals, with reference to the incorporation into Levy's avant-garde fiction of Showalter's historicism. In fact, as the publication data of the book suggests, incorporation is not the right word here. We are told therein that "the diarist has grazed upon, and is indebted to, the research and scholarship of Elaine Showalter's *The Female Malady.*" The result of this grazing, however, is not a faithful reproduction of Showalter's work in the text, for the many "quotations" that it includes are always more or less modified, never quoted directly, as if they have been ruminated, digested, and finally excreted in the explosion of grotesque textuality that is *Diary of a Steak*. The diarist is, perhaps, more "shitting" than "citing" Showalter's words. Such a Bakhtinian confusion of bodily and intertextual process seems entirely consonant with my foregoing analysis. For were the text to represent faithfully Showalter's words, it would simply install them as the authoritative voice of the text, and Showalter's feminist historicism would be the only way to read hysteria. This, of course, would short-circuit the dialogism of hysterical performance and desiring reader with which the text makes space for the recognition of the animals' deaths. Instead, if we recognize that *Diary of a Steak* is forged of a corrupted amalgamation of other texts—for it quotes many other sources than just Showalter—we can see in that corrupt amalgamation a way forward. It suggests that although we must always consume representations of animals, of their lives and their deaths, the possibility remains that out of such consumptions might appear new corrupted meanings that are more attuned to animals' existence.

Notes

1. For statistics pertaining to BSE, see http://www.defra.gov.uk/animalh/bse/statistics/incidence.html; for vCJD, see http://www.dh.gov.uk/PolicyandGuidance/HealthandSocialcaretopics/CJD/fs/en. Figures in this chapter are accurate for June 29, 2005, when all Internet sites were accessed.

2. According to a poll published by the Vegetarian Society, in 1997 5.4 percent of Britons considered themselves vegetarian while 14.3 percent avoided red meat (http://www.vegsoc.org/info/realeat.html).

3. As reported by the Humane Slaughter Association (http://www.hsa.org.uk/farm.html).

4. For an analysis of the media coverage of the BSE crisis in the UK and USA, see J. Gregory Payne, Daniel Dornbusch, and Veronica Demko, "Media Coverage of the Mad Cow Issue," in *The Mad Cow Crisis,* ed. Scott C. Ratzan (London: University College London Press, 1998).

5. Richard Kerridge, "BSE Stories," *Keywords* 2 (1999): n.p.

6. Harriet Ritvo, "Mad Cow Mysteries," *American Scholar* 67 (1998): 119.

7. Elaine Showalter, *Hystories: Hysterical Epidemics and Modern Culture* (London: Picador, 1998), 28.

8. Stephen Dealler, *Lethal Legacy: BSE; The Search for Truth* (London: Bloomsbury, 1996); Richard Rhodes, *Deadly Feasts: Tracking the Secrets of a Terrifying New Plague* (New York: Simon and Schuster, 1997).

9. See http://www.bse.org.uk/report/volume1/chapte68.htm#64614.

10. See http://www.bse.org.uk/report/volume1/execsum2.htm#66959.

11. Hugh Pennington, "The English Disease," review of *The BSE Inquiry,* by Lord Phillips, June Bridgeman, and Malcolm Ferguson-Smith, *London Review of Books* 22, no. 24 (2000): 6.

12. See Vicki Raymond's "Mad Cow's Song" in *Selected Poems* (London: Carcanet, 1993); Simon Armitage's film-poem *Killing Time,* directed by Brian Hill (London: Cen-

tury Films/Channel 4, 2000); Jo Shapcott's "Mad Cow Poems" in *Her Book: Poems 1988–1998* (London: Faber, 2000); and Neil Astley's *The End of My Tether* (London: Scribner's, 2003).

13. Joan Leach, "Madness, Metaphors and Miscommunication: The Rhetorical Life of Mad Cow Disease," in Ratzan, *Mad Cow Crisis*, 128.

14. Kerridge, "BSE Stories"; Barbara Adam, *Timescapes of Modernity: The Environment and Invisible Hazards* (London: Routledge, 1998).

15. See Pam Morris, ed., *The Bakhtin Reader* (London: Arnold, 1994).

16. Deborah Levy, *Diary of a Steak* (London: Bookworks, 1997), 49. All quotations will be transcribed exactly, including the unusual typography that characterizes the text.

17. Levy has written several plays and published a number of novels, books of poetry, and short stories through Vintage; see www.deborahlevy.co.uk.

18. Levy, *Diary*, 11.

19. Ibid., 6–8. For the original report of the *leçons,* see Axel Munthe, *The Story of San Michèle,* quoted in Elaine Showalter, *The Female Malady* (London: Virago, 1987), 148.

20. Showalter, *Hystories,* 15.

21. Sigmund Freud, *Standard Edition of the Complete Psychological Works of Sigmund Freud,* ed. and trans. James Strachey (London: Hogarth, 1953–1974), vol 2.

22. *Zoophilist* 7 (1887): 110, quoted in Elaine Showalter, "Hysteria Feminism and Gender," in *Hysteria Beyond Freud,* ed. Sander Gilman, Roy Porter, and Elaine Showalter (Berkeley: University of California Press, 1993), 311.

23. See Showalter, *Female Malady,* 149.

24. Levy, *Diary,* 8.

25. Elizabeth Bronfen, *The Knotted Subject: Hysteria and Its Discontents* (Princeton: Princeton University Press, 1998), 190.

26. Showalter, *Female Malady,* 149.

27. Levy, *Diary,* 9, 11, 19, 32.

28. Ibid., 34.

29. Ibid., 36–37.

30. Mary Jacobus, *Reading Woman: Essays in Feminist Criticism* (New York: Columbia University Press, 1986), 205. She is quoting from Josef Breuer and Sigmund Freud, *Studies on Hysteria* (London: Hogarth, 1955), 25, vol. 2 of Sigmund Freud, *Standard Edition of the Complete Psychological Works of Sigmund Freud,* ed. and trans. James Strachey (London: Hogarth, 1953–74).

31. Levy, *Diary,* 5.

32. Jacques Derrida, "The Animal That Therefore I Am (More to Follow)," *Critical Inquiry,* trans. David Wills 28 (2002): 417.

33. Levy, *Diary,* 28.

34. Luce Irigaray, *This Sex Which Is Not One,* trans. Catherine Porter (Ithaca: Cornell University Press, 1985), 76.

35. Luce Irigaray, *Speculum of the Other Woman,* trans. Gillian C. Gill (Ithaca: Cornell University Press, 1985), 142.

36. Judith Butler, *Bodies That Matter* (London and New York: Routledge, 1993), 48–49.

37. Levy, *Diary,* 12.

38. Ibid., 14.

39. See the introduction to Peter Stallybrass and Allon White, *The Politics and Poetics of Transgression* (London: Methuen, 1986).

40. John Berger, *About Looking* (New York: Vintage International, 1991), 1–28, esp. 21.

41. Stallybrass and White, *Politics and Poetics,* 200–201.

42. Levy, *Diary,* 30–31. See Showalter, *Female Malady,* 148, 150, 152, 154.

43. Bronfen, *Knotted Subject,* 191.

44. Ibid., 201.

8 Killing Animals in Animal Shelters

CLARE PALMER

Introduction

Domestic cats and dogs (the two species from which the vast majority of pets are drawn) are frequently said to be members of the family.[1] And they are immensely popular. Jennifer Wolch notes that more US households have pets than children. Recently, ways of understanding this practice of pet-keeping seems, in some circles at least, to be shifting. For instance, there have been changes in the language of pet-keeping—in particular, a decline in use of the term "pet" itself. The use of "companion animal" is increasingly popular. The state of Rhode Island passed legislation in 2001 introducing "guardian" as a substitute for "owner" in the context of "companion animals." The term "guardian" was used to designate "a person who possesses, has title to or an interest in, harbors or has control, custody or possession of an animal and who is responsible for an animal's safety and well-being."[2]

The use of both the terms "companion animals" and "guardians" is significant. Some discomfort with the more traditional word "pet" is implied—perhaps because of a perception that it demeans those to whom it is attributed. Animals are to be regarded as companions, not as beings to whom we condescend.[3] The use of the term "guardian" for "owner" in Rhode Island appears to emphasize that having a pet entails a serious responsibility, a duty of care, a concern for safety and well-being not dissimilar to that owed by guardians to children.

Yet this concept of pet-keeping as the benign guardianship of companion animals sits uneasily with other figures about human-pet relations. Although no completely reliable statistics exist, it is estimated that between 6 and 10 million dogs and between 7 and 10 million cats were humanely killed in pet shelters in the United States in 1990.[4] This is somewhere between one-tenth and one-quarter of the total US dog and cat population.[5] Yi-Fu Tuan points out that on average, households keep their pets for only two years.[6] So, alongside the social recognition of cats and dogs as companions and family members lies the social treatment of them as expendable individuals that can be killed en masse at human will—or even whim. In Arnold Arluke and Clinton Sanders's study of animal shelters, for instance, shelter workers recall days when, in a single shelter, more than fifty cats and dogs were killed.[7]

Apparent contradictions in human relations with animals have, of course, been widely noted—in particular that between eating members of some mammal species and cherishing members of other mammal species. But what is particularly interesting here is that the apparently contradictory treatment of the animals concerned is not differentiated by species membership, nor by perceived closeness to or distance from humans (in the way, for instance, noted by Edmund Leach in his classic anthropological paper on terms of animal abuse).[8] It is, after all, members of the very same species of animals—indeed, on occasions, the very same individual animals—that are both cherished and killed. I want, in this essay, to consider the painless killing of healthy animals (primarily cats and dogs) in animal shelters.[9] In particular, I will be exploring the ethical debate around this practice, not with the intention of proposing any definitive "solution," but in order to clarify existing arguments and to suggest some new perspectives on the issues raised. It should also be noted that this essay focuses on ethical, rather than economic, issues about killing animals in animal shelters. Clearly, there is a sense in which financial expedience is the primary reason for the killing of such animals. It would be extremely expensive to house indefinitely all the healthy animals that currently come into animal shelters. But that such killing is accepted and tolerated socially is an ethical issue worthy of investigation in its own right.

Animal Shelters: Context and Practices

Animal shelters take several forms. Some are provided and run by local or city authorities, others by animal protection charities. Almost all of the former, and many of the latter, regularly humanely kill healthy animals. A small number of animal charity shelters and adoption organizations have no-kill policies (except in cases where animals are seriously ill and suffering). Organizations of this kind often select "adoptable" animals from local authority pounds and hold them until they can place them in a home. However, the majority of animal shelters do kill. Statistics suggest that on average, six out of ten stray dogs and eight out of ten stray cats never make it out of an animal shelter alive.[10]

The animals that enter animal shelters fall into three main groups. The first group is composed of short-term, accidental strays, for which owners may well be searching and for which reclaim is possible. The second group is made up of those brought to the shelter by people for a variety of reasons: the animal has been left them by friends or relatives; they can no longer keep the animal due to their own age, infirmity, or impoverishment; they are moving to accommodations with "no pet" policies; the animal has various behavioral problems—it urinates or defecates inappropriately; it is destructive to the fabric of a property; it is aggressive; it doesn't get on with other humans or animals in the household. (Joanna Newby notes, "The number one cause of death of dogs in the Western world is not parvovirus, it is not being hit by cars; it is bad behavior.")[11] The third group is composed of abandoned animals that may have become feral and learned to survive on the streets; some may even have been born into ferality. The outlook for these different groups in animal shelters varies. Those in the first group, provided that their owners get to them in time, will be reclaimed.[12] Those in the second group will be assessed for their adoptability. If they are considered to be unadoptable, they will be humanely killed immediately; if they are regarded as adoptable, a period of grace will be allowed (this usually ranges from several days to several weeks). If the animal is not adopted in this period, it will be humanely killed. Members of the third group are likely to be considered to be unadoptable, since their feral behavior means that they will be difficult to place in a home; they are likely to be quickly killed.

Several different methods of humane killing are routinely used in animal shelters. The most widely advocated and commonest method is by injection of barbiturates. The Report of the American Veterinary Medical Association (AVMA) Panel on Euthanasia in 2000 recommended this as the preferred method of humanely killing dogs and cats (some animal welfare organizations consider this to be the only acceptable way)[13] on the grounds that it works very quickly with minimal discomfort to the animals and is relatively inexpensive. There are disadvantages: those administering the barbiturate injection must be trained and skilled in doing so; a second member of staff is always required to restrain the animal; the drugs are dangerous to humans; the animal may produce "an aesthetically objectionable terminal gasp"; and the drugs linger in the carcass and may be hazardous if eaten by another animal. The other main alternatives used for humane killing in animal shelters are gases, primarily carbon monoxide and carbon dioxide.[14]

Animals may be gassed together in larger numbers in gas chambers (though it is recommended that animals be separated from one another during the process) and no specialist training is required, though correct gas flow levels must be maintained. Carbon monoxide is particularly effective; the AVMA reports that it "induces loss of consciousness without pain and with minimal discernible discomfort" and that at correct levels, death follows rapidly. However, the chambers must be well maintained and sealed, both to get the flow level right and to avoid affecting nearby humans.

The AVMA report—although contested in some quarters—maintains that these methods of killing, if correctly administered, are painless to animals. For the purposes of this essay, I am going to accept this judgment and assume that killing in animal shelters can be carried out without pain or significant distress to the animals. This, obviously, does not mean that no ethical issues are involved; indeed, it is these issues that I will now move on to consider more closely.

Common Claims about Humane Killing

Arguments in support of humane killing in animal shelters tend to maintain that it is the best option for unadopted or unadoptable animals, given the complex of circumstances that brought them there. Specifically, such arguments usually put forward some or all of the following claims (they may be mutually reinforcing):

1. Humane killing is best for the individual animal concerned.
2. Humane killing of such individual animals is required because of animal overpopulation.
3. Humane killing of such individual animals is best for human beings.

Claim 1, that humane killing is best for the individual animal concerned, rests on the judgment that continued life for that animal would be worse than death. Such arguments are commonly found among those who surrender animals to shelters and among shelter workers. Stephanie Frommer and Arnold Arluke report that many who surrender animals to animal shelters "consider euthanization a better solution for their pets than allowing them to live in poor situations. . . . Death was preferable to sacrificing the quality of life that the animal deserved and had come to expect."[15] Similarly, Frommer and Arluke found that shelter workers also used this argument: "By assuming that animals would meet a worse fate as a stray or with uncaring people, shelter workers enable themselves to view euthanasia as merciful."[16] Some shelter workers also maintained that the lives of animals in shelters are of such low quality that humane killing just helps along a process of dying already under way. Although Frommer and Arluke consider these responses only in the context of guilt-displacement strategies, they may be taken as ethical arguments in their own right. That is to say, in terms of the animal's own welfare, humane killing in animal shelters is ethical because it is in the interests of the animal concerned. The alternatives are likely to be poor living conditions that may include abandonment, ferality, hunger, lack of shelter, and ill-health or killing that might be far less humane than that practiced in the animal shelter. Any of these things, so the argument runs, would be worse for the animal than a painless, if premature, death. I will return to this claim later.

Claim 2, that humane killing of individual animals is required because of animal overpopulation, is usually located in the context of a broader discourse about animal overpopulation. The fundamental problem is understood as being the constant production of surplus dogs and cats—more than there can be homes for with human beings. Such surplus animals are likely to be unsterilized and to have a high fecundity rate, thus multiplying the problem.[17] Overpopulation of dogs and cats, it is argued, leads to the creation of feral cat colonies and dog packs (this rests on the assumption that those who take unwanted animals to animal shelters would abandon them if shelters were not available). Alongside poor individual welfare (as in claim 1), diseases and infestations may be carried beyond feral populations into homed populations (though homed populations can at least be vaccinated against some diseases). Even as it is, as fast as animals are killed in animal shelters, new animals are produced to take their place. Without animal shelters, feral populations would rapidly expand, and without killing, animal numbers in animal shelters would quickly grow far beyond the ability of the shelters to deal with them. This view tends to rest on the idea of total animal population welfare rather than on the welfare of specific individuals, as in claim 1. It may thus be argued that even if in the case of any particular individual animal, humane killing may not seem to be in its interests, from the perspective of the total, accumulated welfare of all the individual animals in that population—say, cats in New York—humane killing is required to keep the remaining cats reasonably healthy and with sufficient access to food and shelter. Some individuals must be sacrificed for the welfare of the cat population as a whole.

Claim 3, that humane killing of individual animals is good for human beings, is a further step from claim 2—now the limiting of animal populations is good for humans as well as for animal populations. This is usually explained in terms of hygiene, possible disease, and nuisance. Abandoned and feral animals and colonies of such animals are often seen as health hazards to humans as well as to homed animals. Dog and cat waste, for instance, may harbor parasitic diseases such as toxoplasmosis, which can cause eye or brain damage to infants and the immunosuppressed. The animals may also be considered as the cause of mess and noise and to be of unsightly appearance.

Arguments from claims 1–3 here may be cumulative (humane killing is necessary for the sake of individuals, for the sake of animal population welfare, and for the sake of humans), or, equally, claim 3 might override the others. That is to say, even if humane killing might be argued not to be in the interests of an individual animal or the animal population, human physical and psychological well-being may be thought to prevail over the interests of the animal and the animal population.

Claim 3 also has a further manifestation in relation to particular individual animals regarded as posing a special threat to human well-being. Paradigmatically, this is used for individual aggressive dogs and explains why a number of homed (that is, nonsurplus) dogs are brought to animal shelters. The threat to the owners' or other humans' (or, indeed, animals') welfare from being bitten or attacked by the aggressive individual means that the owners of the animal will no longer house it. The animal is, for the same reason, unadoptable at the animal shelter and hence is humanely killed. This kind of humane killing seems to be underpinned by a judgment about the importance of comparative welfares: the actual or potential harm to human welfare from animal aggression is regarded as being of more significance than the life of the animal.

These common arguments are consequentialist in nature: that is, they rest on the view that humane killing in animal shelters brings about the *best consequences* for individual humans and animals and/or for human and animal populations. Central to this kind of consequentialist position is the idea of *welfare,* construed with particular attention to the avoidance of pain to individual animals and to the health of populations as a whole. Humane killing is seen as maximizing animal and human welfare. Although not usually couched in philosophical terms, these arguments assume a form similar to classical utilitarianism, sometimes used as a basis for philosophical arguments for "animal liberation." Utilitarian arguments of this kind usually maintain that the ability to feel pain is the basic characteristic that determines whether a being should be taken into account when making moral decisions and that the central principle of moral decision-making should be the minimization of total pain in the world, whether that pain is human or animal.[18] Such arguments, while militating against the painful transportation and killing of animals for food and against pain inflicted in experimentation, have nothing obviously negative to say about painless killing in animal shelters. Indeed, guided by pain-minimization alone, practices involving painless killing with a view to promoting total welfare would seem (at first sight, at least) morally laudable. If no pain is involved, and if the continuing life of the animal would be a painful one or contribute to greater pain in animal or human populations, the killing feeds nothing negative into a decision-making calculus.[19] So the common claims I have outlined above and philosophical utilitarian positions associated with animal liberation can be, paradoxically, quite close to one another.[20]

However, very different ethical perspectives can be taken on humane killing in animal shelters. I want now to move on to consider just one, the animal rights position taken by philosopher Tom Regan.

Regan, Rights, and Humane Killing

Tom Regan's book *The Case for Animal Rights,* published in 1984, is a sustained philosophical defense of the argument that we should think of animals (he focuses primarily on mammals) as bearers of particular kinds of rights, primarily rights to respect and to freedom from harm. These rights, he argues, rest on the inherent value possessed by animals, independent of their usefulness to or relationships with human beings; this value is equally present in all animals (and humans). Animals possess such value by virtue of being "subjects of a life"—that is, in Regan's words, as beings displaying the following characteristics:

> beliefs and desires; perception, memory and a sense of the future, including their own future; an emotional life together with feelings of pleasure and pain; preference and welfare interests; the ability to initiate actions in pursuit of their desires and goals; a psychophysical unity over time and an individual welfare in the sense that their experiential life fares well or ill for them, logically independently of their utility for others and logically independently of their being the object of anyone else's interests.[21]

Resting on this theoretical basis, Regan's view is thus rather different from the pain-minimizing, consequentialist positions considered above. He argues that an animal's (or, indeed, a human's) welfare can be harmed without causing pain. Harms to welfare may involve deprivations, even where the individual concerned does not know that or of what they are being deprived.[22] One might, for instance, rear a child in a cage from birth while maintaining the child in a pain-free state; the child would still be harmed, even if he or she did not know what he or she was missing (and, Regan points out, part of the harm is actually *that* the child does not know what he or she is missing). Further, Regan goes on to argue, killing painlessly is just such a harm by deprivation. Indeed, it is fundamental and irreversible; it forecloses all possibilities of finding future satisfaction; it is thus "the ultimate harm because it is the ultimate loss" (although it may not be the worst harm there is—living a life of relentless physical agony would be worse).[23] So, he maintains, "to bring about the untimely death of animals will not hurt them if this is done painlessly; but they will be harmed."[24] Thus there is an immediate contrast with the earlier view, where, since pain is all that is to be taken into account, painless killing does not seem to be a harm at all.[25]

Regan's view that painless killing is a harm clearly has a bearing on the killing of animals in animal shelters. He does not explicitly discuss moral decision-making in this context. However, he makes one point about such killing very clear: the killing of healthy animals in animal shelters should not be regarded as euthanasia (a term I have avoided using until now for just this reason). Regan maintains that euthanasia of animals must have the following characteristics: (a) killing must be by the most painless means possible; (b) killing must be believed to be in the animal's interests, and this must be a true belief; and (c) the one who kills must be motivated out of concern for the interest, good, or welfare of the particular animal involved.[26] Even where (a) applies in animal shelters, according to Regan (b) and (c) usually do not. As we have seen, often the reasons offered for painlessly killing animals are based on the consequences for whole populations, not on the interests, good, or welfare of the particular animal being killed. This may, Regan suggests, be called "well-intentioned killing," but it is not appropriately called euthanasia. However, Regan argues, even when it is genuinely believed (by those surrendering animals or by shelter workers) that killing a healthy animal in an animal shelter is in the animal's own interests, that belief is not a true belief, so (b) does not apply. It is not the case, Regan maintains, that the only alternative for the animal is worse than death (I will return to this later); there are other possibilities, including that the shelter take proper care of the animal until it is homed. Even if—taking the interests of other humans or animals into account—it is argued that, overall, humanely killing an animal in this situation is better than keeping it in the shelter, nonetheless it cannot be argued that the killing is in the interests of the animal being killed. So, whatever one might think about whether or not one should kill such animals, by Regan's definition the correct term for such killing is not euthanasia.

Although Regan's discussion of killing in animal shelters primarily concerns the (in)appropriate use of the term euthanasia, the arguments of his book as a whole imply a strong moral position against such killing. As a nonconsequentialist, Regan takes the view that some actions are morally unacceptable, even if they are aimed at bringing about a greater good. And killing any being with inherent value and a right to respect in order to further any other purpose at all, including minimizing the pain of other animals, humans, or populations of animals and humans, is just such an unacceptable action. For Regan, the only grounds on which killing an animal is morally acceptable is if it is in the interests of the animal concerned, and that could only be if the animal were to be in acute pain with no prospect of that pain ever ceasing.[27] Humane killing of healthy animals in animal shelters does not fall into this category; it is thus an ethically unacceptable practice and should be ceased.

A Relational Approach

Two conflicting ways of thinking about painless killing in animal shelters have so far been identified. One is the broadly consequentialist view that painless killing is the best solution, in terms of minimizing pain, to the perceived problem of dog and cat overpopulation. The second is that painless killing is an unethical, harmful practice that takes the lives of beings entitled to respect. Yet there seems something troubling about both perspectives, taken alone. On the one hand, looking at the issue from a consequentialist, pain-minimization perspective, painless killing does not seem problematic at all. And yet surely the killing of cats and dogs on such a scale does merit, at least, some ethical unease. The rights view, on the other hand, seems excessively demanding, both philosophically, in terms of human responsibilities for animal lives, and in practice, with its implication that all abandoned cats and dogs should be treated, in terms of the provision of essentials, as members of what is almost an animal welfare state.

As I said at the beginning, the purpose of this essay is not to propose any straightforward "solution" to the problem of killing animals in animal shelters. Rather, I want to suggest another possible perspective that I think is at least worth considering alongside the two I have already outlined. This perspective could be thought of as a "relational approach." That is to say, rather than focusing on the outcomes of particular actions or on the value-giving qualities or abilities possessed by animals in themselves, the focus is on the nature of the relationships *between* humans and animals. While not denying the significance of the pain-minimizing, consequentialist view and the rights view, such a relational approach can highlight other moral questions that arise. It can look broadly at the context of human relationships with domestic cats and dogs, seeing painless killing in animal shelters as emerging from a whole nexus of historical and cultural relationships and practices. This is not to say that those adopting pain-centered, consequentialist views or rights views see the animals in animal shelters in a totally decontextualized sense, as if they had suddenly appeared there by magic, independent of human society. This is plainly not the case. Many animal welfare organizations, including those that run animal shelters, advocate and often initiate educational programs for owners and potential owners of cats and dogs. Such programs stress the long-term responsibility of taking on a pet, the need to have it de-sexed and microchipped (for identification purposes), and the need for certain kinds of training. The ignorance, negligence, and failure of pet-owners to take responsibility in these ways, they often argue, form the context in which high numbers of animals come into animal shelters. If people were better informed about what keeping a pet entailed and how best to manage a pet once that pet has been acquired, numbers of animals entering animal shelters would fall substantially.

It may be the case that educational programs have some effect on the number of animals entering animal shelters. But—adopting a relational approach—I want to suggest that there is more to be said here, both in terms of what domestic cats and dogs are owed and how they are regarded, than such an educational strategy can take into account and that these aspects serve to complicate ethical issues around painless killing in animal shelters.

Dependence and Independence

Dogs and cats kept as pets are domesticated species, bound into historical relationships with human beings. Exactly how such relationships began is contested, and how "domesticated" should be defined is also an area of dispute.[28] But it is undisputed that one key element of domestication is human intervention in animal breeding, in particular in the selection of mates in order to produce offspring that manifest characteristics desired by humans. Domesticated dogs and cats bear witness to these human desires in the shape and form of their bodies and in particular in their neotonization (that is, their retention of infantile characteristics). One consequence of this intervention in breeding is the diminished ability of many domesticated dogs and cats to live independently of humans.

It is, though, important to be careful here. Only some dogs and cats are fully dependent on humans (especially when bred in particular bodily shapes that make hunting, scavenging, or reproducing difficult). If abandoned, they would die, perhaps in painful ways. But other dogs and cats can survive partially, or wholly, independent of human beings. Studies of feral dogs, for instance, have suggested that they can live reasonably well, although they are indirectly dependent on scavenging from human settlements.[29] Colonies of feral cats may also scavenge but can live by hunting for birds and rodents. Certainly, such animals may be more vulnerable to disease and injury than homed animals and do not have access to veterinary care; but nonetheless their lives in general do not seem to be ones of unremitting pain such that they might be considered to be lives not worth living.

Significant issues arise from these relations of dependence/independence. First, where domestic cats and dogs are wholly dependent on humans, a special relationship, created by humans, has been established. By relationship here, I do not mean a relationship of affect, though such a relationship may exist in some cases. Rather, I mean that humans have acted to create animals that are constituted such that they are unable to be independent. This is a special kind of relationship, and it is widely accepted that special relationships of this kind bring ethical obligations. For instance, in the case of parenthood, few would object to the claim that "a child is wronged by his parents if adequate care is not given him, and the parent violates a duty if he or she neglects to give such care" because "they bring their children into existence—or they adopt them—and it is this act that imposes duties on the parent."[30] Children are created by adults initially as dependent beings; to refuse to meet the needs of a being one has created to be dependent is, on this account, to deny a duty.

In the case of keeping pets, there seems to be a parallel argument, working on two levels. At the individual level, one could maintain that along with an individual's decision to produce or adopt pets comes a duty to care and provide for them.[31] (This is a commonplace, of course, which often forms one part of an animal welfare organization's educational campaign.) The second level, though, follows a broader, social obligation arising out of the social creation of dependent domesticated animals. That there is a population of domestic dogs and cats, whether homed, unwanted, abandoned, or feral, is due to human action and human relations with these animals. On this basis, it can be argued that humans have *acquired* ethical responsibilities toward humanly originating dependent animals that do not exist toward, say, urban rat populations (where the rats are wild in origin).[32] The existence of animal shelters at all may indicate some basic recognition of this (after all, no such shelters exist for urban rat populations, for which painless killing is rarely considered to be of ethical significance). But it is questionable whether painless killing is an appropriate way of discharging responsibilities to unwanted but dependent animals humans have themselves created.

On the other hand, though, some domesticated cats and dogs do manage to live lives that appear to be satisfactory, outside the context of a home with an owner. They may live as individual hunters and scavengers; they may form colonies and packs with others; they may take up residence in abandoned buildings or the grounds of institutions, allotments, cemeteries, and other backwaters of human development. For these animals, either indirectly reliant on human beings or largely independent of them, being taken to an animal shelter for painless killing seems to be a denial of their *lack* of relationship with particular human beings rather than the failure, as in the previous case, to recognize the ethical force of dependence. Animals that have strayed for some time, or which are feral, are regarded as "unadoptable"; they are likely to be quickly dispatched in a shelter.

The question then arises whether it is better to live a life of ferality, provided that it is not one of interminable agony, or to be painlessly killed. How one answers this question depends on a number of factors, including whether cats and dogs are thought of as the kinds of beings that have any sense of themselves as beings that exist over time and whether they have nonmomentary future-oriented desires that entail continued existence in order to be fulfilled.[33] (Regan obviously thinks they do, and Peter Singer, a utilitarian, suggests in recent editions of *Practical Ethics* that dogs and cats may be self-conscious with a sense of themselves as beings that exist over time, such that killing them, however painlessly, is wrong).[34] In any case, it may be that some sort of double-bind is in operation here. Domestic dogs and cats are recognized in Western urban settings, in particular, as properly living in relationship to particular human owners. This relationship is not regarded as so binding that painless killing—often merely for convenience—is thought of as morally unacceptable, not just by the individuals who surrender animals but at a broader social level where the collective and historical responsibility for having created dependent animals is not taken seriously. But, on the other hand, the relationship is regarded as binding enough that individual animals living outside such a relationship are regarded as inevitably unable to cope, out of place, and (perhaps) better off dead.[35] On both counts, this leads to an increase in the number of animals being humanely killed in animal shelters.

So I am suggesting that greater *collective* responsibility needs to be taken for the existence of all domestic animals (rather than the responsibility being regarded as one attaching solely to individual owners). This may mean both that there are duties of provision and care for dependent domesticated animals and obligations to respect the independent lives of those cats and dogs that succeed in surviving outside the context of a human home; their lives should not be regarded as lives not worth living. These domesticated animals are in particular situations substantially as a result of their relationships to humans and human society; having deliberately put animals into these situations, the appropriate ethical response is to do what is best for the animals concerned within the context in which they are located.

Power and Instrumentalism

A further issue also seems to be raised here. In *Dominance and Affection: The Making of Pets,* Yi-Fu Tuan argues that human relations with pets are appropriately understood as ones of absolute human domination, tempered by affection.[36] This model of pet-keeping seems to me to be unhelpfully monolithic, obscuring the diversity of practices and interactions in the power relationships involved in pet-keeping. There are many circumstances in which pets are able to transgress, or even to resist, human attempts to control or manipulate them, thus tempering human domination not only by affection but also by animals' own active responses.[37] But, having said this, a broader question is raised about how human-pet relations are understood and framed both by individual pet-owners and by society at large. As was mentioned at the beginning of the essay, there have been attempts recently to frame the relationship as one of mutual companionship between the species. I suggested that this idea of companionship stood in tension with the high numbers of pets that end up in animal shelters. Here, I want to make a more general point about the framing of human-pet relations. I want to suggest that pets are, generally, viewed with what might be called an "attitude of instrumentalism." Of course, this attitude is to be expected in the relations humans have with animals kept for food and experimental purposes. But it is unsettling in a relationship described, as we have seen, in terms of companionship or the familial. Yet this attitude not only seems widespread with respect to pets but also is at least plausible that educational campaigns about responsible pet-ownership can actually promote just such a perspective. At the same time, it is this attitude of instrumentalism that makes the surrender of dogs and cats to animal shelters more, rather than less, likely.

One good example of how this attitude of instrumentalism plays out is with respect to de-sexing. Almost all animal welfare organizations advocate de-sexing; they pay for it, encourage it, and campaign for it. The main arguments presented in favor of it are that it prevents the production of unwanted offspring and reduces roaming and other unwanted behaviors in pets themselves. That is to say, it is better both for animal populations and for human owners if pets are de-sexed. But what of the animal itself? We cannot know whether de-sexing matters to a cat or dog, and if it does, how much and in what ways. But it might be the case that there is a way in which de-sexing harms animals, even if it does not matter to them in the sense of being aware of what they are missing. Perhaps the pursuit of sex and the interactions involved in that pursuit, the practice of sex, and the process of producing young would be rich experiences for cats and dogs, so that once de-sexed their lives are less rich, even though they do not know it.

However one might regard animals' *loss* by de-sexing, it is rarely the case that de-sexing is carried out solely for the *benefit* of the animal concerned. When animals are de-sexed, they are, in most cases, being treated as instruments, as a means to an end, where the end is the good of the whole population or, more frequently, an easier life with the owner. So, animals are anesthetized and made to undergo surgery that will change their lives, a process of human domination—understood here as a power relation that they are unable to resist—for reasons not usually to do with their own welfare but as instrumental to other ends. And while there are occasions in many dependent relationships where dominating behavior toward the dependent being seems ethically appropriate or necessary, such occasions are usually in the interests of the one being dominated; that is to say, they are a form of paternalism. This, however, is rarely the case with pet de-sexing, where domination combines with instrumentalism, not paternalism.[38]

But this description—a process of human domination that they are unable to understand or resist, for reasons not to do with their own welfare but as instrumental to other ends—might equally be used to describe much painless killing in animal shelters. What I am suggesting is that both de-sexing and killing in animal shelters flow from the same underlying attitude toward pets. This attitude is one of willingness to adopt dominating practices that treat animals as means to other ends. If this is right, campaigns to promote de-sexing, while at one level being successful in reducing the number of kittens and puppies born,[39] at another level actually promote dominating and instrumentalist underlying attitudes and relationships that make people more likely to surrender animals to animal shelters. Removal of the sex of a domesticated animal (unless that sex can be used for other instrumentalist purposes, such as pedigree breeding) is seen as being good for animal populations and as making the animal into a better, more amenable companion. Precisely the same arguments, as I have already maintained—the need to manage animal populations and problems in "companionship" with animals—lead to the surrender of animals to animal shelters. Rather than seeing the killing of animals in animal shelters as an aberration resulting from overpopulation and some irresponsible owners, it can be viewed instead as the inevitable outcome of a widespread set of human-pet relationships, flowing from an underlying human attitude of instrumentalism, an attitude sometimes promoted by animal welfare organizations themselves.

Conclusion

In this essay, I have considered some of the ethical issues around the practice of painless killing of cats and dogs in animal shelters. I have looked at the most prominent ethical approaches to such killing—that is, a kind of pain-minimizing consequentialism and an animal rights approach. I have suggested that another way of framing the situation would be to explore aspects of the human-animal relations involved, focusing on the relations of dependence/independence between humans and domesticated cats and dogs, and the underlying human relational attitude toward these animals. I have suggested, first, that the ethical responsibilities of the creation of dependence where it exists should be taken more seriously; second, that, on the other hand, relative independence where it exists should be respected; and third, that an underlying cause of the high death toll in animal shelters is an attitude toward pet animals of instrumentalism, an attitude that can actually be promoted by some attempts to reduce the number of animals coming into animal shelters.

Only the second of these points constitutes any kind of practical recommendation at all: that cats and dogs leading feral lives that do not seem to be lives of interminable pain should be left alone to live out their lives, even if their presence seems messy and unhygienic to nearby humans.[40] Aside from this, I have merely attempted to think through some of the underlying relationships, attitudes, and responsibilities that lead to the painless killing of so many animals in animal shelters. Such deep-seated relationships and attitudes are not amenable to simple educational campaigns about "snipping and chipping"—indeed, as I have suggested, such campaigns may serve to reinforce, not undercut, existing attitudes. To change the practices of killing in animal shelters will require a substantial cultural change in attitudes toward those animals humans increasingly like to call "companions."[41]

Notes

1. A survey by A. O. Cain, "A Study of Pets in the Family System," cited in *New Perspectives on Our Lives with Companion Animals,* ed. Aaron Katcher and Alan Beck (Philadelphia: University of Pennsylvania Press, 1983), 77, established that 87 percent of people

with pet cats and dogs regarded them to be members of the family. The claim that the majority of pets are cats and dogs comes from Jennifer Wolch, "Zoöpolis," in *Animal Geographies: Place, Politics, and Identity in the Nature-Culture Borderlands*, ed. Jennifer Wolch and Jody Emel (London: Verso, 1998), 133. The emphasis in this essay is on domestic dogs and cats in a US context. The issues discussed here may not map exactly onto the situation in Europe and may be quite far removed from how dogs and cats are regarded in developing countries.

2. The details of this legislation, from which this quotation is drawn, come from the following Web page at Michigan State University: http://www.animallaw.info/statutes/stusri2000housebill6119.htm.

3. See Yi-Fu Tuan, *Dominance and Affection: The Making of Pets* (New Haven: Yale University Press, 1984).

4. P. N. Olson and C. Moulton, "Pet (Dog and Cat) Overpopulation in the United States," *Journal of Reproduction and Fertility,* supp. 47 (1993): 434. These statistics, though, are contested. See Bernard Rollin and Michael Rollin, "Dogmatisms and Catechisms: Ethics and Companion Animals," *Anthrozoos* 14, no. 1 (2001): 6. I am using the expression "humanely killed" rather than "euthanized" because, as will be seen later, some object to this name for the practice.

5. Olson and Moulton, "Pet Overpopulation," 433.

6. Tuan, *Dominance and Affection,* 88.

7. Arnold Arluke and Clinton Sanders, *Regarding Animals* (Philadelphia: Temple University Press, 1996), 103.

8. Edmund Leach, "Anthropological Aspects of Language: Animal Categories and Verbal Abuse," in *New Directions in the Study of Language,* ed. Eric Lenneberg (Cambridge: MIT Press, 1966).

9. I am, in this essay, interested in the special case of killing healthy animals rather than sick and suffering animals. There is a degree of ambiguity about this, but the broad distinction will suffice here.

10. SAFE 2003 at http://www.safeanimals.com/euthanasia.

11. Joanna Newby, *The Pact for Survival* (Sydney: Australian Broadcasting Corporation, 1997), 250.

12. This can be problematic if shelters have a short turnover time before killing. Where only twenty-four or forty-eight hours are allowed, especially in cities with many shelters, owners may have difficulty locating their dog or cat in time.

13. See the "2000 Report of the AVMA Panel on Euthanasia," *Journal of the AVMA,* 218, no. 5 (March 2001): 669–96. The US Animal Protection Institute, for instance, maintains barbiturate injection to be the only acceptable method of animal euthanasia in a shelter. See Jean Hofve, "Euthanasia and the Animal Shelter," *Animal Issues* 32, no. 2 (Summer 2001), http://www.api4animals./org.

14. Methods deemed unacceptable by the AVMA still seem to be used in some places: there is, for instance, a report that in Enoch, Utah, stray animals are killed by exhaust fumes from a truck.

15. Stephanie Frommer and Arnold Arluke, "Loving Them to Death: Blame-Displacing Strategies of Animal Shelter Workers and Surrenderers," *Society and Animals* 7, no. 1 (1999): 5.

16. Ibid., 8.

17. Olson and Moulton, "Pet Overpopulation," 434.

18. This view is often associated with Peter Singer in *Animal Liberation* (1975; repr., London: Jonathan Cape, 1984). Although Singer is well known for being a utilitarian (though more recently a preference utilitarian rather than a classical utilitarian), as has been pointed out by Keith Burgess-Jackson, the book *Animal Liberation* is not explicitly utilitarian. It is compatible with utilitarianism but does not presuppose it. See Burgess-Jackson's Web log at http://analphilosopher.blogspot.com/2003_12_01_analphilosopher_archive.html.

19. Of course, this is a somewhat simplified position, since there are a range of other factors involved—for instance, the well-documented distress caused to those working in animal shelters at having to carry out the humane killing. I will discuss other possible consequentialist verdicts later.

20. This, though, is not the only possible utilitarian "take" on the situation. See Peter Singer, "Killing Humans and Killing Animals," *Inquiry* 22 (1979): 145–55, and his more recent discussion in Peter Singer, *Practical Ethics,* 2nd ed. (Cambridge: Cambridge University Press, 1993), 132, where he suggests that dogs and cats may be self-conscious and, if so, should not be killed, however painlessly, as noted on p. 181.

21. Tom Regan, *The Case for Animal Rights* (London: Routledge, 1984), 243. Obviously, very many difficulties exist with this argument at all stages; it is not necessary to go into these difficulties here.

22. Ibid., 98–99. This is a view that could be shared by some utilitarians, since one would expect deprivation to mean that an individual's experiences were less happy or less rich than they would otherwise be.

23. Ibid., 100, 113, 117.

24. Ibid., 103.

25. Painless killing, though, ends the possibility of a particular individual having future happy experiences, which (unless replaced) would matter in some forms of utilitarianism as affecting the total happiness in the world. There isn't space to pursue this issue here; Singer discusses it further in *Practical Ethics.*

26. Regan, *Case for Animal Rights,* 114.

27. Regan, in fact, does make a couple of exceptions to this, in particular in what he calls the "miniride" principle. I do not think that the miniride principle applies in this case, though it would be an interesting study to explore this in more detail. See ibid., 305.

28. See, for instance, Stephen Budiansky's *Covenant of the Wild: Why Animals Chose Domestication* (London: Wiedenfeld and Nicholson, 1992), where it is argued that animals connived in their own domestication, a view that is in contrast with more traditional accounts where domestication is presented as humans capturing or confining animals (that is to say, humans were the only active agents in the process).

29. See Newby, *Pact for Survival,* 61.

30. Norman Daniels, *Am I My Parents' Keeper?* (Oxford: Oxford University Press, 1998).

31. Just this case has already been convincingly argued by Keith Burgess-Jackson, and I will not argue for it further here. See Keith Burgess-Jackson, "Doing Right by Our Animal Companions," *Journal of Ethics* 2 (1998): 159–85.

32. I recognize that significant philosophical difficulties exist with the idea of collective or social responsibilities and that many philosophers will find this claim unsatisfactory. There is not, however, space to consider expanded senses of responsibility in more detail here.

33. Nel Noddings raises this question as part of her discussion of caring. She asks, "Does one who cares choose swift and merciful death for the object of her care over precarious and perhaps painful life?," and answers that "it depends on our caretaking abilities, on traffic conditions where we live, on the physical condition of the animal." See Nel Noddings, *Caring* (London: University of California Press, 1984), 13.

34. Peter Singer, *Practical Ethics,* 110–34.

35. The idea that feral animals—specifically cats—are often regarded as being "out of place" is explored by H. Griffiths, J. Poulter, and D. Sibley in "Feral Cats in the City," in *Animal Spaces, Beastly Places,* ed. Chris Philo and Chris Wilbert (London: Routledge, 2000), 56–70.

36. Tuan, *Dominance and Affection,* 2.

37. I have argued this elsewhere; see, for instance, Clare Palmer, "Taming the Wild Abundance of Existing Things: Foucault, Power and Animals," *Environmental Ethics* 23, no. 4 (2001): 339–58.

38. A recent study of Web sites advocating spaying and neutering in fact does uncover paternalistic arguments. It is claimed that de-sexed animals are less susceptible to disease (since they are not mating), are less likely to be harmed by fighting, and do not suffer from thwarted sexual urges. See, for instance, http://www.ktvu.com/family/2003733/detail.html. I don't think that the presence of such paternalistic arguments invalidates my claims here, since the same kinds of paternalistic arguments also exist for humane killing, as I have pointed out.

39. Though this may not be achieved: see Olson and Moulton, "Pet Overpopulation," 43.

40. It might be, for instance, that development of the policy implications of ideas in this essay would lead to advocacy of a much more stringent licensing scheme for pet ownership.

41. Thanks to Francis O'Gorman, Emily Brady, and other contributors to this volume for helpful comments on earlier versions of this paper.

Conclusion:
A Conversation

Throughout the planning of this book, the nature of its conclusion was one of the hardest matters to resolve. This was not a matter of disputing the argument of the individual contributors; we had never entertained the idea that our diverse concerns and perspectives could lead us to reach a single identifiable "conclusion" about animal killing. The challenge was to find a way to draw out common themes and thoughts and to reflect on them as a group, making the whole book more than the sum of its parts.

The practical solution of recording a "round table" discussion was agreed upon, and in the summer of 2003—having already exchanged extensive written comments on each chapter—the group recorded over four hours of conversation in a seminar room at Middlesex University in north London. Some of us took the view that a suitably edited version of the discussion was the only realistic format for eventual publication; others felt strongly that the points raised should be synthesized into an argument with a single authorial voice. In the end, the round table format survived, and what follows—at less than a quarter of the length of the original transcript—is an edited version that aims to preserve both the shape and the tone of that summer afternoon's conversation.

Touching on points raised in a number of the essays, our discussion ranged across topics such as the nature of hunting, ambivalent representations of animal death, animals as killers, visible and invisible killings, killing and conscience, the business of slaughter, and "humane" killing.

The Nature of Hunting

Erica Fudge: Shall I start with a question that comes from reading your chapter, Garry, which is: Is there ever a way in which humans killing animals is "natural"? That is, are all of the ways in which we kill animals and the reasons for killing them cultural?

Garry Marvin: Well, I would claim that all human killing is necessarily cultural because humans are cultural creatures. I can't think what any non-cultural killing of animals might be. So I would argue that we have to understand the cultural context of all killing in order to make sense of those actions. A person hunting is very different from an animal hunting. However much hunters like to say, "We're enacting something natural," I don't think they're doing that at all.

Steve Baker: If we can come at this from a slightly different angle: the idea that hunting and killing are cultural activities doesn't sound too controversial, but you also claim that violence has the effect of a creative force in social relations. I wonder whether you could say something about that idea, if this is what you were saying?

Garry Marvin: Oh, I think it can be creative, because it seems to me that all human relations with animals end with killing them, and therefore that killing must be a key defining relationship. [John] Abbink, whom I quote at the beginning [of my essay], suggests that in human societies, violence comes in and reconstitutes social relations. I actually wanted to turn around that proposition and say that, at least in some sense, human relationships with animals are constituted by the fact that these animals are going to be killed. Whether it's creative . . . well, I think it could be creative in a sense. I am thinking about Jonathan's material on slaughterhouses: that an animal is killed and re-created, or created as meat and transformed in various ways—as are the animals you are dealing with, Steve, that are turned into artworks or images. So how I would use the word "creative" I'm not sure; but I think there is something there.

Diana Donald: When you say that all the killing of animals by humans is "cultural," don't you mean something more than that? Culture implies a kind of normalization, which is perhaps bred of bad conscience, for lack of a better word. It seems to me that the ritualization you stress in relation to hunting is a way of making it acceptable and giving it a kind of legitimation, which is peculiar to human beings.

Garry Marvin: Well, I do puzzle about that because the anthropological literature seems to suggest, in particular from North American native societies, that it's not a kind of guilt but a notion of "We have to do this in the right way; we have to ask the permission of the animals." One can say that's merely disguising, but then I think that doesn't explain anything. So I'm not sure whether guilt is going on, though it might be, say, with slaughtering. *Animal to Edible,* Noëlie Vialles's study of French slaughterhouses, shows the division of labor: no one actually knows who has done the killing. This is my paradox. There seems to be a pleasure in hunting, but neither subsistence hunters nor sports hunters seem to express a pleasure in the act of killing itself.

Jonathan Burt: Isn't there another dimension to this, though, which is that a lot of hunting is privileged, isn't it? I mean, in Africa there are whole traditions of people not being allowed to own guns, and licensing is also linked to the business of animal population control. It's phenomenally expensive for people to hunt in the United Kingdom with shotguns. So therefore this business of getting a license to hunt is cultural but with economic and political constraints.

Steve Baker: I want to bring us back to the issue of the three kinds of death that you talk about, Garry—the cold death, the hot death, and the passionate death. You characterize hunting as being associated with passionate deaths. In particular, I wanted to ask you to say more about the idea of the hunter's emotional bond or emotional closeness with the animal. You make it clear that the point of that closeness is to get close enough to kill the animal, but I suspect that what you are saying about the emotional experience of the hunter amounts to more than that.

Garry Marvin: I'm thinking of the sort of narratives where hunters describe how they've followed the animal, or how it's gone over the mountain and they are trying to cut around, or keep up- or keep downwind of it, or whatever. I think there is a buildup of an incredibly complex relationship between the human and that *particular* animal. It lessens when animals become, as it were, mere targets.

Steve Baker: As I understand it, you are using the term "relationship" in an anthropological sense. I understand, I think, your notion of the hunter's meaningful engagement in the activity. But it seems to me that in all probability, the animal's experience is so alien to the hunter's experience that it's not just an asymmetrical relationship; it's almost as though the hunter is trying to get closer and the animal is trying to get further away. What does that do to the idea of it being a relationship?

Garry Marvin: Yes, I'm using the term "relationship" sociologically or anthropologically. I think we can have relationships with strangers or even people whom we don't know. Sure, the hunted animal might be unaware of a person's presence, and that unawareness is exactly what the hunter is trying to maintain. The hunter closing in is almost like a film photographer making a natural history documentary. I would argue that there is a relationship between the hidden cameraperson and the animal that is being filmed, just as there is between the hunter and the hunted. This is true even if the hunted animal is unaware that it's been hunted, and the relationship is only recognized by the human.

Robert McKay: I wonder whether the hunter's primary relationship is with the animal or with other hunters and with that hunter's community. It seems to me that trophies of the kind you see on the front cover of angling magazines are obviously designed to be shown to other anglers, and the trophy on a wall is creatively mounted to be shown to visitors. Hunting at that point has become a performance. It seems to me that the animal becomes the canvas for the hunter to display or perform his or her prowess upon, that the rules of hunting are simply the correct forms or media used to make the best kind of performance.

Diana Donald: Could I just put in another word: I'm very uncomfortable with this idea of a "relationship" with the hunted animal. It seems to me a kind of delusion, not to put too fine a point on it. Leaving aside any possible anthropological meanings attached to the idea of relationship—surely a relationship, as commonly understood, is voluntary on both sides, and it seems to me that the hunted animal's relationship with the hunter is wholly involuntary. Therefore, to suggest that the hunter has some kind of a rapport with the creature he's chasing seems to be . . .

Garry Marvin: Well, I think I'm using it in a different sense, Diana. I would argue, for example, that a tortured person has a relationship with the torturer. The tortured doesn't want to be tortured, but there is a social relationship between the two of them, as there is between a warder and a prisoner. Although I insist on calling it a relationship in the context of hunting, I don't want to claim anything more than that. For me, "relationship" is a neutral term: it is full of meaning for both parties concerned, but I certainly do not claim it is necessarily good.

Chris Wilbert: Could I add a question? Is this Westerners' "passion for hunting" distinct from the attitude of indigenous peoples? They are hunting for food but certainly do have a relationship with the animals that is strongly cultural, often animistic. I know there are people who try to equate hunting in developed societies, where it is just a leisure sport, with indigenous peoples' hunting. But are there not big differences there, especially in the relationship with the hunted animal?

Garry Marvin: I couldn't see very much difference between the attitude of huntsmen I have spoken with and that of indigenous peoples, knowing or having a close connection with the natural world. I would make the claim they do something very similar.

Steve Baker: I think it is important that, in this project, we want to investigate the nature of killing animals *close to home,* as it were. We want to understand what our own society is doing when it's engaging in killing animals.

Erica Fudge: That leads us on to Diana's chapter, because she's dealing with canonical works of art that arguably reverse the process of distancing we've talked about. These are paintings that draw the viewer in. It's interesting that there seems to be a distinction between the distancing techniques used in actual hunting and representations of hunting that might work against that distancing.

Ambivalent Representations of Animal Death

Diana Donald: I suppose another difference is that, although artists like Landseer and Ansdell were very closely connected with the hunting class, their pictures were public, very public, in the sense that they were not only exhibited but also very widely reproduced in prints. Therefore they opened themselves to a great diversity of reactions, including those of people who were deeply unsympathetic toward blood sports. It seems to me that there is often ambivalence in the image itself: that it is polysemous, presumably reflecting some kind of divided consciousness in the mind of the artist and even of the hunter himself.

Steve Baker: Diana, there's one point where you say, "The representation of a hunt can never bear a direct relationship to the experience it commemorates: it embodies a *concept* rather than a record of the chase." Can you elaborate on that distinction a little?

Diana Donald: Never having taken part in a hunt, I can't actually ascertain the relationship of hunting imagery to the live hunting experience. But I assume that the experience of hunting is highly variable; it's dispersed; the experience of each hunter will be different. The structure would be there but would be liable to be disrupted in all sorts of ways, whereas the image of the hunt is a kind of embodiment of the ideal, of the perfect hunt, as it were. In that way it differs from the actual experience, which I assume is always imperfect.

Steve Baker: The messiness of the thing isn't actually recorded pictorially.

Garry Marvin: Aren't there some nineteenth-century pictures that capture the actual things going on, people falling off their horses, being thrown over hedges?

Diana Donald: I think that's part of the ideal, you see. The popular journalism of that time emphasizes the sort of masculine recklessness that's involved, treating it as a positive virtue. So the thrills and spills were all part of the ideal, actually, and I would even argue that they are a form of mental or moral distancing from the kill. It was axiomatic that the joy was in the riding and the falling and the competition between the horses rather than in actually being there when the fox was dispatched.

Steve Baker: So what would it be to show the messiness? What sort of portrayal would that be?

Diana Donald: I can think of one painting that does show that, and again it's by Landseer. He painted a picture of a fox at the moment before it's killed called *The Last Run of the Season.* In a sense it's an ironic title. The fox is filthy, it's exhausted, it's snarling, it's a sordid image in every way, which I see as Landseer being very honest. I think you could say he was sadistic, but he was also very aware of what he and people like him were doing. It seems to me that that picture was a challenge to those people who were engaged in precisely the kind of distancing which I described— as though to say: this is what hunting *truly* is. What changes over time is not the view of animals but the view of *men*; the idea develops that the human is a super-predator, like any animal predator. This notion certainly becomes current in the nineteenth century, doesn't it? As I understand it, earlier hunting pictures, like those of Rubens in the seventeenth century, were emblems of moral courage. Humans were then thought of as the superior species, morally and intellectually superior, and the hunted animals could therefore be regarded almost as though they were the human's lower self. By killing animals, the human is expelling the animal side of him/herself or triumphing over the world of sensuality or of baser instincts. In the nineteenth century, however, things were seen quite differently because of the greater understanding of the kinship of humans with other species.

Erica Fudge: One of the things that comes really clearly from Diana's chapter is the possibility of ambivalence in the reading of paintings. Steve, you also talk about ambivalence, about people having different responses to works of art. But you also talk a lot about what the artists themselves have said and written about their art. How significant is the latter when we are judging those works of art?

Steve Baker: I don't think we have to accept what they say, as though it offered an authoritative reading. But we need to take their words seriously if we want to question whether contemporary art is a medium in which one can, to put it crudely, lobby for an anti-killing position. This is a terribly difficult question but an important one. And in that sense I agree absolutely with Diana when she asks, "Does a 'masterly' picture by Landseer disturb the spectator by presenting him or her with the cold fact of an intolerable reality? . . . Or does it seek to exculpate the perpetrators of a morally obnoxious practice by dignifying it as high art?" What I am trying to explore with my examples is simply a contemporary version of that same dilemma. If we move away too quickly or too readily from the artist's intentions, it becomes terribly easy to claim that certain works are pro-animal, or that they further the cause of animal rights, or whatever. And yet somebody else can come to those same works and feel something quite, quite different. Because they look so gory, so horrible, or so ugly, they almost have the opposite effect, and they come across as being at some level anti-animal works.

Jonathan Burt: Well, it seems to me that your reading of the problems of interpretation and Diana's reading are quite close in lots of ways.

Steve Baker: Yes, I think so.

Diana Donald: Are there any limits to what an artist can properly show, in defiance of public taste or the sensibilities of the people who may look at the work?

Steve Baker: I want to give a slightly indirect answer to that. Because contemporary art is a field in which artists will push at various kinds of boundaries, it seems to me that there is an opportunity there for an absolutely serious engagement with the forms and limits and the inconsistencies of cultural thought about particular issues, including human-animal relations. And, in my view, art is one of those rather neglected spaces outside language in which there's a unique possibility of opening up perceptions of how those relationships work. My experience of talking to artists—even those whose views are very different from my own—is that they are always absolutely serious about what they are doing. They are not engaging in . . .

Diana Donald: . . . sensationalism.

Steve Baker: Yes. And an opportunist latching on to whatever will shock the public and give them more publicity. So I would want to argue that notions of propriety and of ethical limits should not be imposed on such artists. With regard to violent *representations,* as distinct from actual harm done to animals, I would not see considerations of good taste or anything like that as being an appropriate reason for trying to limit what an artist might do.

Animals as Killers

Erica Fudge: Steve's "botched taxidermy" is perhaps not so very far from what Chris is talking about: the man-eater coming to be seen as a hybrid creature that is not wholly animal. But are we even still talking about something that we can call an animal? Or are we entering a sphere where "animal" itself and all that it means cease to be useful? Can these man-eaters be thought of as active agents and not just as objects of human scrutiny?

Chris Wilbert: Yes, in some ways. The man-eater's identity comes from its interactions with other things, really, and that identity is no longer essential in any meaningful sense: it's dispersed and can take different forms. The man-eater is a good example because it is treated weirdly, and, yes, I don't think it is treated like a conventional lion; but this is just one particular way a lion can perform and be performed. The man-eater is one possible way a lion can turn out. Much discussion in science or natural history focuses on why the lion or tiger becomes a man-eater, and it is nearly always claimed it is because the animal has lost the ability to hunt and catch its conventional prey. Or it is down to loss of prey because of environmental factors or due to people excluding these animals' prey. Therefore, man-eating always seems to be portrayed as aberrant, as unnatural even. But recently there has been a turn around, in that animals that attack people are no longer necessarily being seen as monstrous creatures. Their behavior is now blamed on the activities of people, often of people behaving wrongly or going into places where animals see them as prey. But that does not always happen. Agency is attributed to animals in differing, shifting ways.

Steve Baker: But what's fascinating in some of your examples is that it seems almost as though the disobedient animal, the man-eater, is perceived as being in the process of becoming human or becoming more human.

Chris Wilbert: Yes, I think this is very much so in the early stories of man-eaters but also in more recent ones, for example, in attitudes to the dingoes in Australia that I discuss. Human categories of the criminal, or accusations of being lazy, are imposed on the dingoes by the press and the wildlife services after dingoes attack tourists. In the earlier examples, like the Tsavo man-eaters, the lions seem to be viewed as devils, perhaps as having both animal and human characteristics, being just too clever for the white male hunter.

Garry Marvin: How does the term "man-eater" get used? Is it used to identify a particular species, or an individual rogue animal? I ask because, for example, grizzly bears can be man-eaters, or pythons can be man-eaters, or crocodiles, or a number of things. Does the term only apply to big cats? Polar bears will kill and eat people if they come across them, but you don't really hear about man-eating polar bears.

Jonathan Burt: Sharks. You can have man-eating sharks.

Garry Marvin: So is it a question of an individual animal? All sharks can prey on humans, but you don't regard them as man-eaters in any other sense. Is it always an individual that has gone wrong?

Diana Donald: It has implications of perversion, doesn't it? The animal has turned away from its proper food and proper behavior.

Chris Wilbert: This kind of man-eater discourse seems to me to be very specific to the nineteenth century.

Garry Marvin: And is applied to cats rather than anything else.

Chris Wilbert: Yes, it seems much of it is. And, actually, if you look through Peter Boomgaard's book on tigers—*Frontiers of Fear*—you will see that there have been many people killed at work by tigers in India and in the Malaysian peninsula in the past. Boomgaard writes of 1,200 people a year being killed by tigers in India, according to nineteenth-century records. These man-eaters are usually seen as "rogue" animals, that is, individuals, or so it seems. Animals are not usually individualized in the wild, but they are if they attack people. It seems to me that in developed countries, people are surprised when animals do act violently, defensively, or however we wish to characterize their motivations. Perhaps people are so used to their environments being domesticated, of animals being domesticated, that they are shocked when an animal acts independently, especially if it does something people perceive as dangerous.

Erica Fudge: There is an interesting possibility that you have to demonize the animal because otherwise you, as human, end up being thought of as merely food stuff. We are supposedly above that; we are not just flesh and bones in the same way a cow is flesh and bones and so on. We are human. And therefore to eat a human is not just eating flesh and bones; it is actually doing something which is much more unnatural.

Steve Baker: One of the interesting implications of Chris's examples of animal "propriety" is not only that the animal proper is the animal that humans can control but also that ultimately the animal proper is the being that humans can kill. But as soon as the action is reversed, it no longer works, apparently, to call the killer an animal.

Garry Marvin: Again we are focused on Western culture, and these might be particularly blinkered Western notions. Other peoples go into the jungle knowing that there are dangerous animals there. They do not necessarily regard these animals as perverse or unnatural—they just have to take care.

Chris Wilbert: Absolutely. And they do try to take care. Often peoples can seemingly accept these dangers and accept the fact of the animals being there. Of course, the situation of many people in the developing world, especially people in rural areas, is often very different from that of Western peoples. Many are exposed to all kinds of animal threats, and we could include here things like mosquitoes and water snails—animals that do not themselves do horrific things but pass on diseases that for these people are horrific in their effects. Then there are larger animal threats such as crocodiles, and occasionally lions and tigers, for example. We can also think of the ways that conservation, national parks, etc., in developing countries cause local people many problems when protected wild animals prey on their livestock. I am trying to think about the differing and changing orderings of human-animal interactions in various cultures and to think through the current fascination with animal attacks on the part of people in the developed parts of the world.

Clare Palmer: Couldn't it be said that in *both* cases—the demonization of man-eaters and when humans are blamed for "creating" animals that kill—there is a denial of animal agency? In the first case, it is not really animals doing the killing, the killing is demonic and something more than animal; while in the second case, it's not really animals doing the killing, it's the humans who created them. The animals themselves never carry responsibility for acting. So it's the opposite of what you were saying.

Chris Wilbert: That question has worried me too. And here I suppose we get to notions of agency and how it is attributed. The animals are actively doing things. But you are right; people are still speaking, interpreting, and arguing about what is happening, and what the roles of the animals are, and what they are doing. I am just saying that the animals do things, are caught up within certain orderings; they provoke actions, or reactions, and are doing things which people seek to interpret and act upon. Often this does involve a disavowal of agency.

Steve Baker: Surely the resonance of this is at the level of cultural rhetoric, really. The reason that an episode of animals eating humans seems much more striking than animals simply killing humans is not just that it's rarer but that it's the inverse of what we are doing to animals. The principal human reason for killing animals is in order to eat them.

Visible and Invisible Killings

Jonathan Burt: I keep thinking about the quotation from Ortega y Gasset in Garry's piece. I think it should be, "One does not hunt in order to kill; one kills in order to represent." I am beginning to think that your material, Steve, and what Diana is talking about and Chris's stuff too are all very much about representation and a certain weird displacement that keeps going on. Why can't we have killing without representation? It seems

we can't. One kills in order to represent. It seems to me that the whole
business of the documentation of killing, the fetishization of the documentation of killing, is common to all these forms of killing.

Clare Palmer: How about killing in laboratories, where it's done undercover and where you're not meant to see it?

Jonathan Burt: But that is recorded in other ways.

Steve Baker: And the issue of representation is still a crucial one. It's just that,
in this case, anti-vivisection activists may be adopting a different perspective and trying against the odds to represent that killing.

Diana Donald: Garry, you try to distinguish three kinds of killing of animals.
But perhaps the absolutely basic distinction is between those kinds of
killing that are willfully invisible, removed from the consciousness of the
perpetrators and excluded from the sight of anyone else, and those that
are in some way commemorated or represented?

Garry Marvin: I think that is an important distinction, commemorated versus noncommemorated.

Steve Baker: I want to come back briefly to this idea of Jonathan's about
"killing in order to represent," which strikes me as having something right
about it. But in the vast majority of cases, I suspect, the intention in "killing to represent" is not to represent the animal that's being killed. What
is striking about the visual examples that both Diana and I have been using, and the literary examples that Robert uses, is that there you have
artists and writers trying to figure out ways in which one might, against
the odds, make the representation of a killing say something about the
animal that's being killed. That's part of the agenda that both artists and
writers are trying to engage with. They recognize what's going on in the
popular rhetoric and try to address something that they find lacking in
that rhetoric. The rhetoric that they are challenging is seen both in Chris's
examples and those discussed in some of our other essays.

Diana Donald: Is it partly the excitement of rebellion? It seems to me that
the shocked reaction to a man-eating animal is a bit like fear of a popular
uprising by the (supposedly) lower orders. If you assume that society and
the order of the cosmos respect the status quo, to find a creature which is
challenging that is a bit like political revolution.

Chris Wilbert: Yes, I think that analogy can be made. There are plenty of
authors who express a "primitivist" anarchism and celebrate animal "resistance," as they term it. But, yes, there is a fear there, and these anarchist
groups today play on such fear, and invert it, seeing the animal as strong
and good: a very Romantic sense of the power of the animal. The violence
is, for them, a kind of return of the repressed, much like the popular up-

risings you mention. These anarchist groups see such animals (in a rather deliberately humorous way) as being engaged in a struggle akin to their own.

Robert McKay: Does the animal have to be, in some sense, unknown in order to be a man-eater? In the sense that the killing has to happen out of the blue?

Chris Wilbert: I think mystery is an essential element, because this "unknowing" prompts efforts to try to interpret and then represent what these animals are doing. But the meaning of their behavior is contested. On the one hand, we have scientists speaking for the animals, telling us why the animal attacks. But then we also have these green anarchist groups arguing that animal attacks are analogous to an attack on capitalism, authority, state institutions. They come up with all kinds of examples, such as bats invading courtrooms in Texas and criminals escaping the justice system because of them. They are making a rather anthropomorphic insinuation, that the animals are on their side, and they are on the animals' side. In doing so they are making similar claims to those of the scientists, to be able to speak for and interpret the motives of animals that attack humans. But they want to disturb our conceptions by playing on mystery.

Steve Baker: Like having God on your side, only different.

Erica Fudge: With sharper teeth.

Jonathan Burt: "When Animals Attack Capitalists"; I love that.

Killing and Conscience

Erica Fudge: I would like to ask a question stemming from my own essay. Does the difference between a "good life" and a "good self" hold up in terms of how we live with animals now?

Jonathan Burt: Are you thinking about the notion that the idea of civility is universal, and so if we treat animals well and we live well then we will be civilized rather than simply good?

Erica Fudge: No, I don't think it's about civility at all. The key model that existed in the early modern constructions of morality is the "good self," which is based upon the classical distinction that is made between the reasonable self and the animal. But the animal is also the animal that is within the self. What the "good self" has to do in that Renaissance argument is ensure that the animal self is kept down. And so when writers of the period discuss cruelty, their interest is not in the victim of cruelty, the animal in this instance. They are concerned with what happens to a person who becomes cruel: you lower yourself to the status of your animal self by becoming enraged, by giving in to passion.

Clare Palmer: If the cruelty was being displayed toward humans rather than animals, would it be seen differently?

Erica Fudge: No, in this discourse you never pay attention to the object of cruelty, even if it's human. But Montaigne argues against this attitude. For him the crucial moral issue is sentience, not the power of reason. The animal is not the human's lower self, because the animal also feels. In this new model "good life," you're not just interested in controlling yourself but you are also interested in yourself in relation to the world around you. Clare might associate this with her relational model because it's not just about self-control.

Diana Donald: I take it that, if you had asked somebody in the seventeenth century, "How alike are human beings and animals?," they would have said that they were not alike at all. Human beings were created in the image of God and had an immortal soul, whereas animals were not and did not. And yet if one looks in the anatomical and medical works of the time, it's freely assumed that animals are sufficiently like humans, in physique anyway, for animal dissection to have medical value. It can throw light on the treatment of human diseases and so on. Can that ambiguity be related to your theme?

Erica Fudge: By the seventeenth century, differentiating humans and animals involves assumptions that you can never actually put your finger on. You can never, say, open up the human head and find the soul: it is inorganic and therefore its presence is not provable by dissection. This means you can dissect animals in place of humans because actually you are never looking for that intangible essence. What you are looking at is mechanical: how the heart pumps, things like that. But to return to the first part of your question: if you had asked early modern people what they thought of animals, I think there would be differences between the literate response, which is what I'm dealing with in my chapter, informed by a classical philosophy, and the response based on experience at a day-to-day level, where people knew their animals. What was happening in the case of Montaigne and the Protestant writers I'm looking at is that ethics seemed to move from a very theoretical position to a more practical one: instead of abstract categories of *the* animal and *the* human, they were concerned with individuals in real situations confronted by real animals.

Diana Donald: But would more typical thinkers of that time have said that the human's possession of that immaterial something, that immaterial soul, gave him/her the right to exercise powers of life and death over other species?

Erica Fudge: Absolutely. There were nuances in the permissible scope of that power: someone like Joseph Hall would say that it was justifiable to use animals as servants—eat them, use their skin as clothes—but not to kill them for pleasure. But ultimately, yes, humans have dominion. Wildness and animals that turn on humans—the bear eating the child—is, within the Christian framework, regarded as a punishment of humans for Adam and Eve's fall. Animals become wild after the Fall because humans have sinned.

Diana Donald: It's very interesting that the license to kill doesn't belong to the part of man which is animal. Is that right? Is that a paradox? Is he spiritually superior to the animal because he has soul, which they do not have? Which gives him carte blanche.

Erica Fudge: Not quite carte blanche. There was a distinction between activities like killing in the Bear Garden, which would be regarded as sinful and a descent to the animal self, and sports like hunting, which would conventionally be praised as conducive to military training and riding prowess. To kill in that activity would not be deemed bestial: it would be deemed an enhancement of your humanness. But I'm coming more and more to think that the emphasis on absolute human dominion in the early modern period is not the whole picture. You can find numerous writers who are concerned about the fact that a stag can experience pain, about the fact that on Judgment Day you might be questioned about how you treated your horse as well as how you treated your son and daughter. However, I don't think that the Montaignean model that I outlined should be read as equivalent to our current environmental ideas, although some of the shift in early modern thought does anticipate the kind of debate that we're still having. I also wanted to say that Jeremy Bentham was not the first to emphasize sentience. It's earlier than that, and I think what is interesting about finding it earlier is that you can therefore make the case that concern about animals does not emerge only in modernity. It emerges in a period when it would be very easy not to be concerned about animals because there is a dominant discourse that allows for a lack of concern. So our modern questions about ethics and right and wrong are actually not merely a production of modernity, although they take certain forms in modernity. The crucial thing we talked about with hunting is the issue of distancing, and in a sense it might be easier to be distanced nowadays, when you go to the supermarket and buy your prepacked bit of thing called meat and forget that it was actually a part of something living at some point. But if you were living with animals on a day-to-day basis, whether it was your dog or cat or flock of sheep, you would have had an understanding which was very different from a simple notion of dominion, because you were looking into an eye and it was looking back at you.

Diana Donald: Can I ask a question which some readers might want to raise? We assume that superstitions gradually disappear in human history and that through culture and education we all become more rational or reasonable. But actually there is nothing obvious or inevitable about this process. I would ask, similarly: why is it that in the sixteenth and seventeenth centuries, educated or cultured people experienced no distress in seeing animals being tortured, whereas a century or two later this was considered obnoxious, repellent, and something which was assumed to be only in the province of the "uncouth"? Why does that change happen?

Erica Fudge: It's really difficult. Historians have argued that if you walked down the street near the Bear Garden in late-sixteenth-century London, you might see all sorts of other unpleasant and unhealthy things—like open sewers and diseased people. You would smell disgusting smells. And so in those terms, the Bear Garden was not as shocking as it would appear to our modern sensibility. I think that's true to a certain extent. But I actually think that the Bear Garden was popular because even then people knew that they shouldn't enjoy it.

Diana Donald: Does that mean that we are *kinder* people now, in the twenty-first century?

Erica Fudge: It goes back to the question of visibility. The things that are done to the animals now are done out of sight and out of mind. It's the slaughterhouse. It's the putting down of animals in animal shelters. Only when killing becomes something visible and pleasurable does anyone get upset—in dogfighting and hunting and so on. So, we might not be kinder; we just don't necessarily have such clear and frequent reminders that we're cruel.

Clare Palmer: This resembles the kind of trajectory that Foucault talks about in *Madness and Civilization* and *Discipline and Punish*. In these books, he discusses periods when those thought of as mad, or as criminals, were treated very harshly. The mad were displayed publicly, and executions were public rituals. These periods were followed by more recent practices where madness was medicalized and the mad hospitalized, and criminals were locked away from the public gaze. These more recent practices formed part of new "humanitarian" regimes and allowed for the view that society had become kinder. But Foucault argues, controversially of course, that these humanitarian regimes were themselves highly disciplinary and controlling. Similarly, perhaps, it might be argued now that, in the absence of the public display of animal torture and slaughter, society has become kinder and more humanitarian. But, in fact (as Jonathan's chapter reminds us), absolutely huge numbers of animals are killed away from the public gaze. One might also argue that high levels of selective breeding and genetic modification of animals are introducing new forms of disciplining animals from the inside—altering their very constitutions in order to make them more docile.

Steve Baker: Erica, you discuss the differences between use and pleasure, and that's still crucial to the killing which is not seen because there is still, in the view of many people, the notion that experimenting on animals for cosmetics is a bad thing but for medical advances it's a good thing. But in those experiments, and the subsequent killing that happens out of sight, no account at all is taken of the experience of the experimented-on and then killed animal. The experience is actually identical, whatever the human purpose, whether it's cosmetic research or medical research. What actually happens to the animal is the same in both cases, so it's a convenient rationalization that we can justify one kind of killing, but there is another that we prefer with our current sensibilities not to justify.

Erica Fudge: That is why the argument that things have improved becomes very difficult to maintain. When you see someone kicking a dog, that is perhaps more shocking than reading the statistics in the introduction, because it happens in front of you. But these statistics make it impossible to propose that feeling pity for the kicked dog and anger toward the person show how much kinder we have become over time.

The Business of Slaughter

Steve Baker: Jonathan's chapter is particularly useful in establishing a distinction between a specific instance of the act of killing and the system to which it belongs. You say, Jonathan, that it's understandable that the focus has been on the so-called humanity, or lack of humanity, of the killing of the individual animal within slaughterhouse practices, because what is unthinkable is the scale of the whole industry and all its economic, social, and cultural ramifications. That's too big a thing to take on, so it's rather convenient to look at the method of slaughter of the individual animal and what might be done about that. That apparent contradiction seems to be a particularly useful thing to attend to. While some of us argue that, by focusing on the act of the kill, or the representation of that act, one creates something that might jolt people out of their complacency, you say, here is one instance where a focus on the nature of individual deaths is precisely the way in which the culture manages to excuse itself from looking at the scale of those deaths.

Jonathan Burt: Well, you've said it for me! But to answer you—I think that in the case of the meat industry, there are two factors. First, a focus on individual killing in terms of regulating slaughterhouses and making them humane is bound up with the language of efficiency. The aim is to make the whole thing work smoothly so that animal welfare and efficient killing get confusedly bound up together. But the second point comes back to the problem of representation: where do you find the center of the meat industry? It's really like some crazed Deuleuzian network, because there is nothing that is not touched by it. As Eric Schlosser showed in *Fast Food Nation,* you can look at transport systems; you can look at the computerization; you can look at the pathogens in meat, at the migrant labor that makes up the meat industry, and the tremendous corruption of the meat industry in America—there is just a tale of poison and horror that completely infects the whole social network we live in.

Diana Donald: As I understand it, you are not saying that focusing on an individual death heightens awareness of the killing in total. You are saying it has a kind of diversional role, as a false alibi. By blaming some kind of killings, you validate others and remove the sense of guilt. It happens in rather the same way in the hunting ethic—if you say it's wrong to kill female deer, then it makes it all right to kill stags.

Jonathan Burt: Well, I think my version of it is a bit darker than this. I'm saying that the language of animal welfare has corrupted, for understandable reasons, the institutions that deal with animal welfare and slaughterhouses. Those concerned with welfare see themselves as not being able to tackle the moral case for meat. In fact, a report that came out in 2003 actually said that all the moral questions in relation to slaughter are not their province: all they wanted was for the animal to die as painlessly as possible, and they suggested various ways in which it could be done. But that really doesn't make sense. You either have no meat industry at all, or you don't surround the language of efficiency with the language of welfare.

Steve Baker: This brings us back to issues in Jonathan's essay around the question of intention. There are a couple of fascinating passages you quote from parliamentary debates—discussions about whether Jewish slaughter practices should be regulated—and at the end of those debates the decision was made not to act to improve the animal welfare provision because MPs feared that their good intentions would be misunderstood.

Jonathan Burt: As anti-Semitism.

Garry Marvin: Haven't Jews and Muslims argued that their form of slaughter is sacred—a sacralization of this process—and that they are actually treating the animal with greater respect through their process?

Jonathan Burt: They have said that it's Christians who have lost the sense of importance of the animal and that it's the Muslims and Jews who recognize that the animal is provided by God as part of his creation: when you kill it you have to remember its sacredness, even in a slaughterhouse. Can I make one more point? The reason that I wrote this piece was merely to show that slaughter in a sort of secular, "high-tech" society is full of residues, religious sentiments, and all sorts of other things.

Steve Baker: A good deal of your essay, Robert, is about how the inventive novelist might find ways of putting language into animals' mouths in these kinds of circumstances. What's your perspective on this?

Robert McKay: It's not quite that Deborah Levy wants to put language into animals' mouths, if that implies giving them a subjectivity that they've been denied by the agricultural process or by being killed. That approach would raise similar concerns to those you raise in your essay, Steve, about just how comfortable we should feel in reading a work of art as the embodiment of a political message when that seems to go against the way that art works. In fact, literary works that raise questions about animal ethics—works I would distinguish from, say, Richard Adams's books (*Watership Down* and so on)—will tend either to shy away from this idea of literature "speaking for animals" or will complicate it. J. M. Coetzee is a good example of this because he's known to be a vegetarian and to support animal causes, and in at least one of his books, *Elizabeth Costello,* he very self-consciously creates a character who is a novelist with pro-animal attitudes. The experience of reading the book is one of never being able to know whether we are reading the author's or the character's opinions about the ethics of killing animals. Coetzee notoriously avoids commenting on the politics of his own writing, but his reticence and unwillingness to speak for animals or to polemicize against killing them is also present in the works of writers who have openly engaged in pro-animal and environmental activism, like Brigid Brophy and Maureen Duffy in Britain or Margaret Atwood and Alice Walker in North America.

Chris Wilbert: So politics and aesthetics can't be separated?

Robert McKay: Well, all these writers find ways to complicate the type of realistic representation that underpins most explicit animal rights polemic: the idea that if you can expose viewers or readers to the true sight of animal exploitation, they'll give up meat, or whatever. I think that, when it comes to how Deborah Levy represents the meat industry, her aesthetic is not at all to "cut to the truth" of this situation but to make it explicit just how far ideology and presumption condition our conception of animals. Because she wants you to recognize this, to make it part of the experience of reading the book, she actually makes it *difficult* to make sense of the representation of animals or of meat, whereas an undercover animal rights film of a slaughterhouse, by making it so easy to see the killed animal, really doesn't address questions about how ideas of animal use and abuse are legitimated in society.

"Humane" Killing

Erica Fudge: On this question of animal use and abuse: could we talk a little about the consequences of the strategic interventions discussed in Clare's chapter? If it is better to allow the development of colonies of feral animals rather than continue to permit their "humane" killing in animal shelters, how would this work? What would the logical outcome of this be for us, say, living in London, if all abandoned dogs and cats were allowed to remain on the streets so long as they did not in some way interfere with the health and safety of human populations or other animal populations?

Clare Palmer: I think that no uniform policy toward feral animals could be adopted. It would really depend on the situation of the animals concerned. Obviously some of them wouldn't be able to cope. But others, for example some feral cat colonies, seem to be able to keep themselves going. Those are the kinds of situations where I think that one could argue that they should be left alone. There may be volunteer human feeders—that is probably fine—but if the feral animals become dependent on the feeders, those feeders must be willing to take responsibility for the relationship. There would be more feral animals than at present, but many countries already have more than Britain anyway. Indeed, I understand that Italy now has a law forbidding the euthanasia of healthy feral cats and dogs except in the case of dogs that are a danger to the public.

Erica Fudge: Actually, you are saying that, if this Italian model was taken up here, we would just live slightly differently with feral animals.

Clare Palmer: There has to be a higher tolerance of messiness so that there are different cultural ways of thinking about what's tidy and what's messy and what is acceptable or not.

Steve Baker: Is this something like a living animal equivalent of Mary Douglas's notion in *Purity and Danger* of dirt as "matter out of place"?

Garry Marvin: But it is also about space and the ways that animals occupy spaces. In Tirana, Albania, until recently there were packs of dogs which dominated urban territories: people didn't go down certain streets so as to avoid them. I think they dealt with them by just shooting them. So I think packs of feral dogs moving through central London would be a bit more problematic than cats. Feral cats disperse, but, as "matter out of place," a pack of feral dogs in the city becomes highly charged: they might well hurt you. For me the question raised by Clare's chapter was: shouldn't you just prohibit the pet industry? I think you wouldn't then have the problem that Clare raises, because the animals would not be there. Should these pets exist anyway just for human satisfaction, as utilitarian objects?

Clare Palmer: I think that's a real question, but I suppose I am unhappy with this conclusion as well. There seems to me to be a cleft stick here. One argument tends toward the view that there is something wrong with pet-keeping, and that's the problem. But on the other hand, for many people, living with an animal is the only opportunity to interact with animals in general. Derrida recently wrote about his relationship with his cat—his reflections were based on his cat gazing at him. Many people living in urban areas might see the odd fox running around, but they are never going to have close contact with a member of another species except as a pet-owner. And I don't think I want to say that it would be good to live our lives divorced from the lives of other animals. Perhaps the very day-to-day interaction with animals causes us to reflect on our own lives in relation to those animals—and to other animals, animals with whom we do not interact when they are alive, including those we might eat, wear, hunt.

Steve Baker: It's not as if people living with pets don't recognize that it's a compromised relationship. Nevertheless, I think it is, or at least it can be, a real relationship and deserves to be recognized as such.

Garry Marvin: But the end of pet relationships is often that humans have to kill, or to hand the animal over to someone else to kill for them. Is this acceptable?

Jonathan Burt: The pet industry is like the meat industry, in that one in four people wants to own a pet, so there are going to be millions of pets. It then becomes a question of population control, doesn't it? And somehow it seems to me we have to embed the question of pets into this mass of human-animal relations rather than individualizing it. The question as to whether we should or should not have a pet because it might be euthanized seems very different from this broader view.

Diana Donald: I think the real moral problem about pet-keeping is not just the fate of pet animals but the fact that it makes one complicit in killing, because pets are fed animal food. It makes people, even vegetarians, complicit in the death of other animals, unless a cat maintains itself by catching mice, which is probably unlikely. And a separate point: if feral animals were left to go their own way, the survival of the fittest would take over, and one would see them dying of starvation or fighting each other for the last scrap, and that would offend the context of values in which human society is now lived, wouldn't it? So do we not find it easier that they should be, as people say, "painlessly put away" rather than face up to that hard fact of nature?

Erica Fudge: All of our essays are dealing with material that is in some ways shocking. But in a sense the most shocking contribution I think is Clare's, because when you think about pet-ownership, you are thinking about companionship, you are thinking about love, you are thinking about anthropomorphism, but actually what comes out of Clare's essay is this endless supply of unnecessary animals being slaughtered.

Garry Marvin: And also shocking was what you said about the length of time that most people keep a pet. You said the average was two years? Now that really struck me as dreadfully shocking. "We're going to have a dog but only keep it a couple of years." Would that apply in Britain as well?

Clare Palmer: I can't find any figures on Britain; those were statistics from the US. Yes, for some reason or other, after two years on average, people found they could no longer keep the animal that they had taken on. It reminds me of an attack on Peter Singer's philosophy that said something like this: suppose there's an organization called "DisposaPup." Every year it gives a family a playful puppy, and they keep it until they go on their summer holiday the next year. But what they really prefer is just a playful puppy; so, come the summer, they give the puppy—which has now become a dog—back, and DisposaPup painlessly kills it and gives them a new puppy on their return from vacation. Everyone's happy—the company makes a profit, the dog doesn't suffer, a new life is generated to replace the one that's lost, the family gets a new playful puppy, and they don't even have to pay to kennel it during the vacation. How could there be an objection if the concern is only with suffering?

Steve Baker: But this is why your Tom Regan quotation—about harm being done to the animal even if it is killed entirely painlessly—provides, at the very least, an interesting perspective.

Clare Palmer: I think you have to maintain something like Regan's position if you want to get around the utilitarian argument about suffering; you must argue that, even if there is not suffering, there is still harm or a wrong of some other kind. And that, I think, is the only argument that will work here.

Diana Donald: Another issue that comes out of this discussion is the fact that the different attitudes to killing—killing one kind of animal but not another, doing it in one way but not another—suggest that there is actually no single framework of moral values that will accommodate our relationship to animals. So are we saying that cultural relativity is the only thing there is? Human beings are so inconsistent that we can never say that something is absolutely right or absolutely wrong?

Jonathan Burt: The issue of cultural relativity makes me think of the different levels of this conundrum about consistency that you raise, because we are accounting for both private attitudes on the one hand and attitudes and practices toward animals that are defined by, say, one's religion or profession on the other. Of course, the two are interlinked. But there seems to me a difficult tension between respecting cultural difference on the one hand and acknowledging the fact that the end result is that animals are killed en masse whatever the method used.

Steve Baker: Yes, it struck me that you said in your chapter, Jonathan, that slaughter is more than killing, and Garry quotes something to the effect of hunting being more than killing. Both of which are clearly true, but in the end the experience that the animal has of it is of the killing.

Diana Donald: It seems to me we've skirted the fact that it's quite impossible to enter into animal subjectivity or to express things from an animal's viewpoint. But we've tried, haven't we? Many of the authors of major recent books on human-animal relations are not the slightest bit interested in animals, not the slightest; they are interested in human social history. They read off phenomena relating to the treatment of animals and say this is about imperialism or that is about evangelical religion in the nineteenth century.

Jonathan Burt: Yes, absolutely.

Robert McKay: Whereas what we've tried to do in this project, to an extent, is to make the animal available for thinking about: to make it morally and intellectually visible and to make the obfuscations in much thinking about animals available for thinking about.

Jonathan Burt: In your Deborah Levy example, Robert, as well in many of the other examples we've discussed, it's almost as though the closer and closer you get to animal killing, the more everything begins to fall apart, perspective and everything.

Steve Baker: And language . . .

Jonathan Burt: . . . and language, and in the end you're left with . . .

Erica Fudge: . . . a blank page . . .

Jonathan Burt: . . . with nothing to say.

Index

STEVE BAKER is a reader in contemporary visual culture at the University of Central Lancashire and is the author of *The Postmodern Animal* and *Picturing the Beast* and the guest editor of a special issue of *Society and Animals* on "The Representation of Animals." He has lectured on his research at the New Museum of Contemporary Art in New York, the Museé d'art contemporain de Montréal, and the Natural History Museum in London. He has essays in recent edited collections, including Nigel Rothfels's *Representing Animals* and Cary Wolfe's *Zoontologies,* and has contributed to books and catalogs on the work of individual artists such as Catherine Chalmers, Eduardo Kac, Lyne Lapointe, and Olly and Suzi.

JONATHAN BURT is a freelance writer and the editor of Reaktion's *Animal* series and other works concerning animals in late-nineteenth- and early-twentieth-century culture. He has published a number of essays, including "Violent Health and the Moving Image: The London Zoo and Monkey Hill," in *Dead or Alive—Animals and Human Culture,* edited by Mary Henniger-Voss and William Jordan, and also writes a regular review feature on animal films for *Society and Animals.* He is the author of *Animals in Film* and *Rat.*

DIANA DONALD was formerly head of the Department of History of Art and Design at Manchester Metropolitan University. She has published several works on caricature and popular prints, including *The Age of Caricature.* She is now completing a book on animal imagery in British art, *A Divided Nature: The Representation of Animals in Britain, c. 1750–1850.* Her article "Beastly Sights: The Treatment of Animals as a Moral Theme in Representations of London, c. 1820–1850" appeared in *Art History.*

ERICA FUDGE is a reader in literary and cultural studies in the School of Arts at Middlesex University and is the author of *Perceiving Animals: Humans and Beasts in Early Modern English Culture* and *Animal.* She edited the collection *Renaissance Beasts: Of Animals,*

Humans and Other Wonderful Creatures and has essays in Nigel Rothfels's *Representing Animals* and Wendy Wheeler's *The Political Subject*. She is associate editor of *Society and Animals*.

GARRY MARVIN is a reader in social anthropology at Roehampton University and is the author of *Bullfight* and coauthor (with Bob Mullan) of *Zoo Culture*.

ROBERT MCKAY is a teaching fellow in English literature at the University of Sheffield, where he completed a PhD on the representation of animal ethics in contemporary fiction. His publications include work on Margaret Atwood and Alice Walker.

CLARE PALMER is an associate professor in philosophy and environmental studies at Washington University in St. Louis and is the author of *Environmental Ethics* and *Environmental Ethics and Process Thinking*. She has published a number of articles on animals and ethics, including "Placing Animals in Urban Environmental Ethics" in the *Journal of Social Philosophy*, and is the editor of the journal *Worldviews: Environment, Culture, Religion*. She recently moved to the United States from Lancaster University, UK.

CHRIS WILBERT is a lecturer in geography, planning, and tourist studies at Anglia Ruskin University and is joint editor (with Chris Philo) of *Animal Spaces, Beastly Places: New Geographies of Human-Animal Interactions*. More recently, he has published two essays on animal geographies with Jennifer Wolch and Jody Emel: "Animal Geographies," in *Society and Animals*, and "Re-animating Cultural Geographies," in *Handbook of Cultural Geography*, edited by Kay Anderson et al.

The University of Illinois Press
is a founding member of the
Association of American University Presses.

———————————————————

Composed in 10.5/13 Adobe Minion
with Meta display
at the University of Illinois Press

University of Illinois Press
1325 South Oak Street
Champaign, IL 61820-6903
www.press.uillinois.edu